Lecture Notes in Computer Science 9111

Commenced Publication in 1973
Founding and Former Series Editors:
Gerhard Goos, Juris Hartmanis, and Jan van Leeuwen

More information about this series at http://www.springer.com/series/7408

Juan Antonio de la Puente · Tullio Vardanega (Eds.)

Reliable Software Technologies – Ada-Europe 2015

20th Ada-Europe International Conference
on Reliable Software Technologies
Madrid, Spain, June 22–26, 2015
Proceedings

 Springer

Editors
Juan Antonio de la Puente
Universidad Politécnica de Madrid - UPM
Madrid
Spain

Tullio Vardanega
Università di Padova
Padova
Italy

ISSN 0302-9743   ISSN 1611-3349   (electronic)
Lecture Notes in Computer Science
ISBN 978-3-319-19583-4   ISBN 978-3-319-19584-1   (eBook)
DOI 10.1007/978-3-319-19584-1

Library of Congress Control Number: 2015939828

LNCS Sublibrary: SL2 – Programming and Software Engineering

Springer Cham Heidelberg New York Dordrecht London

Printed on acid-free paper

Springer International Publishing AG Switzerland is part of Springer Science+Business Media
(www.springer.com)

Preface

The 20th edition of the International Conference on Reliable Software Technologies (Ada-Europe 2015) took place in the city of Madrid, 26 years after the successful conference *Ada: The Design Choice*, which marked the start of Ada-Europe as an international organization. This was the fourth time that the conference was hosted in Spain, after Santander in 1999, Palma de Mallorca in 2004, and Valencia in 2010. Previous editions of the conference were held in France (Toulouse, 2003, Brest, 2009, and Paris, 2014), the UK (London, 1997, York, 2005, and Edinburgh, 2011), Switzerland (Montreux, 1996, and Geneva, 2007), Sweden (Uppsala, 1998, and Stockholm 2012), Germany (Potsdam, 2000, and Berlin, 2013), Belgium (Leuven, 2001), Austria (Vienna, 2002), Portugal (Porto, 2006), and Italy (Venice, 2008).

The conference series is run and sponsored by Ada-Europe, in collaboration with local organizations. This year Ada-Spain led the organizing team, with the support of the hosting institution, ETSIT-UPM, a top-rank engineering school in information and communications technology at the Universidad Politécnica de Madrid. This was a very appropriate choice as ETSIT-UPM celebrated the 50th anniversary of its current location in Madrid, with a wide range of special events, including the Ada-Europe conference among the most prominent ones.

This year's conference fell on the year in which the informatics and engineering communities worldwide and the Ada community in particular celebrate the 200th anniversary of Lady Ada Lovelace's birth, December 10, 1815. Ada Lovelace, the namesake of the Ada Programming Language, was the visionary who anticipated the advent and creative power of computer programs, long before Alan Turing published his most famous "Computing Machinery and Intelligence" paper. The conference included a display of oeuvres on Ada Lovelace's work and correspondence, while the *Ada User Journal* devoted the full contents of its December 2015 issue to celebrating her figure.

The conference took place during June 22–26, 2015, with a rich program on both the technical and social sides. The scientific part of the conference program featured 12 presentations selected among 36 peer-reviewed papers, which were grouped into four regular sessions spread on the central days of the conference. The program also included nine industrial presentations, split across three industrial sessions. A special session on "Advances in Methods" with three presentations, and one vendor session with an accompanying vendor exhibition, completed the core program. In addition to this rich set of material, nine tutorials for the equivalent of 12 half-day sessions were scheduled on Monday and Friday, together with two full-day workshops on subjects of high relevance, one on the engineering of "Dependable Cyber-Physical Systems" (Monday), and the other on "Architecture Centric Virtual Integration" (Friday).

Each day of the core conference program opened with a keynote talk centered on topics high in the interest of the conference focus:

- *EC-61508 Certification of Mixed-Criticality Systems Based on Multicore and Partitioning.* Jon Pérez, from IKERLAN, presented an authority-approved certification strategy to achieve conformance with EC-61508, a cross-domain standard for functional safety, in the development of a wind-turbine mixed-criticality system running on a modern multicore processor.
- *Software Development of Safety-Critical Railway Systems.* Javier Rodríguez, Siemens Rail Automation, provided insight into the development of safety-critical systems, focusing on the review of the software lifecycle activities.
- *The Central On-Board Computer of the Philae Lander in the Context of the Rosetta Space Mission.* Andras Balázs, from the Wigner Research Centre for Physics in Budapest, Hungary, presented an overview of the major hardware and software design aspects of the central on-board computer of the Philae lander, which traveled over 10 years as the precious payload of the Rosetta spacecraft that recently made the historical encounter with the comet 67P/Churyumov-Gerasimenko.

The proceedings contained in this volume cover two of the three keynote talks, and the full set of peer-reviewed papers. The remainder of the conference proceedings were published, in successive instalments, in the *Ada User Journal*, the quarterly magazine of Ada-Europe.

The 36 submissions to the peer-reviewed track of the conference program came from 19 countries and 87 distinct authors, from Europe, Asia, North America, and Africa. The selection was very competitive and resulted in the making of four technical sessions, on topics ranging from critical systems to multi-core and distributed systems via language technology and real-time applications.

The tutorial program covered a wide range of topics in the scope of the central themes of the conference, as follows:

- "Access Types and Memory Management in Ada 2012", Jean-Pierre Rosen, Adalog, France.
- "Designing and Checking Coding Standards for Ada", Jean-Pierre Rosen, Adalog, France.
- "Parallelism in Ada, Today and Tomorrow", Brad Moore, and Stephen Michell, General Dynamics and Maurya Software, Canada.
- "Probabilistic Timing Analysis", Francisco Cazorla, Tullio Vardanega, Jaume Abella, and Mark Pierce, Barcelona Supercomputing Center, Spain, University of Padua, Italy and Rapita Systems, UK.
- "Ada 2012 (Sub)types and Subprogram Contracts in Practice", Jacob Sparre-Andersen, JSA Research & Innovation, Denmark.
- "When Ada Meets Python: Extensibility Through Scripting", Emmanuel Briot and Ben Brosgol, AdaCore, France and USA.
- "Software Measures for Dependable Software Systems", William Bail, MITRE, USA.
- "Software Design Concepts and Pitfalls", William Bail, MITRE, USA.
- "Real-Time and Embedded Programming with Ada 2012", Patrick Rogers. AdaCore, USA.

The industrial sessions featured nine presentations centered on various aspects of reliable software development:

- "From Ada 83 to Ada 2012" Philippe Gast and David Lesens, Airbus Defence and Space, France.
- "Automated Trading with Ada" Duncan Sands, DeepBlueCapital, France.
- "WCS Warehouse Control System in Ada" Björn Lundin, Consafe Logistics AB, Sweden.
- "Early Experiences in the Industrial Application of Spark 2014" Angela Wallenburg, Florian Schanda, Stuart Matthews, Alan Newton, Stephen Williams and Neil White, Altran, UK.
- "System Integration in a Railway Setting" Theodor Norup, Rambøll, Denmark.
- "Model Based Engineering of an Unmanned Aerial System" Jose Luis Fernández, Juan López, and J. Patricio Gómez, Universidad Politécnica de Madrid and Unmanned Solutions, Spain.
- "Multi-core Testing and Code Coverage" Ian Broster and David George, Rapita Systems, UK.
- "Deriving Reusable Process-Based Arguments from Process Models in the Context of Railway Safety Standards" Barbara Gallina and Luciana Provenzano, Mälardalen University and Bombardier Transportation, Sweden.
- "Source Code Analysis of Flight Software Using a SonarQube Based Code Quality Platform" Maurizio Martignano, Andreas Jung, Christian Schmidt, and Tobias Lehmann, Spazio IT - Soluzioni Informatiche, European Space Agency, Airbus Helicopters, and Inopus, Italy, The Netherlands, and Germany.

The program also included a special session on *Advances on Methods*, which was designed to allow the presentation of work in progress, not yet finalized to make the conference proceedings, but mature enough to be orally exposed to the conference crowd:

- "A Task-Based Concurrency Scheme for Executing Component-Based Applications" Francisco Sánchez-Ledesma, Juan Ángel Pastor, Diego Alonso and Bárbara Álvarez, Universidad Politécnica de Cartagena, Spain.
- "Persistent Containers with Ada 2012" Jacob Sparre Andersen, JSA Research & Innovation, Denmark.
- "Effective Worst-Case Execution Time Analysis of DO178C Level A Software" Stephen Law, Andrew Coombes, Michael Bennett, Ivan Ellis, and Stuart Hutchesson, Rolls-Royce Controls & Data Services, and Rapita Systems, UK.

We would like to acknowledge the work of all the people who have contributed, with various responsibilities and official functions, to the making of the conference program. First of all, the authors of the presentations, who were largely responsible for the success of the conference. Then the members of the Program Committee, who worked hard to review and select a high-quality set of papers, both for the Springer LNCS volume in the case of peer-reviewed papers and the *Ada User Journal*, the industrial presentations, the special session papers, and the workshops. Finally, the group of organizers who made the conference program a reality: Local Chair Juan Zamorano; Conference Chair

Alejandro Alonso; Industrial Co-chairs Jørgen Bundgaard and Ana Rodríguez; Publicity Chair Dirk Craeynest; Exhibition Chair Santiago Urueña; Tutorial Chair Jorge Real. They all deserve our gratitude for their effort.

We hope that the attendees enjoyed the conference, in both its technical and social program, as much as we did in organizing it.

June 2015   Juan Antonio de la Puente
                                                                            Tullio Vardanega

Organization

The 20th International Conference on Reliable Software Technologies, Ada-Europe 2015, was organized by Ada-Europe and Ada-Spain, in cooperation with ACM SIGAda, SIGBED, SIGPLAN, Ada Resource Association, and ETSIT-UPM (Escuela Técnica Superior de Ingenieros de Telecomunicación, Universidad Politécnica de Madrid).

Conference Chair

Alejandro Alonso   Universidad Politécnica de Madrid, Spain

Program Co-chairs

Juan Antonio de la Puente   Universidad Politécnica de Madrid, Spain
Tullio Vardanega   Università di Padova, Italy

Industrial Co-chairs

Jørgen Bundgaard   Rambøll, Denmark
Ana Rodríguez   ASSystem Iberia, Spain

Tutorial Chair

Jorge Real   Universitat Politècnica de València, Spain

Exhibition Chair

Santiago Urueña   GMV, Spain

Publicity Chair

Dirk Craeynest   Ada-Belgium and KU Leuven, Belgium

Local Chair

Juan Zamorano   Universidad Politécnica de Madrid, Spain

Sponsoring Institutions

AdaCore
Rapita Systems Ltd.

Program Committee

Mario Aldea	Universidad de Cantabria, Spain
Ted Baker	US National Science Foundation, USA
Johann Blieberger	Technische Universität Wien, Austria
Bernd Burgstaller	Yonsei University, Korea
Alan Burns	University of York, UK
Maryline Chetto	University of Nantes, France
Juan Antonio de la Puente	Universidad Politécnica de Madrid, Spain
Laurent George	ECE Paris, France
Michael González Harbour	Universidad de Cantabria, Spain
J. Javier Gutiérrez	Universidad de Cantabria, Spain
Jérôme Hugues	ISAE Toulouse, France
Hubert Keller	Institut für Angewandte Informatik, Germany
Albert Llemosí	Universitat de les Illes Balears, Spain
Franco Mazzanti	ISTI-CNR Pisa, Italy
Stephen Michell	Maurya Software, Canada
Jürgen Mottok	Regensburg University of Applied Sciences, Germany
Laurent Pautet	Telecom ParisTech, France
Luís Miguel Pinho	CISTER/ISEP, Portugal
Erhard Plödereder	Universität Stuttgart, Germany
Jorge Real	Universitat Politècnica de València, Spain
José Ruiz	AdaCore, France
Amund Skavhaug	NTNU, Norway
Sergio Sáez	Universitat Politècnica de Valencia, Spain
Tucker Taft	AdaCore, USA
Theodor Tempelmeier	University of Applied Sciences Rosenheim, Germany
Elena Troubitsyna	Åbo Akademi University, Finland
Santiago Urueña	GMV, Spain
Tullio Vardanega	Università di Padova, Italy

Industrial Committee

Roger Brandt	Roger Brandt IT Konsult AB, Sweden
Ian Broster	Rapita Systems, UK
Jørgen Bundgaard	Rambøll Danmark A/S, Denmark
Dirk Craeynest	Ada-Belgium and KU Leuven, Belgium
Peter Dencker	ETAS GmbH, Germany
Ismael Lafoz	Airbus Defence and Space, Spain
Ahlan Marriott	White Elephant, Switzerland
Steen Palm	Terma, Denmark
Paolo Panaroni	Intecs, Italy
Paul Parkinson	Wind River, UK
Eric Perlade	AdaCore, France
Martyn Pike	Embedded Consulting UK Ltd.
Ana Rodríguez	Assystem Iberia, Spain
Jean-Pierre Rosen	Adalog, France
Florian Schanda	Altran UK
Jacob Sparre Andersen	JSA Consulting, Denmark
Claus Stellwag	Elektrobit AG, Germany
Jean-Loup Terraillon	European Space Agency, The Netherlands
Rod White	MBDA, UK

Contents

Critical Systems

Multicore and Distributed Systems

Keynotes

A Safety Concept for an IEC-61508 Compliant Fail-Safe Wind Power Mixed-Criticality System Based on Multicore and Partitioning

Jon Perez[1]([✉]), David Gonzalez[1], Salvador Trujillo[1], and Ton Trapman[2]

[1] Embedded Systems Group, IK4-IKERLAN Technology Research Centre,
Mondragon, Spain
{jmperez,dgonzalez,strujillo}@ikerlan.es
[2] ALSTOM Renewables, Software and Performance, Barcelona, Spain
anton-aart.trapman@power.alstom.com

Abstract. The development of mixed-criticality systems that integrate applications of different criticality levels (safety, security, real-time and non-real time) in a single embedded system can provide multiple benefits such as product cost-size-weight reduction, reliability increase and scalability. However, the integration of applications of different levels of criticality in a single embedded system leads to several challenges with respect to safety certification standards. This research paper describes a safety concept for a fail-safe wind turbine mixed-criticality control system based on multicore partitioning that meets IEC-61508 and ISO-13849 industrial safety standards. The safety concept has been positively assessed by a certification body.

1 Introduction

In multiple domains the embedded systems architecture follows a federated approach, in which the system is composed of multiple interconnected subsystems where each of them provides a well defined functionality. The ever increasing demand for additional functionalities leads to an increase in the number of subsystems, connectors and wires leading to an increase in the the overall cost-size-weight-power and complexity [25] that in some cases limits the scalability of this approach. For example [32,33]:

- Wind power: A modern off-shore wind turbine dependable control-system manages up to three thousand inputs / outputs, several hundreds of functions are distributed over several hundred nodes grouped into eight subsystems interconnected with a field-bus and the distributed software contains several hundred thousand lines of code [32,33].
- Automotive: The software component in high-end cars currently totals around 20 million lines of code, deployed on as many as 70 ECUs (Electronic Control Unit) that accounts for 30% of overall production costs [7]. The Volkswagen Phaeton has 61 ECUs, 11.136 electrical parts, 2.110 cables and 3.860 meters of cables with a weight of 64 kg [28].

J.A. de la Puente and T. Vardanega (Eds.): Ada-Europe 2015, LNCS 9111, pp. 3–17, 2015.
DOI:10.1007/978-3-319-19584-1_1

– Railway: The ever increasing request for safety, better performance, energy efficiency and cost reduction in modern railway trains have forced the introduction of sophisticated dependable embedded systems [13]. The number of ECUs within a train system is in the order of a few hundred [8,24].

In addition to this, the overall system reliability can be decreased due to electrical failures caused by an increasing number of connectors and wires. For example, in the automotive domain field data has shown that between $30 - 60\%$ of electrical failures are attributed to connector problems [38]. In the aerospace domain interconnection problems are also a major cause of aircraft electrical equipment failures with a percentage of 36% [16] / 43% [35].

The integration of applications of different criticality (safety, security, real-time and non-real time) in a single embedded system is referred to as mixed-criticality system[32,33]. This integrated approach could improve the overall system scalability and reliability by reducing the amount of systems-wires-connectors and associated cost-size-weight-power. However, safety certification according to industrial standards such as IEC-61508 becomes a challenge because sufficient evidence must be provided to demonstrate that the resulting integrated system is safe for its purpose.

This publication contributes with the safety concept description of an IEC-61508 and ISO-13849 compliant fail-safe wind turbine mixed-criticality control system based on Commercial Off-The-Self (COTS) multicore partitioning. The safety concept is based on the strategy described in [32] and updates the safety concept described in [33], which summarizes the complete safety concept document positively assessed by a certification body [34].

The paper is organized as follows. Section 2 introduces basic concepts and Section 3 analyses related work. Section 4 describes the wind turbine control, the safety protection system and a safety concept based on well tried safety principles and solutions (common practice). Section 5 describes the equivalent safety concept based on multicore partitioning. Finally, Section 6 draws the overall conclusion and future work.

2 Background

2.1 Certification Standards

IEC-61508 [19–21] is a generic safety standard used as a reference standard by multiple domain specific standards (e.g., automotive ISO-26262, railway EN-5012X). Safety Integrity Level (SIL) is a discrete level corresponding to a range of safety integrity values where 4 is the highest level and 1 is the lowest. As a rule of thumb, the highest the SIL the highest the certification cost.

2.2 Fail-Safe and Fail-Operational

Safety systems can be classified as either fail-safe or fail-operational [32,33]. A system is fail-safe if there is a safe state in the environment that can be reached in case of a system failure either by the safety function or diagnostics, e.g., a process plant can be safely stopped, a train can be stopped. A system is fail operational if no safe state can be reached in case of a system failure, e.g., drive by wire in a car.

2.3 Hypervisor

Hypervisor is a layer of software (or a combination of software / hardware) that allows running several independent execution environments in a single computer platform. Hypervisor solutions such as XtratuM [9] have to introduce a very low overhead compared with other kind of virtualizations (e.g., Java virtual machine); the throughput of the virtual machines has to be very close to that of the native hardware.

3   Related Work

As stated in [32], multiple reports [2–4,6,10,11], research projects [39] and publications [12,26,29,32,33] indicate that is likely to be a significant increase in the use of multicore processors over the next years replacing applications that have traditionally used single core processors. Multicore and virtualization technology, independently or in combination, can support the development of integrated architectures in mixed-criticality platforms by means of software partition, or partition for short.

IEC-61508 safety standard does not directly support nor restrict the certification of mixed-criticality systems. Whenever a system integrates safety functions of different criticality, sufficient independence of implementation must be shown among these functions [19,20,32]. If there is not sufficient evidence, all integrated functions will need to meet the highest integrity level. Sufficient independence of implementation is established showing that the probability of a dependent failure between the higher and lower integrity parts is sufficiently low in comparison with the highest safety integrity level [20]. As stated in IEC-61508-2 Annex F, spatial and temporal independence are key to ensure the independence of execution ("that elements will not adversely interfere with each other's execution behaviour such that a dangerous failure would occur").

Widely available COTS multicore processors were not designed with a focus on hard-real time applications but towards the maximal average performance. This is the source for multiple temporal isolation / independence issues [27,30,32,33] and a challenge for the development of safety critical embedded systems as stated by different experts in the field [5,15,36,37]. In general, providing sufficient evidences of isolation / independence among safety and non-safety related functions distributed in a multicore processor is not a trivial task [27,30,32,33].

The avionics industry has widely adopted the Integrated Modular Avionics (IMA) [1] architecture, which allows integrating several applications on a single processing element. However, the migration of an existing set of pre-certified single-core avionics IMA systems into a multi-IMA multicore system is not a trivial task, because it is required to ensure that the temporal and spatial isolation of the partitions will be maintained without incurring in huge recertification costs [3,10,11,14,17,22,23,31].

4   Wind Turbine Control and Protection

A wind park is composed of interconnected wind turbines and a centralized wind park control centre as shown in Figure 1. As previously explained current wind turbine control unit follows a federated architectural approach and provides three major functionalities:

- 'Supervision': wind turbine real-time control and supervision.
- 'SCADA': Non real-time Human Machine Interface (HMI) and communication with SCADA system
- 'Safety Protection': Safety functions that ensure that design limits of the wind turbine are not exceeded

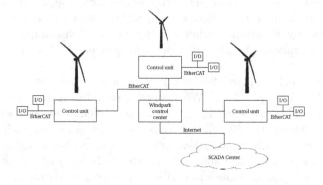

Fig. 1. Simplified wind park diagram [32,33]

As shown in Figure 2, there is a safety chain composed of safety relays in serial that activates the 'pitch control' safety function whenever the chain is opened. The 'pitch control' safety function leads the wind turbine to a safe state: protects the mechanical integrity of the wind turbine by moving the blades to anti-aerodynamic position. The 'safety protection' function must ensure that design limits of the wind turbine are not exceeded (e.g., over speed) and if exceeded output safety relays connected to the safety chain must be opened. The 'safety protection' and 'pitch control' functions must meet 'PLd' level of ISO-13849 [18] and IEC-61508 SIL2/3. Table 1 shows most relevant safety requirements to be met by this simplified example safety concept [32,33].

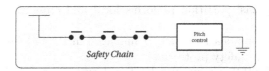

Fig. 2. Wind turbine safety chain [32,33]

Table 1. Wind turbine control and 'safety protection' requirements (most relevant) [32,33]

ID	Requirements
SR_WT_4	The 'safety protection' function must activate the 'safe state' if the 'rotation speed' exceeds the 'maximum rotation speed'
SR_WT_5	The 'safety protection' function must ensure 'safe state' during system initialization (prior to the running state where rotation speeds are compared)
SR_WT_6	'Safety protection' function must be provided with a SIL3 integrity level (IEC-61508)
SR_WT_7	The safe state is the de-energization of output 'safety relay(s)'
SR_WT_8	Output 'safety relay(s)' is(/are) connected in serial within the safety chain
SR_WT_9	A single fault does not lead to the loss of the safety function: HFT=1 and Diagnostic Coverage (DC) of the system $>= 90\%$ (according to IEC-61508).
SR_WT_10	The reaction time must not exceed PST
SR_WT_11	Detected 'severe errors' lead to a 'safe state' in less than PST (SW_WT_14)
SR_WT_12	The 'rotation speed' absolute measurement error must be equal or below 1 rpm to be used by 'safety protection'. If measurement $error \geq 1\ rpm$ it must be neglected
SR_WT_13	The 'maximum rotation speed' must be configurable only during start-up (not running)
SR_WT_14	The Process Safety Time (PST) is 2 seconds

4.1   Safety Concept- Common Practice

This section describes a simplified safety concept for the fail-safe 'wind turbine control and protection' using well tried safety principles and solutions (common practice). The 1oo2 (D) dual channel architecture shown in Figure 3 is based on two independent processors, two shared diverse input sources (rotation speed) and two output relays connected in serial to the safety chain.

The safety node (SCPU) has a Hardware Fault Tolerance of one (HFT = 1) based on two independent processors. Each processor controls one independent safety relay that can be de-activated (safe state) either directly commanded by 'safety protection' or indirectly by 'diagnosis' function. If the 'diagnosis' detects a fatal error, it does not refresh the associated watchdog and this leads to a reset of the node. As a summary:

- P0 and P1 are independent single core processors:
    - P0 processor only executes safety related functions and diagnosis techniques ('safety protection' and 'diagnosis')
    - P1 processor executes all types of functions, safety related and non-safety related
    - Each processor controls one independent safety relay
    - Each processor is monitored by one independent watchdog and a watchdog reset (e.g., due to time-out) implies de-energization of all safety relays

- The 'diagnosis' partition performs local and cross-channel monitoring diagnosis
- EtherCAT 'communication stack' is managed in P1 and the safety communication layer in 'safety protection'
- An IEC-61508 SIL2 system with HFT = 1 requires a Safe Failure Fraction (SFF) of $90\% > SFF >= 60\%$

The number of integrated functionalities will continue to increase and the future scalability of this approach is limited as previously described, e.g., limited by the computation power of single core processor(s) and reliability restrictions (e.g., usage of fans is not allowed). If processor P1 does not provide sufficient computation power new processors / nodes will be needed. Adding new processors / nodes and their associated communication buses leads to additional reliability and availability issues (e.g., material reliability, EMC).

5   Safety Concept- Multicore Partitioning

This section describes the multicore partitioning based safety concept for the fail-safe 'wind turbine control and protection', which aims to reach the same integrity level while providing a suitable solution that overcomes limitations of the current federated approach. The safety concept is based on the strategy described in [32] and updates the safety concept described in [33], which summarizes the complete safety concept document positively assessed by a certification body [34]. It is structured as follows:

- The fault hypothesis identifies the assumptions regarding faults that the fault-tolerant safety system must tolerate (Section 5.1)
- The general description provides a textual description of the safety concept (Section 5.2)

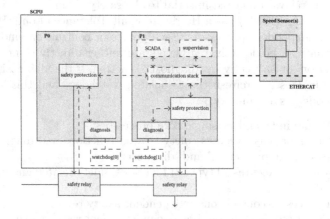

Fig. 3. Safety concept ($1oo2$; 2 processors) [32,33]

- Most relevant safety techniques used to support the safety concept are described in Section 5.3
- The hypervisor compliant item is described in Section 5.4
- The overall diagnosis strategy is described in Section 5.5

5.1 Fault Hypothesis

The fault hypothesis of this strategy [32] consists of the following assumptions:

- FSM: The system and safety relevant subsystems are developed with an IEC-61508 Functional Safety Management (FSM)
- Maximum SIL, HFT and DC: Considered up to IEC-61508 SIL3 safety function(s). A single fault does not lead to the loss of the safety function: HFT = 1 and Diagnostic Coverage (DC) of the system $>= 90\%$ (according to IEC-61508).
- Node: The node (SCPU) forms a single Fault-Containment Region (FCR) and can fail in an arbitrary failure mode.
- Processor:
  - The permanent failure rate is assumed to be in the order of $10 - 100$ FIT (i.e., about one thousand years) and the transient failure rate is assumed to be in the order of 100.000 FIT (i.e., about one year).
  - Complete temporal isolation might not be assured among cores (if the processor does not provide enough guarantees with sufficient evidences), but bounded temporal interference can be provided.
  - The multicore processor (ASIC) is developed taking fault avoidance measures required for the targeted SIL (as described in IEC-61508-2 Annex E/F) into account.
- Hypervisor: The hypervisor provides interference freeness (bounded time and spatial independence) among partitions, can fail in an arbitrary failure mode when it is affected by a fault and it is a compliant item as defined in section 5.4.
- Partition: A partition can fail in an arbitrary failure mode when it is affected by a fault, both in the temporal as well as the spatial domain.
- EtherCAT: Safety over EtherCAT provides a safety communication layer with the required integrity level (SIL3) according to IEC-61784-3.

5.2 General Description

The safety concept is described in a top-down approach with more detailed description of safety techniques at later refinement stages. Figure 4 shows a partitioned solution allocated to a heterogeneous quad-core processor selected for public demonstration purposes, based on two 'LEON3 FT' soft core processors (FPGA) and two 'x86' cores (Atom processor). The core allocation is equivalent to the processor allocation described in the previous safety concept (Section 4.1, Figure 3). Each functional group from Section 4.1 corresponds to one or more partitions, e.g., 'supervision' functional group is divided in multiple partition(s).

The hypervisor is considered to be a software compliant item (see Section 5.4) that guarantees temporal and spatial independence among partitions (IEC-61508-2 Annex F), ensuring interference freeness among safety and non safety partitions, and interference freeness among safety partitions. Partitioning and multicore allocation is used to support a reasonable balance between performance (e.g., 'supervision' functional group is divided in multiple partition(s)) and temporal interference due to shared resources.

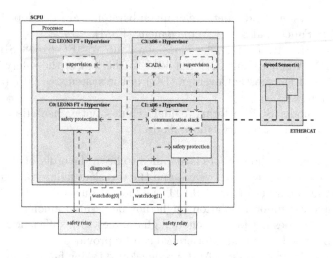

Fig. 4. Simplified safety concept (1oo2), multicore) [32,33]

Figure 5 shows the most detailed representation of the partitioned solution allocated to a heterogeneous quad-core processor with all hardware resources of relevance: communication buses, memory, shared resources, clocks and synchronization mechanisms, etc.

– The safety node (SCPU) supports / provides:
  • Two independent watchdogs with different clock sources controlled by the processor. They reset the SCPU if not refreshed correctly.
  • Two external shared memories ('External Shared Memory' and 'External Shared Memory 2')
  • Additional safety techniques and diagnosis for a IEC-61508 SIL3 (HFT = 1 and DC >= 90%), e.g., Power Failure Monitor (PFM)
  • A heterogeneous multicore processor
  • The multicore processor meets IEC-61508-2 Annex E in order to claim HFT=1. (Note: If the (COTS) multicore processore would not meet IEC-61508-2 Annex E, the core dedicated to safety partitions should be and independent processor within the same node)

– The processor supports / provides:
  • The processor is quad-core, two 'LEON3 FT' cores and two 'x86' cores (diverse). 'LEON3 FT' and x86 cores are connected via PCIe gateway to AHB bus
  • Each 'LEON3 FT' core has internal L1 memory, not shared ('LS MEM'). An AHB bus connects 'LEON3 FT' cores and an external shared memory ('External Shared Memory')
  • Each 'x86' core has internal L1 cache memory. All 'x86' cores share an L2 memory cache and an external shared memory ('External Shared Memory 2')
  • The processor has an internal synchronization hardware that generates a periodic interrupt of configurable period to all cores.

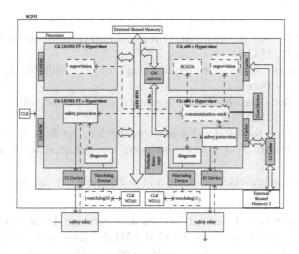

Fig. 5. Safety concept (1oo2), multicore and shared resources [32,33]

A certifiable hypervisor according to Section 5.4 supports the processor and the configuration of the hypervisor ensures that:

– 'Safety Protection' partitions control associated safety relays (command digital output and confirm state with digital input) and performs reciprocal comparison of results by software
– 'Diagnosis' partitions perform checks of the cores and possibly of I/Os in case they are not dedicated (exclusive access) to other partitions, using reciprocal comparison of results by software and control associated watchdog. Diagnosis partitions also manage health monitoring diagnosis information.
– The 'communication stack' partition manages the EtherCAT communication bus
– Inter-partition communication is supported by the hypervisor using shared communication buses (e.g., PCIe¡-¿AHB) and external shared memories.

- The system configuration is static and defined during the design stage: e.g., the allocation of 'partitions' and 'system partitions' to the platform; the configuration of 'partitions', 'system partitions' and 'hypervisor'; the scheduling of partitions and resources.

5.3 Safety Techniques

The safety concept [34] includes a detailed selection and analysis of safety techniques. This section summarizes most relevant safety techniques used to support the safety-concept.

Measures to Reduce the Probability of Systematic Faults: The usage of a Functional Safety Management (FSM) compliant with IEC-61508 and required SIL level:

- The overall system is conceived, developed and certified using a SIL3 FSM compliant with IEC-61508
- The hypervisor meets the requirements of a certifiable hypervisor as described in section 5.4
- Safety partitions are conceived, developed and certified using a SIL3 FSM compliant with IEC-61508
- Tools associated to the development, validation, verification, configuration and parametrization of safety partitions are qualified tools according to IEC-61508-3
- The system configuration is static and defined during the design stage

FMEAs, Measures to Control Errors and System Reaction to Errors: The safety concept [34] includes detailed FMEAs, measures to control errors, error reaction definitions and it is complemented with a detailed assessment of the platform. The overall diagnosis is based on the diagnosis strategy described in Section 5.5.

Spatial independence was positively assessed. However, it was concluded that temporal characteristics of partitions could be influenced by different loads scenarios in other partitions due to shared resources. For example:

- Shared memory: 'x86' cores use shared-memory and 'LEON3 FT' cores use shared memory for inter-partition communication. Maximum temporal interference suffered by a partition is estimated and measured
- Shared cache: Atom processor (dual core 'x86') does not support temporal interference freeness in shared cache, the maximum temporal interference suffered by a partition is measured
- Interrupts: Some interrupts in the Atom processor cannot be rerouted and this can influence the timing behaviour of the hypervisor, the maximum temporal interference suffered by a partition is measured

- Communication channel: Complete decoupling of sender and receiver partitions connected with a communication channel require temporal independence

Different solutions are defined in order to avoid and control failures due to previously described temporal interferences.

- Example fault avoidance techniques:
  - Shared-resources: 'Safety protection' and 'diagnosis' partition Worst-Case Execution Time (WCET) are measured for each core type ('x86' and 'LEON3 FT'). Both partitions are scheduled at the beginning of each periodic cycle with a pre-assigned timeslot bigger than the maximum estimated execution time, which considers both the WCET and maximum estimated time interference due to shared resources.
  - Interrupts: All unused interrupts are routed to 'diagnosis' or health monitoring
  - Communication channel: The communication among 'safety protection' and 'diagnosis' partitions in different cores is delayed one execution cycle, which it is considered sufficient to diminish temporal interferences due to shared resources.
- Example fault control techniques:
  - Shared-resources: Safety partitions are executed in two diverse cores ('x86' and 'LEON3 FT') with different hypervisor configuration. Each 'diagnosis' partition refreshes an independent watchdog if monitored-time constraints are met.
  - Interrupts: 'Diagnosis' partition traps unused interrupts and decides whether to refresh an independent watchdog based on the severity of the error
  - Communication channel: Safety partitions monitor communication channel time-outs.

5.4 Hypervisor Compliant Item

The strategy [32, 33] assumes that the hypervisor ported to the given platform is provided as a single certified compliant item according to IEC-61508. The safety manual should state that the compliant item provides the techniques and properties described in Table 2.

5.5 Diagnosis Strategy

In order to manage the complexity management arising from the safe integration of multiple mixed-criticality partitions, the diagnosis strategy defined in [32, 33] was taking into consideration:

- The partition should be self contained and should provide safety life-cycle related techniques (e.g., IEC-61508-3 Table A.4 defensive programming) and platform independent diagnosis (e.g., IEC-61508-2 Table A.7 input comparison voting) abstracted from the details of the underlying platform

Table 2. Selected safety techniques and functions of an hypervisor compliant item [32,33]

Safety technique / function	Description
Startup and initialization	The hypervisor must start up and initialize in a known and repeatable state within a bounded and known time.
Configuration	A hypervisor needs to be configured with the guest environment state before a guest environment can be run
Spatial independence	To prevent one partition from overwriting data in another partition, or a memory address not explicitly assigned to this partition
Temporal independence	To ensure that a partition has sufficient processing time to complete its execution
Exclusive access to peripherals	Protect access to peripherals used by safety a safety partition
Virtualization of resources	Provide a virtual environment in a safe, transparent and efficient way. The main components to be virtualized are processor core(s), memory and I/O devices
Hypervisor Execution Integrity	The hypervisor execution should be isolated and protected against software faults.
Health monitoring	To control random and systematic failures of the system in software based measures. Diagnostic measures for safety techniques / functions, such as: exclusive access to peripherals, spatial and temporal independence, configuration integrity, soft-error detection of the hypervisor program and data memories. To control random and systematic failures of the platform (e.g., hardware) using the hypervisor privileged mode
Time Synchronization	Fault-tolerant time synchronization that provides a 'global notion of time' to the hypervisor partition scheduler
Inter-partition communication	The hypervisor must provide mechanism(s) to support safe data exchange between two or more partitions.
Shutdown	A non critical partition shutdown should not affect a critical partition

- The hardware provides autonomous diagnosis (e.g., IEC-61508-2 Table A.9 Power Failure Monitor (PFM)) and diagnosis components to be commanded by software (e.g., IEC-61508-2 Table A.10 watchdog)
- The hypervisor and associated diagnosis partitions should support platform related diagnosis (e.g., IEC-61508-2 Table A.5 signature of a double word)
- The system architect specifies and integrates additional diagnosis partitions required to develop a safe product taking into consideration all safety manuals

6   Conclusion and Future Work

While mixed-criticality paradigm based on multicore and partitioning provides multiple potential benefits, it is clear that the safety certification of such systems based on COTS multiprocessors not designed for safety is a challenge. This paper has contributed with a safety concept for a fail-safe wind turbine mixed-criticality control system based on multicore partitioning.

IEC-61508 based safety critical embedded systems must be developed with a safety life-cycle that aims to reduce the probability of systematic errors and ensure that sufficient fault avoidance and fault control techniques are implemented. Regarding temporal independence, this means that independence needs to be systematically guaranteed (or give safe worst case bounds) and diagnosis techniques must be used to detect temporal independence violations (e.g., watchdog , logic execution, etc.). If unexpected violation occurs, diagnosis should lead the system to safe state . Therefore, the lack of complete temporal isolation (due to temporal interference) would reduce the availability of the system but should not jeopardize safety.

The assumptions and analysis considered at this stage will be reviewed in the following design stages and validated at the final stage of the case-study.

Acknowledgments. This work has been supported in part by the European projects FP7 MultiPARTES and FP7 DREAMS under project No. 287702 and No. 610640 respectively and the national INNPACTO project VALMOD under grant number IPT-2011-1149-370000. Any opinions, findings and conclusions expressed in this article are those of the authors and do not necessarily reflect the views of funding agencies.

References

1. RTCA DO-297 integrated modular avionics (IMA) development guidance and certification considerations (2005)
2. Mixed criticality systems. Tech. rep., European Comission, February 3, 2012
3. MULCORS - use of multicore processors in airborne systems (research project easa.2011/6). Tech. rep., EASA, December 16, 2012
4. 2013 - embedded market study. Tech. rep., UBM Tech (2013)
5. Abella, J., Cazorla, F.J., Quinones, E., Grasset, A., Yehia, S., Bonnot, P., Gizopoulos, D., Mariani, R., Bernat, G.: Towards improved survivability in safety-critical systems. In: IEEE 17th International On-Line Testing Symposium (IOLTS), pp. 240–245 (2011)
6. Balacco, S., Rommel, C.: Next generation embedded hardware architectures: Driving onset of project delays, costs overruns and software development challenges. Tech. rep., Klockwork, Inc. September 2010
7. Buttle, D.: Real-time in the prime-time - ecrts keynote talk. In: Report, ETAS Gmbh (2012)
8. Corbier, F., Kislin, L., Forgeau, E.: How train transportation design challenges can be addressed with simulation based virtual prototyping for distributed systems. In: 3rd European Congress ERTS - Embedded Real-Time Software (2006)
9. Crespo, A., Ripoll, I., Masmano, M.: Partitioned embedded architecture based on hypervisor: the XtratuM approach. In: European Dependable Computing Conference (EDCC), pp. 67–72 (2010)
10. EASA: Development assurance of airborne electronic hardware (2011)
11. EASA: Certification memorandum - software aspects of certification - easa. Tech. rep. March 9, 2013
12. Ernst, R.: Certification of trusted MPSoC platforms. In: MPSoC Forum (2010)
13. ERRAC: Joint strategy for european rail research. Report, The European Rail Research Advisory Council (2001)
14. Fisher, S.: Certifying applications in a multi-core environment: a new approach gains success. Tech. rep., SYSGO AG (2013)
15. Fuchsen, R.: How to address certification for multi-core based IMA platforms: Current status and potential solutions. In: IEEE/AIAA 29th Digital Avionics Systems Conference (DASC) (2010)

16. Galler, D., Slenski, G.: Causes of aircraft electrical failures. IEEE Aerospace and Electronic Systems Magazine **6**(8), 3–8 (1991)
17. Huyck, P.: ARINC 653 and multi-core microprocessors - considerations and potential impacts. In: IEEE/AIAA 31st Digital Avionics Systems Conference (DASC), pp. 6B41-6B47 (2012)
18. IEC: ISO 13849-1: Safety of machinery - safety-related parts of control systems (2002)
19. IEC: IEC 61508-1: Functional safety of electrical/electronic/programmable electronic safety-related systems - part 1: General requirements (2010)
20. IEC: IEC 61508-2: Functional safety of electrical/electronic/programmable electronic safety-related systems - part 2: Requirements for electrical / electronic / programmable electronic safety-related systems (2010)
21. IEC: IEC 61508-3: Functional safety of electrical/electronic/programmable electronic safety-related systems - part 3: Software requirements (2010)
22. Jean, X., Gatti, M., VBerthon, G., Fumey, M.: The use of multicore processors in airborne systems. Tech. rep., Thales Avionics (2011)
23. Kinnan, L.M.: Use of multicore processors in avionics and its potential impact on implementation and certification. SAE Technical Papers (2009)
24. Kirrmann, H., Zuber, P.A.: The iec/ieee communication network. IEEE Micro **21**(2), 81–92 (2001)
25. Kopetz, H.: The complexity challenge in embedded system design. In: 11th IEEE International Symposium on Object Oriented Real-Time Distributed Computing (ISORC), pp. 3–12 (2008)
26. Kopetz, H., Obermaisser, R., El Salloum, C., Huber, B.: Automotive software development for a multi-core system-on-a-chip. In: Fourth International Workshop on Software Engineering for Automotive Systems (ICSE Workshops SEAS), pp. 2–9 (2007)
27. Kotaba, O., Nowotsch, J., Paulitsch, M., Petters, S.M., Theilingx, H.: Multicore in real-time systems - temporal isolation challenges due to shared resources. In: Workshop on Industry-Driven Approaches for Cost-effective Certification of Safety-Critical, Mixed-Criticality Systems (WICERT) (2013)
28. Leohold, J., Schmidt, C.: Communication requirements for automotive systems. In: 5th IEEE Workshop in Factory Communication Systems (WCFS) (2004)
29. Mollison, M.S., Erickson, J.P., Anderson, J.H., Baruah, S.K., Scoredos, J.A.: Mixed-criticality real-time scheduling for multicore systems (2010)
30. Nevalainen, R., Slotosch, O., Truscan, D., Kremer, U., Wong, V.: Impact of multicore platforms in hardware and software certification. In: Workshop on Industry-Driven Approaches for Cost-effective Certification of Safety-Critical, Mixed-Criticality Systems (WICERT) (2013)
31. Nowotsch, J., Paulitsch, M.: Leveraging multi-core computing architectures in avionics. In: 2012 Ninth European Dependable Computing Conference (EDCC), pp. 132–143 (2012)
32. Perez, J., Gonzalez, D., Nicolas, C.F., Trapman, T., Garate, J.M.: A safety certification strategy for iec-61508 compliant industrial mixed-criticality systems based on multicore partitioning. In: 17th Euromicro Conference on Digital Systems Design (DSD), Verona, Italy (2014)
33. Perez, J., Gonzalez, D., Nicolas, C.F., Trapman, T., Garate, J.M.: A safety concept for a wind power mixed-criticality embedded system based on multicore partitioning. In: 11th International Symposium - Functional Safety in Industrial Applications (TÜV Rheinland), Cologne, Germany (2014)

34. Perez, J., Trapman, A.: Deliverable d7.2 (annex) - wind power case-study safety concept - v03.00 (fp7 multipartes). Report (2014)
35. Sullivan, S., Slenski, G.: Managing electrical connection systems and wire integrity on legacy aerospace vehicles (2001)
36. Salloum, C.E., Elshuber, M., Hoftberger, O., Isakovic, H., Wasicek, A.: The ACROSS MPSoC - a new generation of multi-core processors designed for safety-critical embedded systems. In: 2012 15th Euromicro Conference on Digital System Design (DSD), pp. 105–113 (2012)
37. Schneider, J., Bohn, M., Röbger, R.: Migration of automotive real-time software to multicore systems: First steps towards an automated solution. In: 22nd EUROMICRO Conference on Real-Time Systems (2010)
38. Swingler, J., McBride, J.W.: The degradation of road tested automotive connectors. In: Forty-Fifth IEEE Holm Conference on Electrical Contacts, pp. 146–152 (1999)
39. Trujillo, S., Obermaisser, R., Gruettner, K., Cazorla, F., Perez, J.: European project cluster on mixed-criticality systems. In: Design, Automation and Test in Europe (DATE) Workshop 3PMCES (2014)

The Central On-Board Computer of the Philae Lander in the Context of the Rosetta Space Mission

A. Balázs[1] ([⊠]), A. Baksa[2], H. Bitterlich[3], I. Hernyes[1], O. Küchemann[5], Z. Pálos[1], J. Rustenbach[3], W. Schmidt[4], P. Spányi[1], J. Sulyán[2], S. Szalai[2], and L. Várhalmi[1]

[1] Wigner Research Centre for Physics, Budapest, Hungary
balazs.andras@wigner.mta.hu
[2] SGF Co. Ltd., Budapest, Hungary
szalai@sgf.hu
[3] Max-Planck Institute for Solar System Research (MPS), Göttingen, Germany
[4] Finnish Meteorological Institute (FMI), Helsinki, Finland
[5] Zentrum für Deutsche Luft- und Raumfahrt (DLR), Cologne, Germany

Abstract. The Rosetta-Philae space mission is an unprecedented venture. After a ten-year journey across the Solar System and many complicated manoeuvres, the Rosetta spacecraft smoothly approached a small (2-4 km in diameter) celestial body, comet CG/67P. Furthermore, the spacecraft executed additional fine manoeuvres to fly a multitude of low and high altitude orbits around the comet, mapping its shape and surface in detail never seen before, and has continued to observe it for a year since then. The Rosetta spacecraft is equipped with scientific instruments that deliver a wealth of new knowledge about the CG/67P comet, in addition to spectacular pictures. Delivering the Philae lander onto the surface of the comet 500 million km away from Earth was also a remarkable technological success. The direct measurements made by the Philae lander on the surface of the comet provided significant new knowledge. The first half of this paper gives a brief overview of the objectives and highlights of the Rosetta-Philae mission. In the second half the major hardware and software design aspects, including the conceptual design and implementation of the central on-board computer (CDMS) of the Philae lander are outlined. It focuses on the implementation of fault tolerance, autonomous operation and operational flexibility by means of specific linked data structures and code execution mechanisms that can be interpreted as a kind of object oriented model for mission sequencing.

Keywords: Critical embedded systems · Hybrid architectures · Fault tolerance · Object oriented model for mission sequencing · Operational flexibility

1 The Rosetta-Philae Mission

1.1 Mission Objectives

The Rosetta-Philae mission is a cornerstone project of the European Space Agency (ESA). It is of Europe-wide significance in terms of technological and research organisation, and of worldwide significance in scientific terms. Several short-term

© Springer International Publishing Switzerland 2015
J.A. de la Puente and T. Vardanega (Eds.): Ada-Europe 2015, LNCS 9111, pp. 18–30, 2015.
DOI: 10.1007/978-3-319-19584-1_2

close observations have delivered valuable data about other comets in recent years, typically via one-shot, high-speed fly-bys. The Rosetta-Philae mission is unique in many aspects, however, and has already provided much more information than previous missions. A comet is not a passive, dead chunk of matter. As it moves closer to the Sun in its Keplerian orbit, it becomes increasingly more active. Complex physical and chemical processes take place at an increasing rate in the comet's nucleus, on its surface, in the gas and dust atmosphere surrounding its nucleus, and in its coma and tail. As scientists interpret, analyse and evaluate the large amount of data gathered, old comet models may prove to be incorrect or need some upgrading. An explanation of the in-situ measurement results may call for the development of new methods and modelling approaches.

1.2   Rosetta's 10-year Flight in the Solar System to the Comet CG/67P

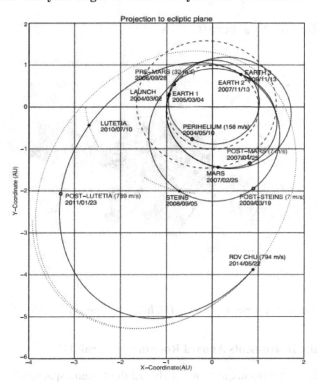

Fig. 1. Rosetta's journey to comet CG/67P. Image by courtesy of ESA [1].

Mission event	Date
Launch	2 March 2004
First Earth Gravity Assist	4 March 2005
Mars Gravity Assist	25 February 2007
Second Earth Gravity Assist	13 November 2007
Steins Flyby	5 September 2008

Third Earth Gravity Assist	13 November 2009
Lutetia Flyby	10 July 2010
Rendezvous Manoeuvre 1	23 January 2011
Start of Hibernation	July 2011
Hibernation Wake Up	January 2014
Rendezvous Manoeuvre 2	22 May 2014
Between 4.5 and 4.0 AU	
Start of Near-Nucleus	22 August 2014
Operations at 3.25 AU	
PHILAE Delivery	12 November 2014
Start of Comet Escort	16 November 2014
Perihelion Passage	August 2015
End of Nominal Mission	31 December 2015

2   The Rosetta Spacecraft

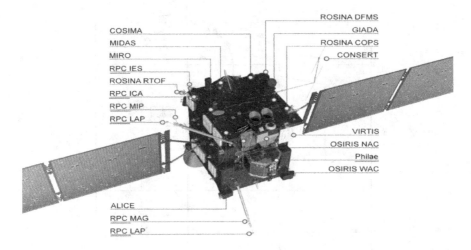

Fig. 2. The Rosetta spacecraft [1]. Image by courtesy of ESA [1].

2.1   Scientific Instruments Aboard Rosetta Spacecraft [1]

Eleven scientific experiments are carried aboard the Rosetta spacecraft: multicolour imaging equipment with narrow and wide angle cameras; UV spectroscope; IR spectroscope; a microwave spectroscope; neutral gas, ion mass spectroscope and gas pressure sensor; dust mass spectrometer; grain morphology with an atomic force microscope; radio sounding and nucleus tomography; dust velocity, impact and contamination monitor; plasma monitoring package, comprising Langmuir probe, ion and electron sensor, flux gate magnetometer, ion composition analyser, mutual impedance probe and plasma interface unit; radio science experiment.

3   The Philae Lander, a Scientific Mini-Laboratory

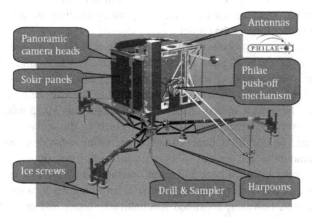

Fig. 3. The Philae lander [2]. Image by courtesy of DLR [2].

Philae lander properties [2]:

Size: main structure 1.1×1.0×1.0 m3
Mass: 100 kg
Landing system: 3 unfoldable legs and anchoring system with 2 harpoons
Radio link: ~16 kbps
Primary battery: ~1300 Wh
Rechargeable battery: ~100 Wh
Solar array output: ~10-12 W at 3 AU

3.1   Scientific Instruments and Subsystems Aboard Philae Lander [2]

The Philae comet science operations were partitioned into three mission phases: Separation-Descent-Landing (SDL), First Comet Science Sequences (FSS) and Long Terms Science operations (LTS).

The Philae lander carries ten scientific instruments: panoramic, stereoscopic and descent camera; α-p-x-ray spectrometer; evolved gas analyser for elemental, molecular and isotopic composition; infrared microscope; comet acoustic surface and sounding experiment; permittivity probe; dust impact monitor; multi-purpose sensor for surface and sub-surface science; magnetometer; plasma monitor; comet nucleus sounding experiment; drill and sample distribution system.

The Philae subsystems are as follows: central on-board computer (dual modular, in some parts triple redundant), power distribution subsystem (in some parts dual redundant); thermal control (dual redundant); landing gear; fly-wheel; anchoring (dual redundant); active descent subsystem; radio telecommunication (dual redundant) units.

3.2   Landing on Comet CG/67P

Comet CG/67P turned out to have an astonishingly irregular shape and a large variety of surface patterns. Although the scientific objectives were the major driver in the

Philae landing site selection process, the flight dynamics requirements of the Rosetta spacecraft and the comet's thermal and solar illumination conditions also had to be taken into account. The location chosen as the primary landing site for Philae was on the top of the smaller lobe of the comet.

The Philae separation process was initiated in an accurately pre-calculated lander delivery flight track of the Rosetta spacecraft at distance of 22.5 km from the comet, with a push-off velocity of 0.17 m/s. Philae then entered a ballistic descent phase for ~7 hours. The lander hit the comet at the target landing site with an accuracy of a few tens of metres. The impact velocity relative to the comet was ~0.35 m/s. Upon touching down, however, the lander could not attach itself to the comet due to an unexpected systematic failure in the dual redundant anchoring subsystem and a fatal error in the non-redundant active descent subsystem. Instead of staying at the initial touchdown site, the lander bounced back and made one big and two further smaller bounces over the surface before finally coming to rest at an unknown location on the rocky terrain. The lander, however, remained mechanically intact and proved to be functional even during the triple bouncing period, keeping radio contact alive with the Rosetta spacecraft. Afterwards, the lander was able to start its science programme on the comet. In order to cope with the unexpected situation and to obtain as many scientific results as possible, the nominal sequence of comet operations had to be largely - and quickly - reshuffled by assessing risks and goals, and giving first priority to the less risky investigations before scheduling those that required mechanical movements. During the radio visibility periods, Philae autonomously reported all of the data measured by the scheduled experiments. The probe's primary energy sources delivered energy for doing science on the surface for roughly 50 hours.

Philae happened to finally land in a somewhat unfortunate orientation, and some of its solar panels seem to be partially shadowed by nearby obstacles. Consequently, the solar panels are illuminated for a shorter period than anticipated, and do not provide sufficient power for charging the battery. However, hope is not lost that Philae may return to life in the coming months when the comet approaches the Sun.

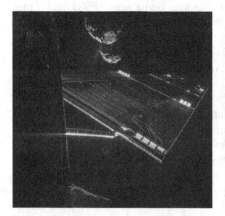 

Fig. 4. Comet CG/67P 500 million km from Earth, 18 km from the Rosetta spacecraft in the field of view of the CIVA panorama camera aboard Philae still aboard Rosetta (left), and by the Rosetta navigation camera

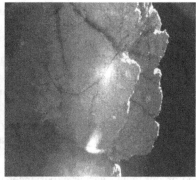

Fig. 5. Surroundings of the Philae lander after landing on the comet. One of the feet of Philae is seen on the left-side image. Images taken by the CIVA panorama camera.

4   The Central On-Board Computer of Philae

4.1   Basic Technical and Operational Requirements

The starting times and duration of the radio visibility time-windows for the Rosetta spacecraft to establish a radio link with the Philae lander depended on numerous circumstances and factors, such as the executed flight track of the Rosetta spacecraft, the 12.6 hours rotation period of the comet, the landing site, and the orientation of Philae on the comet. Although these time-windows were nominally calculable, Philae had to be prepared also for the worst-case, if there was any deviation from the predictions.

The amount of available energy in the primary and in the rechargeable batteries and the produced solar power to perform all anticipated science programmes was very limited (especially far from the Sun), thus the periods of falling back into stand-by mode and waiting for operator instructions had to be minimized.

4.2   Operating System and Application Tasks

The Rosetta mission imposed very strict requirements on the flight hardware. The electronic components had to withstand a high radiation dose during the more than 10- year flight and had to operate within a wide temperature range and with low power consumption.

In order to meet these expectations, the central on-board computer (CDMS) was built around a microprocessor type, which has a long track record in space. The RTX2010, manufactured by Harris Semiconductor at that time, although was not a new and fast processor, but it had been especially designed for embedded control tasks in military and aerospace applications. It is a radiation-hardened stack machine processor that implements the Forth programming environment in hardware.

The software had to meet the following low-level requirements (these do not cover the actual functionality described later).

- Real-time behaviour: Low granularity in task switching and predictable response times to external events, especially in critical mission phases (e.g. at comet touchdown).
- Flexibility, reprogrammability: This criterion is self evident if we consider the 10 year flight time. The software was not fully ready at launch, and had been updated several times during the mission.
- Fault tolerance: See below.
- Small memory footprint: 16 kBytes PROM for compressed bootstrap; 4*64 kBytes RAM for code, data and variables; 4*64 Kbytes EEPROM for code and tables.

Based on our team's earlier experiences with similar projects, we decided to develop a purpose-built proprietary operating system from scratch, for the following reasons:

- Full control of design allowed us to utilize the unique features of the RTX2010 processor. The whole onboard software was written in Forth, the native language of the processor. Forth results a rather compact code which is easy to modify during runtime by patching.
- The proprietary hardware required special drivers for the interfaces to the instruments, the communication links, the background data memory (Mass Memory) and the onboard clock.
- Due to the memory limitation, only features and services essential for our purposes were implemented. Consequently, the entire operating system occupied not more ~4.5 kBytes.

The operating system provides pre-emptive multitasking scheduling, ensuring that no task can hold the CPU resources longer than a fixed time period defined by the real-time clock tick. The stack-oriented Forth system uses two stacks: a Data and a Return stack. These are integrated in the RTX2010 processor (each having the size of 256 words), and optionally can be split in multiple independent pieces, to support multitasking. This feature is also utilized: 8 tasks can run in parallel with two priority levels. Stack overflow or underflow events are handled in interrupt routines and so do not lead to memory corruption. To further reduce the danger of memory overwriting, dynamic memory allocation is not used. The operating system API is implemented via software interrupt system calls, which provide I/O device reservation, read/write, task management, onboard time setting, etc.

The application program is divided into tasks, and the distribution of the application-level functions among the tasks is static. Each task has a special role, and the most important tasks are.

- TC/TM: Telecommunication link establishment and maintenance with the Rosetta orbiter
- EXP: Experiment control, commanding and telemetry data collection from the Philae instruments and subsystems
- AMST: Autonomous operational sequencing of the Philae instruments
- PWTH: Power and thermal control of the Philae lander
- ADS: Active Descent System for anchoring and touch-down control
- RDM: Self-diagnostics and redundancy management of functional subunits

4.3   Fault Tolerance, Challenge and Related Dilemmas

Common sense tells us that the simpler a system is (i.e. the less components it is composed of), the more reliable it is. However, redundant components (and/or modules, in modular redundant systems) along with all the critical decision mechanisms for selecting functionally intact modules make the system more complex. This seems to challenge the usefulness of redundant systems. On the other hand, it is well known that "anything that can go wrong will go wrong". Thus these apparently self-evident statements are mutually contradictory. It is a contradiction which needs to be resolved in practice, especially in critical systems in extremely expensive and mostly unrepeatable space missions.

Theory vs. Reality. Further questions and dilemmas arise in the practical implementation of theoretically optimum-solutions. These include considerations like environmental conditions, mass-, volume-, harnessing- and power consumption limitations, parameters of available components (e.g. radiation hardened components), costs of hardware/software development, implementation, manufacturing, functional validation and system integration. The definition of fault-containment regions [4] within a complex system (e.g. Philae lander) is also an important step in preparing the design concept.

Fault tolerance expectations need to be formulated in a way that they do not lead to unrealistic system complexity. Protection is therefore primarily restricted to single point failure, in other words, no single failure at any point should lead to functional degradation of the entire system. Depending on the hardware architecture and software support, multiple errors may lead to either partial degradation or – in the worst case – complete loss of the system. A further typical problem to be prevented in modular redundant systems is the negative – and, potentially fatal – impact of systematic design errors. This can be achieved through design diversity [4] involving different hardware and/or software in redundant modules.

The potential benefits of N-version programming are suggested by Philae's failure to attach itself to the comet upon the first touchdown. This was due to a systematic hardware and/or software design error in the double redundant anchoring subsystem. An improved software process for anchoring control had been uplinked into the flight software after some hardware problems came to light in the anchoring subsystem of the Philae flight model. The improvement was identical for both channels/modules of the redundant subsystem. A better approach would have been to tackle the software control process in the two channels/modules differently, so that one of them might have had a better chance of doing the job. Fortunately, the flexible software mechanisms implemented in the on-board software (see below) may yet provide an opportunity to make a further attempt at shooting Philae's harpoons.

In order to make a system fault tolerant, hardware structures (modules and architecture) and particularly specific software mechanisms need to be implemented to support fault recognition, isolation and system recovery. The first key-consideration here is the method of fault recognition and follow-on decision mechanisms: Whether to disallow any interruption in the operation, or to tolerate short interruptions followed by a system-level recovery at atomic (machine instruction), application task or some higher level of operational context.

The simplest - and poorest - choice for fault tolerant architecture would have been a dual modular redundant system with an external human decision scheme. In case of a failure, this would activate a spare counterpart via high-priority (hardware decoded) telecommanding after behaviour evaluation of off-line data.

Another option might have been the implementation of a triple modular redundant [4] (TMR, fault masking structural redundancy) system with robust majority voting schemes at the actuators. Such systems can be built either with synchronously running processor units and distributed local code/data memories, or asynchronously running processor units with local access to code and shared access to triple redundant data memories. The complexity and hardware demand of such a system architecture is so high, however, that this idea had to be rejected for technical reasons (mass, volume, harness, power consumption, etc.).

If a limited region of a complex system, in particular the intelligent core (the processing unit; fault tolerant multi processor, FTMP) of a system can be built to be fault tolerant with self-repairing capabilities, the extension of fault tolerance towards the entire system may be simply the question of "intention". Intention here means the availability of time, development and validation costs of introducing additional software to improve the fault-tolerance of the entire system. This can be performed by implementing specific software measures and techniques, self-diagnostics routines, algorithms and tricks, context data integrity and code consistency checking techniques, etc. The rest of the system (functional subunits, modules, interfaces) does not necessarily need to be provided with self-repairing capabilities, especially where there are no severe real-time requirements to be met (e.g. if dynamic recovery is allowed). The self-repairing fault tolerant and intelligent core can reliably test, select and finally activate any other intact functional subunit, provided it has its embedded spare counterpart. This concept was the basic design guideline for the central on board computer of Philae.

Central on-board computer of the Philae lander as a fault-tolerant subsystem. The severe technical constraints left no other realistic choice other than hybrid hardware architectural design in the on-board computer along with activity sharing between hardware and software (software supported fault tolerance). Some functional subunits are triple modular redundant (e.g. high priority hardware telecommand decoders and on-board timers at FPGA level are protected against single event upset (SEU) due to radiation in space), some others are dual hot redundant (e.g. processors equipped with Hamming-code protected memories against SEU, on-board timers at unit level, internal serial communication interfaces and units), others are dual cold redundant (e.g. Mass Memory for collected science data; RX/TX radio communication units).

A simple, distributed (triple redundant) hardware logic decides on the current role (primary vs. secondary) of the two identical (dual hot redundant) processor units (DPUs). Both can access and control any other functional subunits, and a serial bidirectional cross-link is established between the two DPUs to keep them in sync.

Both DPUs constantly control the Philae lander, but only the current primary one has effective control. The current secondary DPU can take over the primary role at any time. Role-change and follow-on recovery take place at the level of Elementary Sequencing Items (see below).

A hardware-software watch-dog technique and numerous specific regularly-running self-diagnostic software mechanisms have been implemented to support fault recognition in the local DPU, in the on-board computer, and at all points where it is specifically required, even at the level of the Philae lander. There were also many smart ideas to tackle problematic areas and provide fault tolerance. For example, simply checking a single hardware status signal to determine whether the actively powered RX receiver unit is fully functional is a vulnerable method in terms of fault tolerance. A much more effective approach is to use an algorithm which checks the presence of protocol control and/or data patterns in the received signal, regardless of what the questionable hardware status signal says. Numerous such creative ideas have been implemented in the on-board computer of Philae.

An absolute fall-back measure to handle unexpected emergency situations is a top mechanism involving the triple hot-redundant high-priority hardware telecommand decoders. This provides a means of human intervention to override the internal autonomy and isolate failed modules.

4.4   Autonomous Operation and Operational Flexibility - an Object Oriented Scheme of Mission Sequencing

A three-level scheme has been developed to facilitate autonomous operation and sequencing of measurements, execute system level nominal activities, handle off-nominal cases and provide a high degree of operational flexibility. In order to fit these requirements to the embedded nature of the on-board computer, we defined specific linked data structures and code execution mechanisms. These can be interpreted as a kind of object oriented model for mission sequencing.

- 1st level: Construction of *Elementary Sequencing Items* (ESIs, instances of a specific class stored in CDMS memory) with their
  - Individual attributes and member variables, e.g. active lander units to power on, selectable power converters, unit priorities, data collection rates, data quotas, and also a pointer attribute to the list of relative time-tagged telecommands (TCs) to be executed in conjunction with this ESI. Further attributes define the conditions under which a particular ESI should be deactivated (e.g. terminated upon time-out or/and occurrence of nominal vs. off-nominal events) and the means of carrying on the sequencing (e.g. step to the next ESI, conditional vs. unconditional jump to another ESI),
  - Nominal and off-nominal event handler routines,
  - Common - either "instance" or "static", in Java terminology - methods (e.g. housekeeping and science data collection methods, system relevant nominal activities to perform). The behaviour of methods depends on the individual attributes and member variables of a particular object. *A special feature* is

provided by a set of stored commands, so called *method constructor TC primitives* to the processor. This feature allows for adding new methods to the existing ones during run-time, even during flight (*in-flight methods*), and as such it fits well to the embedded nature of the on-board computer and can provide a high degree of operational flexibility (see below).

- 2nd level: Construction of *Mission Sequencing Objects* (MSOs, instances of another class stored in CDMS memory), as - mostly, but not necessarily - series of Elementary Sequencing Items (ESIs).
- 3rd level: Construction of a *Timeline*. A timeline is composed of parallel-running Mission Sequencing Objects. In practice, we need to differentiate as-planned from as-run timelines. The finally executed as-run timeline is not necessarily a priori predictable; it may change due to nominal-, off-nominal event terminated ESIs and/or condition dependent branching in MSOs, or on the initiation of individual methods of ESIs.

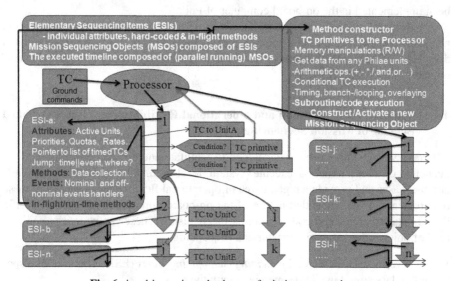

Fig. 6. An object oriented scheme of mission sequencing

The Elementary Sequencing Items, the Mission Sequencing Objects, and the list and contents of relative time-tagged commands - including method constructor TC primitives to the processor - are all changeable, and are pre-stored in the EEPROM memory of the on-board computer by means of structured tables linked together by appropriate pointers. The zero reference time of the relative time-tagged commands attached to a particular Elementary Sequencing Item is the moment of its activation.

The list of relative time-tagged TCs may contain commands both to the Philae lander units (instruments and subsystems) and to the processor unit itself. This latter one is the point where in-flight methods can be introduced in any particular Elementary Sequencing Item in practice, during run-time at any points of the running sequences. A specific set of method constructor TC primitives has been defined to realize such in-flight methods, e.g. providing functions for memory read/write, obtaining data from any Philae unit, executing arithmetic operations on local variables (+, -, *, /, and, or), condition checking and conditional TC execution, timing, branching, looping, code overlaying to make more effective use of the limited code memory space, subroutine execution and constructing/activating a new Mission Sequencing Object. The relative time-tagged TCs for subroutine execution accommodate executable machine code with an integrity checking mechanism.

The object oriented data structures and in-flight methods are not inherent parts of the hard-coded on-board core software. They can at any time be uplinked as stand-alone telecommands. In order not to lose them upon temporary power losses (see below, LTS survival mode), they are stored in reprogrammable EEPROM memory.

The implemented scheme has provided a high degree of flexibility in terms of operational reorganization, rescheduling and running parallel sequences upon either ground commands, or unexpected on-board events and time-outs, both in the software development phase and - if necessary - even after landing on the comet, so that an optimized behaviour can be adapted to the in-situ operational and environmental conditions.

Note that some of the memory manipulator functions of the method constructor TC primitives can also be used as classic code patching tools.

4.5   Philae-Specific Jobs of the Central On-Board Computer

The on-board computer performs some additional tasks specific to controlling Philae, such as

- Support of inter-instrument communication
- Real-time control of anchoring and ADS subsystems upon touching-down on the comet
- Autonomous battery operations control and power flow management, in particular during the Long Term Science (LTS) operational phase on the comet. This involves a specific LTS survival mode for in-situ solar power calculations and optimized power flow control in a closed loop, thermal and re-charging control of the secondary battery, and controlled Philae system shut-down upon Sun-set on the comet.

References

1. Glassmeier, K.H., Boehnhardt, H., Koschny, D., Kührt, E., Richter, I.: Rosetta Mission: Flying towards the origin of the Solar System. Space Science Reviews **128**, 1–21 (2007). doi:10.1007/s11214-006-9140-8
2. Ulamec, S., Balazs, A., Debus, A., Espinasse, S., Feuerbacher, B., Gaudon, P., Maibaum, M., Paetz, B., Roll, R., Szalai, S., Szemerey, I., Willnecker, R.: Rosetta Lander Philae: System overview. Space Science Reviews **128** (2007)
3. Bibring, J.-P., Rosenbauer, H., Boehnhardt, H., Ulamec, S., Balazs, A., Biele, J., et al.: Space Science Reviews **128**, 1–21 (2007). DOI: 10.1007/s11214-006-913-8-2.0
4. Web-link. http://www.cs.ucla.edu/~rennels/article98.pdf

5. Baksa, A., Balázs, A., Pálos, Z., Szalai, S., Várhalmi, L.: Embedded computer system on the rosetta lander, DASIA 2003 data systems. In: Aerospace, SP-532, Prague, pp. 250–256, 2–6 June 2000
6. Szalai, S., Balazs, A., Baksa, A., Tróznai, G.: Rosetta Lander Software Simulator, 57th International Astronautical Congress, Valencia, Spain, (on DVD of 57 IAC) (2006)
7. Balazs, A., Biro, J., Szalai, S.: Transputer based onboard computer; Workshop on Computer Vision for Space Applications, Antibes, France, 22–24 September 1994. ISBN: 2-7261-0811; C-151
8. Balázs, A., Szalai, S., Várhalmi, L.: A multipurpose computer for Mars space missions, Fifth IAESTED Int. Conf. Reliability and quality control, Lugano, pp. 132–143 (1989)
9. Balázs, A., Biró, J., Hernyes, I., Horváth, I., Szalai, S., Grintchenko, A., Kachirine, V., Kozlov, G., Medvedev, S., Michkiniouk, V., Marechal, L.: Locomotion system of the IARES demonstrator for planetary exploration. Space Technology **17**(3/4), 173–182 (1997)

Language Technology

Extensible Debugger Framework
for Extensible Languages

Domenik Pavletic[1]([⊠]), Markus Voelter[2], Syed Aoun Raza[1],
Bernd Kolb[1], and Timo Kehrer[3]

[1] Itemis, Markus-Schleicher-Str. 20, Stuttgart 70565, Germany
{pavletic,raza,kolb}@itemis.de
[2] Independent/Itemis, Stuttgart, Germany
voelter@acm.org
[3] University of Siegen, Siegen, Germany
kehrer@informatik.uni-siegen.de

Abstract. Language extension enables integration of new language constructs without invasive changes to a base language (e. g., C). Such extensions help to build more reliable software by using proper domain-specific abstractions. Language workbenches significantly reduce the effort for building such extensible languages by synthesizing a fully-fledged IDE from language definitions. However, in contemporary tools, this synthesis does not include interactive debugging for programs written with the base language or its extensions. This paper describes a generic framework for extensible debuggers that enables debugging of the language extensions by defining mappings between the base language and the language extensions. The architecture is designed for extensibility, so debug support for future extensions can be contributed with little effort. We show an implementation of our approach for mbeddr, which is an extensible version of the C programming language. We also discuss the debugger implementation for non-trivial C extensions such as components. Finally, the paper discusses the extent to which the approach can be used with other base languages, debugger backends and language workbenches.

Keywords: Debugging · Domain-specific languages · Frameworks

1 Introduction

A program *source* is a description of the program *behavior*. Source and behavior are different: first, the source describes all dynamic execution behaviors of a program as a *static* structure. Second, the source considers all possible sets of input data. However, program execution always happens for a specific set of input values. Debugging helps programmers to *inspect* and *animate* the dynamic behavior of a program for a *specific set* of input values.

The way this is done depends on the language paradigm. Imperative languages, the focus of this work, use the step-through approach. Thus, users single-step through instructions and observe changes to the program state.

Programming languages such as C, Java or Python contain a *fixed* set of language construct and cannot easily be extended. The debuggers for such languages

© Springer International Publishing Switzerland 2015
J.A. de la Puente and T. Vardanega (Eds.): Ada-Europe 2015, LNCS 9111, pp. 33–49, 2015.
DOI:10.1007/978-3-319-19584-1_3

can be hand-crafted specifically for the constructs provided by the language. In contrast, modern language engineering allows the development of *extensible* languages [15,16]. This allows users to add new constructs to a language in an incremental and modular way. These languages are used to describe solutions for technical or domain-specific problems on a higher level of abstraction. This approach supports domain-specific validation and verification of developed system at the same abstraction level as the problem. Thus it delivers improvements in reliability.

The concepts (structure definition) introduced by a language extension are translated to semantically equivalent base language code before compilation. For example, a `foreach` statement that supports iterating over a C array without manually managing the counter variable. This statement would be translated back to a regular C `for` statement. The transformation generates the code that manages the counter (see our example in Section 3).

To make debugging extensible languages useful to the language user, it is not enough to debug programs *after* extensions have been translated back to the base language (using an existing debugger for the base language). A debugger for an extensible language must be extensible as well, to support debugging of modular language extensions *at the extension-level.* Minimally, this means that users can step through the constructs provided by the extension, and see watch expressions (debugger evaluated expressions on execution stop) related to the extensions. In the `foreach` example, the user would see the `foreach` statement in the source code. Furthermore, the generated counter variable would not be shown in the watch window.

In this paper, we contribute a framework for building debuggers for extensible, imperative languages based on the ideas published in [11]. With this framework, each language extension is debugged at its particular abstraction level. We illustrate the approach with an implementation that supports single-thread of control based on mbeddr [15], an extensible C build with the JetBrains Meta Programming System (MPS) [8]. For a non-trivial C extension we show an example debugger extension. Further, we discuss whether and how the approach can be used with other extensible languages and language workbenches.

This paper is structured as follows: Section 2 provides an overview of the mbeddr technology stack which is the basis of our reference implementation. In Section 3, we introduce an example language extension for which we describe the debugger extension in Section 6. Section 4 lists the requirements for our extensible debugger and Section 5 describes the essential building blocks of the architecture. We validate our approach by discussing debuggers for non-trivial extensions of C in Section 7. In Section 8, we discuss the benefits, trade-offs and limitations of our approach. We then look at related work in Section 9 and conclude the paper with a summary and an outlook on future work in Section 10.

2   The mbeddr Technology Stack

mbeddr is an extensible version of C that can be extended with modular, domain-specific extensions. It is built on top of JetBrains MPS and ships with a set of language extensions dedicated to embedded software development. Several software projects have already used mbeddr extensively [14]. Amon those, a pacemaker has been in build in the safety-critical domain. In this section we discuss mbeddr briefly; details can be found in [15].

Fig. 1 shows how mbeddr is organized into layers. The foundation is MPS, which supports language definition. Its distinctive feature is its projectional editor, which unlike textual editors, does not rely on a parser. Instead, the visual notation is a *projection* of the Abstract Syntax Tree (AST). This means, every change performed by the user is *directly* reflected in the AST.

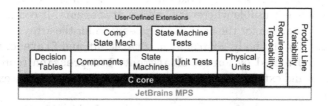

Fig. 1. An overview of the mbeddr stack

The second layer (C Core) provides an implementation of C99[7]. The next layers contain the default language extensions, generally useful for embedded software development. These include languages for specifying test cases, state machines, interfaces/components and decision tables.

3   Language Extension Examples

This section illustrates how to extend mbeddr with a `foreach` statement that allows programmers to iterate over arrays. The code below shows an example:

```
1   int8[] numbers = {1, 2, 3};
2   int32 sum = 0;
3   foreach (numbers sized 3) { sum += it; }
```

Defining a language or extension in MPS comprises the following steps: structure (syntax or meta model), the concrete syntax (editor definition in MPS), the type system (for defining and checking typing rules), a generator (for mapping extensions to the base language), various IDE features such as quick fixes or refactorings, and of course the debugger. This section only discusses aspects important for debugger definition. For a more detailed discussion of language extension we refer to [15]. The debugger extension itself is shown in Section 6.

A particularly important feature of MPS as a language workbench is its support for *modular* language extension, where an extension lives in its own language module. While such a module may depend on (and use concepts from) a base language, it cannot invasively change this base language.

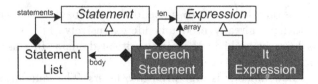

Fig. 2. UML class diagram showing the structure of the language extensions. Concepts from C are colored in white, others from `foreach` are dark grey.

In terms of structure, our `foreach` language consists of a `ForeachStatement` and an `ItExpression` (dark grey boxes in Fig. 2). `ForeachStatement` extends `Statement` to make it usable wherever C allows `Statements`. It consists of three children: an `Expression` for the array, an `Expression` for the array length, and a `StatementList` for the body. `Expression`, `Statement` and `StatementList` are defined in C and reused by `ForeachStatement`. `ItExpression` represents the current element and extends C's `Expression` to make it usable where expressions are expected.

The details on the transformation to C are described in [15]. For implementing the debugger extension in Section 6, it is important to understand the structure of the generated code. The code snippet below shows an example usage of `foreach` (left column) and the corresponding generated C code (right column).

```
1  int8 sum = 0;                              int8_t sum = 0;
2  int8[] sortedNumbers = {1, 2, 3};          int8_t[] sortedNumbers = {1, 2, 3};
3  foreach (sortedNumbers sized 3) {          for (int __c = 0; __c < 3; __c++) {
4                                                 int8_t __it = sortedNumbers[__c];
5      sum += it;                                 sum += __it;
6  }                                          }
```

4   Requirements on the Debugger

Debuggers for extensible languages should provide the same functionality as the corresponding base language debugger. This includes debug commands (stepping and breakpoints) and inspection of the program state (watches and call stack).

In general, the execution of a program is debugged by a base language debugger (e. g., `gdb` in case of C). To enable debugging on the abstraction level of extensions, a mapping must be implemented between the base language debugger and the program as represented on the extension-level. Fig. 3 illustrates the relationship and information flow between the extension and base-level debugging mechanism: stepping must be mapped from the extension-level to the base-level and the program state must be represented in terms of the extension-level. This methodology is also applicable to hierarchical language extensions.

MPS allows the composition of multiple independently developed language extensions in a single program [13]. mbeddr capitalizes on this feature. Hence, programs are typically a mix of code written in C and in several language extensions (the code snippet above uses concepts from C and the `ForeachLanguage`). A debugger for such a language workbench should provide the capability to

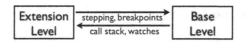

Fig. 3. Debugging interactions between extension- and base-level

debug mixed-language programs. Considering this, a debugger for extensible languages should support the following general requirements GR1 through GR3:

GR1 Modularity: Language extensions are modular, so debugger extensions must be modular as well. This means, to enable debugging for programs developed with a particular language extension, no changes to the base language must be necessary. Also, the debugger definitions for independently developed language extensions must be usable together in a single program.

GR2 Framework Genericity: In addition, implementing debug support for new language extensions must not require changes to the debugger framework or its interfaces (not just to other languages, as described in GR1).

GR3 Ease of Extensibility: Language workbenches make language development relatively simple. So, to make an extensible debuggers fit in, the development of debugger extensions must be comparatively simple as developing the language itself.

Depending upon the nature of the base language and its extensions, there can be additional requirements for a debugger. mbeddr addresses embedded software development, which leads to the specific requirements shown below. In other domains, these concerns may be useful as well, whereas for embedded software they are essential.

ER1 Limited Overhead: In embedded software, runtime overhead is always a concern. So the framework should limit the amount of additional debugger-specific code generated into the executable. Additional code increases the size of the binary, potentially preventing debugging on target devices with small amount of memory.

ER2 Debugger Backend Independence: Depending upon the target device vendor, embedded software projects use different C debuggers. Re-implemention of the debugger logic is cumbersome, hence debugger backend independence is crucial.

5   General Debugger Framework Architecture

The framework architecture can be separated into the specification aspect (Section 5.1) and the execution aspect (Section 5.2). The *specification* aspect declaratively describes the debug behavior of language concepts and enables modular extension of the debugger (GR1). The *execution* aspect implements the extensible debugger framework in a generic and reusable manner (GR2).

5.1   Specification Aspect

The debugger specification is based on a set of abstractions that can be split into four main areas: breakpoints, stepping, watches and stack frames (see Fig. 4). Debuggers are defined by mapping concepts from the base language and language extensions to these abstractions. To map a language concept to any of these abstractions, it implements one or more of these interfaces (other language workbenches may use other approaches [9]). To specify the concept-specific implementation behavior of the interfaces, mbeddr provides a DSL (Domain-Specific Language) for debugger specification (GR3). This way the approach facilitates modularity (GR1) by associating the debug specification directly with the respective language concept. Details on the language structure can be found at the end of the paper in Annex.

Breakpoints. Breakpoints can be set on `Breakables`. In imperative languages, breakpoints can be set on statements so they will be mapped to `Breakable`.

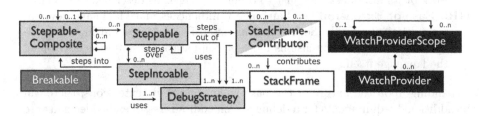

Fig. 4. Abstractions for the debugger specification

Stack Frames. `StackFrameContributors` are concepts that are translated to base-level callables (functions or procedures) or represent callables on the extension-level. They contribute `StackFrames`, each is linked to a base-level stack frame and states whether it is visible in the extension-level call stack or not.

Stepping. `Steppable` concepts support stepping, which is separated into *step over*, *step into* and *step out*. For *step over*, a `Steppable` defines where program execution must suspend next, after the debugger steps over an instance of `Steppable`. Again, statements are the typical examples of `Steppables` in an imperative language. If a `Steppable` contains a `StepIntoable` under it, then the `Steppable` also supports *step into*. `StepIntoables` are concepts that branch execution into a `SteppableComposite`, typically requiring its own stack frame via `StackFrameContributor`. The canonical example in programming languages are function calls (`StepIntoable`) and the corresponding functions (`SteppableComposite`). Once we are in a `SteppableComposite` we may want to *step out*; hence a `StackFrameContributor` contributes *step out* behavior.

All *stepping* is implemented by setting breakpoints and then resuming execution until one of these breakpoints is hit (this approach is adopted from [18]). The actual single-stepping functionality of the underlying debugger is not used, because it slows down the stepping at extension-level. `Steppable`s use `DebugStrategies` that determine where to set the base-level breakpoints to implement a particular stepping behavior for an extension concept. Language extensions can implement their own strategies (GR2) or use predefined ones (GR3). For instance, to prepare for *step over* on the extension-level, the `SingleBreakpoint` strategy retrieves for a node the first line of generated base-level code and sets a breakpoint on it. This way no further dependencies to other extensions are required, and extensions remain modular (GR1).

Watches. `WatchProviders` can contribute entries to the debugger's watch window. For example a local variable declaration whose value can be inspected in the watch window. A `WatchProviderScope` is a nestable context in which `WatchProviders` are declared and are valid e. g., two functions declaring local variables. When suspending within any of them, the corresponding `WatchProviderScope` causes the debugger to only show its local variables.

5.2   Execution Aspect

The framework relies on traces and the AST to provide the debug support. This means no debugger-specific code should be generated into the executable (ER1). Fig. 5 shows the components of the execution aspect and their interfaces (names start with an I, e. g., `IWatches`) to implement this AST/trace-based approach: `ProgramStructure` provides access to the AST via `IASTAccess`. `Trace Data` provides `ITraceAccess` that is used to locate the AST node (base and extension-level) that corresponds to a segment or line in the generated base-language code, and vice versa. The `Low-Level Debugger` represents the native debugger for the base language. It provides the `ILLDebuggerAPI` interface, which is used to interact with the `Low-Level Debugger` (ER2). These interactions include setting breakpoints, finding out about the program location of the `Low-Level Debugger` when it is suspended at a breakpoint and access watches. Languages provide `Debugger Extensions` (GR3), based on the abstractions discussed in Section 5.1. *Those abstractions are translated to Java and integrate with the debugger framework.* The `IDebugControl` interface is used by the `Debugger UI` to control the `Mapper` which integrates the other components. For example, `IDebugControl` provides a `resume` operation, `IBreakpoints` allows the UI to set breakpoints on program nodes and `IWatches` lets the UI retrieve the data items for the watch window. All previously mentioned interfaces are used by the `Mapper`, which controls the `Low-Level Debugger` and is invoked by the user through the `Debugger UI`. The `Mapper` uses the `Program Structure`, the `Trace Data` and the debugging implementation from the `Debugger Extensions`.

To illustrate the interactions of these components, we describe a *step over* scenario. After the request has been handed over from the UI to the `Mapper` via `IDebugControl`, the `Mapper` performs the following steps:

– Ask the current `Steppable` for its *step over* strategies; these define all possible locations where the debugger may have to break after the *step over*.

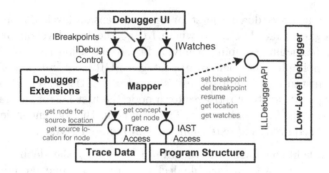

Fig. 5. The components of the execution aspect and their interfaces

- Query `TraceData` for corresponding lines in the generated C code for those program locations.
- Set breakpoints via `ILLDebuggerAPI` on those lines in the low-level code.
- Use `ILLDebuggerAPI` to resume program execution. It will stop at any of the just created breakpoints.
- Use `ILLDebuggerAPI` to get the low-level call stack.
- Query `TraceData` to find out for each C stack frame the corresponding nodes in the extension-level program.
- Collect all relevant `StackFrameContributors` (see next section). The `Mapper` uses them to construct the extension-level call stack.
- Get the currently visible symbols and their values via `ILLDebuggerAPI`.
- Query the nodes for `WatchProviders` and use them to create watchables.

At this point, execution returns to the `Debugger UI`, which then gets the current location and watchables from the `Mapper`. With this information, it highlights the `Steppable` on which execution is suspended and populates the watch window.

6   Example Debugger Extension

This section discusses the implementation of a debugger extension for the language described in Section 3. The specification of the extension resides in the respective language module (GR1). As part of the mbeddr implementation, we have developed a DSL for debugger specification (GR3) that integrates directly with MPS' language definition language. We use some concepts from this DSL for implementing the debugger extension in this section.

Breakpoints. We want to be able to set breakpoints on a `foreach` statement. Since both concepts are derived from `Statement`, we can already set breakpoints on them; no further work is necessary.

Stack Frames. The `foreach` statement does not have callable semantics and is not generated to C functions (see Section 5.1). Hence, suspending the debugger in a `foreach` statement affects not the number of stack frames in the call stack.

Stepping. `ForeachStatement` is derived from `Statement`. Its implementation for *step over* suspends the debugger on the `Statement` following the current one. `Statement` realizes this by delegating the *step over* request to its surrounding `SteppableComposite` (ancestor in the AST). This `SteppableComposite` simply sets a breakpoint on the next `Steppable`, which is again a `Statement`:

```
void contributeStepOverStrategies() { ancestor; }
```

We must overwrite this default behavior for the `ForeachStatement`, since its stepping behavior differs. Consider we suspend our debugger on the `foreach` that is shown in last snippet of Section 3 and perform a *step over*. If the array is empty or we have finished iterating over it, a *step over* ends up on the statement that follows *after the whole* `foreach` statement. Otherwise we end up on the first line of the `foreach` body (`sum += it;`). This is the first line of the mbeddr program, *not* the first line of the generated base program (which would be `int8_t __it = sortedNumbers[__c];`). The debugger cannot guess which alternative will occur since it would require knowing the state of the program and evaluating the expressions in the (generated) `for`. Instead, we set breakpoints *on all possible next statements* and then resume execution until we hit one of them — the created breakpoints are then removed again. The code below shows the implementation: we delegate the request to the surrounding `SteppableComposite`, but we also set a breakpoint on the first statement in the `body` (if not empty).

```
void contributeStepOverStrategies() {
    delegate to ancestor;
    break at this.body.first;  }
```

Let us look at *step into*. Since the `array` and `len` expressions of a `foreach` can be arbitrarily complex and may contain invocations of callables (such as function calls), we have to specify the *step into* behavior as well. This requires the debugger to inspect the expression trees in `array`, `len` and find any expression that can be stepped into. Such expressions implement `StepIntoable`. The following code shows the *step into* implementation:

```
void contributeStepIntoStrategies() { inspect this.array, this.len for StepIntoables; }
```

Watches. By default, the watch window contains all C symbols (global and local variables, arguments) as supplied by the C debugger. In case of `foreach`, this means the `it` expression is not available, but the two generated variables `__it` and `__c` are. This is exactly the wrong way: the watch window should show `__it` as `it` and hide `__c`. The code below shows the implementation in `foreach`:

```
void contributeWatchables() {
    hide local variable with identifier "__c"
    map by name "__it" to "it"
        type mapper: this.array.type
}
```

Line 2 **hides** the C variable `__c`. The rest **maps** a base-level C variable to a watchable. It finds the C variable named `__it` inserted by the `foreach` generator,

hides it and creates a watch variable named it. The type of it is the base type
of the array over which we iterate. This type is responsible for mapping the
value (type mapper), in our example above the int32 type simply returns the
C representation of an int32_t value.

To complete the implementation, we must implement WatchProviderScope
in foreach. This requires an implementation of collectWatchProviders to
collect instances of WatchProviders in a scope. foreach owns a StatementList
which implements this interface already and collects WatchProviders in the top-
level scope of the body. Hence, a foreach simply contributes itself (for hiding
__c and mapping __it), which is expressed with the following implementation:

```
void collectWatchProviders() { collect watch providers: this; }
```

7 Validation

To validate our approach, we have implemented the debugging behavior for
mbeddr C and most of its default extensions (components, state machines and
unit testing). This section discusses some interesting cases we have experienced
during implementation.

7.1 Polymorphic Calls

There are situations when static determination of a *step into* target is not possible e. g., polymorphic calls on interfaces. Our components extension provides
interfaces with operations, as well as components that provide and require
these interfaces. The component methods that implement interface operations
are generated to base-level C functions. The same interface can be implemented
by *different* components, each implementation ending up in a *different* C function. A client component only specifies the *interface* it calls, not the component.
So, we cannot know statically which C function will be called if an operation is
invoked on the interface. However, statically, we can find all components that
implement the interface (in a given executable), so we know *all possible C functions* that may be invoked. A strategy specific for this case (GR2) sets breakpoints on the first line *of each of these functions*. Consequently, we stop in any
of them if the user *steps into* an operation invocation.

7.2 Mapping to Multiple Statements

In many cases a single statement on the extension-level is mapped to several
statements or blocks on the base-level. So *stepping over* the extension-level statement must step over the block or list of statements in terms of C. An example is
the assert statement (used in tests) which is mapped to an if. The debugger
has to step over the complete if, independent of whether the condition in the
if evaluates to true or false. Note that we get this behavior for free: we never
step actually over statements. In contrast, we set breakpoints at all possible code
locations where the debugger may have to stop next. The assert statement sets
a breakpoint on the base-level counterpart of the *next extension-level statement*.

7.3   Datatype Mapping

Language extensions may provide new data types in addition to the existing base language data types. During code generation, these additional data types are translated to the base language data types. In mbeddr, a trivial example for this is the **boolean** type, which is translated to C's **int** type. When inspecting the value of a watchable that is of type **boolean** we expect the debugger to render the **int** value either as **true** or **false**.

For mbeddr's **components** a more complex mapping is needed. As shown in the listing below, **components** can contain declarations for fields (instance variables e. g., *color*) and provided/required ports (interfaces e. g., *tl* and *driver*). The code generator translates each **component** (e. g., *TrafficLights*) to a **struct** declaration (e. g., *CompModule_compdata_TrafficLights*). This **struct** declaration contains members (e. g., *field_color* and *port_driver*) for the declared fields (e. g., *color*) and for each required port (e. g., *driver*).

```
1  component TrafficLights extends
       nothing {
2    provides ITrafficLights tl
3    requires IDriver driver
4    TLC color;
5    void setColor(TLC color) op tl.setColor
       {
6      color = color;   }
7  }
```

```
struct CompModule_compdata_TrafficLights {
    /* fields */
    CompModule_TLC field_color;
    /* required ports */
    void* port_driver;
};
```

When debugging a **component** instance on the extension-level, we expect the debugger to provide watches for the fields. They should have their respective extension-level values and names. However, the members for the ports should not be displayed. In the mapping implementation of **component** we must therefore extract the fields from the respective **struct** instance and map the names and their respective values.

8   Discussion

This section revisits the requirements outlined in Section 4 to evaluate to what extent they are fulfilled:

8.1   Revisiting the Requirements

GR1 Modularity. Our approach requires no changes to the base language or its debugger implementation to specify the debugger for an extension. Also, independently developed extensions retain their independence if they contain debugger specifications. MPS' capability of incrementally including language extensions in a program *without defining a composite language first* is preserved in the face of debugger specifications.

GR2 Framework Genericity. The extension-dependent aspects of the debugger behavior are extensible. In particular, stepping behavior is factored into strategies, and new strategies can be implemented by a language extension. Also, the representation of watch values can be customized by querying the type (e. g., consider our `boolean` type example).

GR3 Simple Debugger Definition. This challenge is solved by the debugger definition DSL. It supports the declarative specification of stepping behavior and watches. However, it does not concern the user with implementation details of the framework or the debugger backend.

ER4 Limited Overhead. Our solution requires no debugger specific code at all (except debug symbols added by compiling the C code with debug options). Instead, we rely on trace data to map the extension-level to the base-level and ultimately to text. This is a trade-off since the language work-bench must be able to provide trace information. Also, the generated C code cannot be modified by a text processor before it is compiled and debugged. This would invalidate the trace data (the C preprocessor works, it is han-dled correctly by the compiler and debugger). On the contrary, we are not required to change existing transformations to generate debugger-specific code. This keeps the transformations independent of the debugger.

ER5 Debugger Backend Independence. We use the Eclipse CDT Debug Bridge [6] to wrap the particular C debugger. This way, we can use any compatible debugger without changing our infrastructure. Our approach requires no changes to the native C debugger itself. However, since we use breakpoints for stepping, the debugger must be able to handle a reasonable number of breakpoints. The debugger also has to provide an API for setting and removing breakpoints and for querying the currently visible symbols and their values. In addition, the API should allow us to query the code location where the debugger is suspended. Most C debuggers support all of this, so these are not serious limitations.

8.2   Other Evaluation Criteria

In addition to the specific requirements from Section 4, our approach can be evaluated with regards to additional criteria.

Sizes and Efforts. The `ForeachLanguage` consists of 70 lines of code. 17 of them (25%) are related to the debugger. For the much more complex components extension, the ratios are similar, although the language is ca. 2.500 lines of code. We do not have numbers for the default extensions itself, since their debugging implementation was mixed with the development of the debugger framework. From these numbers we conclude that we have reached the goal of the debug-ger specification for extensions not requiring significantly more effort than the definition of the extension itself.

Multi-Staged Transformations. The extensions described so far are *directly* transformed to C. However, extensions may also be transformed to other lan-guage extensions. Thus, forming a multi-level stack with high-level languages on top and low-level languages at the bottom. Our current framework implemen-tation provides debug support for such multi-level extensions as well. However, for high-level extensions, the debugger must be specified relative to C and *not* relative to the next lower-level extension. This is a limitation, since all transformations between the extension and the base language must be considered.

Use for other Base Languages. The framework was designed and implemented for mbeddr C. However, it contains no dependencies on mbeddr or on the C implementation. The framework only assumes that the base language and its extensions use the imperative paradigm with statements that can be nested and embedded into callables. Consequently, debug support for other imperative base languages can be implemented using our framework.

Use outside of MPS. Our *implementation* cannot be used outside of MPS since it depends on MPS' APIs. However, the general *approach* can be adapted to other language workbenches. According to Fig. 5, the tool has to provide the following services: a debugger UI that lets users interact with the debugger, access to the program and the language definitions as well as trace data.

9   Related Work

This section provides an overview of related research. We look at compile-time debuggers, extensible debuggers and DSL debuggers.

Compile-time Debuggers. Our approach animates and inspects the execution of a program. Other debuggers inspect the compilation or macro expansion phase. Examples include Porkoláb's debugger for C++ template metaprogram compilation [12]. Furthermore, Culpepper's stepper for the macro expansion process in Scheme [4]. In mbeddr, the equivalent of compile time meta programs or macros is the transformation of extensions to base language code. While not discussed in this paper, MPS provides various ways of debugging the transformation process. This includes retaining all intermediate programs for inspection as well as a debugger for stepping through the transformation process itself.

Cornelissen [3] describes an approach to enable debugging at two meta-levels at the same time. Their work is based on the TIDE debugger framework [2] and the ASF+SDF Meta-Environment [5]. One debugger debugs the execution of a program written in the Pico language. At the same time, the interpreter defining the semantics of the Pico language can be debugged as well. This is different from our approach. We support integrated debugging of programs expressed at different *abstraction* levels (C base language and the various extensions). In contrast, Cornelissen supports debugging at different *meta*-levels.

Extensible Debuggers. Extensibility can address different aspects of a debugger, not just the extensibility of the base language as discussed in this paper. Vraný and Píse describe a debugger that integrates information from multiple different debuggers into a common debugger UI. Consequently, providing an integrated execution flow [17]. This approach is similar to ours in that it considers several languages. However, in our case, the languages are mixed within the same program, extend a common base language and run in a single debug process.

The debugger described by Al-Sharif and Jeffery [1] can be extended with user-defined program execution monitors. These monitors run concurrently, listen to debug events, such as `breakpoint hit`, and process them in user-definable ways. May et al. introduce a debugger for parallel applications [10]. They provide an API to integrate custom views. Those views can also access debug sessions, but additionally, they contribute components to the debugger UI. Both works address extending the *debugging functionality* for a fixed language. However, our debugger provides a fixed functionality, but for extensible *languages*.

DSL Debuggers. Wu et al. introduce a debugging framework for imperative, declarative and hybrid DSLs [18, 19]. They integrate `print` statements into the generated code that output debug symbols, such as values of watches or the current source line. Based on this output, the debugger renders the UI. Our debugger stores the mapping between high-level nodes and generated code in a trace data structure. This information is created during the transformation process. With this approach, we avoid instrumenting the program code, an important requirement for us (ER4). In the same work, Wu et al. also describe a debugger for a simple assembler-like language. To implement step *in* and step *over* in this language, they introduce the idea of using breakpoints. While they use a mix of native stepping and breakpoints, we adapted their approach to use *only* breakpoints. In addition, we add support for *step out*, based on a call stack.

Lindeman et al. introduce a generic debugger framework for DSLs [9]. Using a debugger specification DSL, developers create *event types* and map the syntax and semantics of a language onto an execution model. This is similar to our approach, as we also provide a DSL to map language concepts to a execution model (see Section 5.1). In Lindemann's approach, a preprocessor integrates debug symbols into the DSL program, based on the specified event types. In contrast, our debugger uses external trace data to relate extension-level programs to base-level programs, and ultimately to lines in the generated code.

10   Summary and Future Work

Extensible languages are a good compromise between general-purpose and domain-specific languages because they can grow towards a domain incrementally. In addition, they enable validation and verification on the problem-level, by reducing propagation of possible errors into base language code. To alleviate the rest of the errors, extension-level debugging is helpful. In this paper, we have introduced a debugger framework for an extensible language. Furthermore, we have demonstrated the feasibility by implementing debugging support for non-trivial extensions for the mbeddr C language. The requirements regarding extensibility, modularity and limitation of overhead outlined at the beginning of the paper have all been satisfied. Further, efforts for implementing debugger extensions fit well with the efforts for building the language extensions themselves.

In the future, we will investigate the extent to which multiple alternative transformations for a single language concept require changes to the debugger framework. We will explore synergies between the debugger and other language definition artifacts such as transformations (watches) and the data flow graph (stepping). Finally, we will investigate improved support for multi-staged transformations.

Acknowledgments. We would like to thank our co-author Syed Aoun Raza for his continuous insightful refinements and feedbacks in preparation of this work. This publication would not have been possible without his contribution.

References

1. Al-Sharif, Z., Jeffery, C.: An Extensible Source-Level Debugger. In: Proceedings of the 2009 ACM Symposium on Applied Computing, pp. 543–544. ACM, Honolulu (2009)
2. Van den Brand, M.G.J., Cornelissen, B., Oliver, P.A., Vinju, J.J.: TIDE: A Generic Debugging Framework - Tool Demonstration. In: Electronic Notes in Theoretical Computer Science, vol. 141, pp. 161–165. Edinburgh, UK (2005)
3. Cornelissen, B.: Using TIDE to Debug ASF+SDF on Multiple Levels. Master's thesis, University of Amsterdam, Netherlands (2005)
4. Culpepper, R., Felleisen, M.: Debugging Macros. In: 6th International Conference on enerative Programming and Component Engineering, pp. 135–144. ACM, Salzburg (2007)
5. van Deursen, A., Dinesh, T.B., van der Meulen, E.: The ASF+SDF Meta-Environment. In: Proceedings of the 3rd International Conference on Methodology and Software Technology, pp. 411–412. Springer, Enschede (1993)
6. Eclipse Foundation: Eclipse CDT (2015). http://www.eclipse.org/cdt
7. International Organization for Standardization (ISO): ISO C 99 Standard (1999). http://www.open-std.org/jtc1/sc22/wg14/www/docs/n1124.pdf
8. JetBrains: Meta Programming System (2015). http://www.jetbrains.com/mps
9. Lindeman, R.T., Kats, L.C., Visser, E.: Declaratively Defining Domain-specific Language Debuggers. In: 10th Conference on Generative Programming and Component Engineering, pp. 127–136. ACM, New York (2011)
10. May, J., Berman, F.: Panorama: A Portable, Extensible Parallel Debugger. In: 3rd Workshop on Parallel and Distributed Debugging, pp. 96–106. ACM, San Diego (1993)
11. Pavletic, D., Raza, S.A., Voelter, M., Kolb, B., Kehrer, T.: Extensible Debuggers for Extensible Languages. In: 15th Workshop Software-Reengineering. pp. 33–34. Bad Honnef, Germany (2013)
12. Porkoláb, Z., Mihalicza, J., Sipos, A.: Debugging C++ Template Metaprograms. In: 5th Conference on Generative Programming and Component Engineering, pp. 255–264. ACM, New York (2006)
13. Voelter, Markus: Language and IDE Modularization and Composition with MPS. In: Lämmel, Ralf, Saraiva, João, Visser, Joost (eds.) GTTSE 2011. LNCS, vol. 7680, pp. 383–430. Springer, Heidelberg (2013)
14. Voelter, M.: Preliminary Experience of using mbeddr for Developing Embedded Software. In: Proceedings of the Workshop Model-based Engineering of Embedded Systems X, pp. 73–82. Wadern, Germany (2014)

15. Voelter, M., Ratiu, D., Schaetz, B., Kolb, B.: Mbeddr: An Extensible C-based Programming Language and IDE for Embedded Systems. In: Conference on Systems. Programming, and Applications: Software for Humanity, SPLASH 2012, pp. 121–140. ACM, New York (2012)
16. Voelter, M., Visser, E.: Language Extension and Composition with Language Workbenches. In: Companion to the 25th Annual ACM SIGPLAN Conference on Object-Oriented Programming, Systems, Languages, and Applications, SPLASH/OOPSLA, pp. 301–304. ACM, New York (2010)
17. Vraný, Jan, Píše, Michal: Multilanguage Debugger Architecture. In: van Leeuwen, Jan, Muscholl, Anca, Peleg, David, Pokorný, Jaroslav, Rumpe, Bernhard (eds.) SOFSEM 2010. LNCS, vol. 5901, pp. 731–742. Springer, Heidelberg (2010)
18. Wu, H.: Grammar-Driven Generation of Domain-Specific Language Testing Tools. In: Companion to the 20th Annual ACM SIGPLAN Conference on Object-Oriented Programming. Systems, Languages, and Applications, OOPSLA 2005, pp. 210–211. ACM, San Diego (2005)
19. Wu, H., Gray, J.G., Roychoudhury, S., Mernik, M.: Weaving a Debugging Aspect into Domain-Specific Language Grammars. In: Proceedings of the 2005 ACM Symposium on Applied Computing, pp. 1370–1374. ACM, Santa Fe (2005)

Annex

The debugger framework provides a DSL for specifying the concept-specific implementation behavior of the interfaces described in Section 5.1. This DSL extends MPS' *base language*, which is an extensible version of Java. We have already used the language for implementing the **foreach** debugger in Section 6. It comprises 22 concepts (contained in *com.mbeddr.core.debug.blext* language that ships with mbeddr) from which we describe the implementation of two important concepts in the table below. First, **BreakOnNodeStatement** for setting a breakpoint on a node. Second, **HideByIdStatement** for hiding watches that have no representation on the extension-level.

Concept	BreakOnNodeStatement	HideByIdStatement
Structure		
	consists of an **Expression** that represents a AST node to break on.	consists of an **Expression** for the name of the watch to hide and a **VarKind** which defines the scope.
Type System	`infer typeof(breakOnNode.node)` `:<=: <node<ISuspendableNode>>;`	`infer typeof(hideById.name)` `:<=: <string>;`
	node must be a subtype of **ISuspendableNode**.[1]	accepts only **String** types for *name*.
Generator	```if ($COPY_SRC$ node .isNotNull) { $COPY_SRC$ node .runTo(str); }```	```foreach watch in allWatches { if (watch.getKind().equals($COPY_SRC$ "kind" && watch.getName(). equals($COPY_SRC$ ""))) { watch.hide(); } }```
	In the above code, *node* gets replaced with a reference that will point to a AST node at runtime.	In the above code, *allWatches* contains watches visible in the current scope. Those with the same *name* and *kind* do not appear in the watch window.

Static Backward Program Slicing
for Safety-Critical Systems

Husni Khanfar[✉], Björn Lisper, and Abu Naser Masud

School of Innovation, Design, and Engineering,
Mälardalen University, SE-721 23 Västerås, Sweden
{husni.khanfar,bjorn.lisper,masud.abunaser}@mdh.se

Abstract. *Static program slicing* is a technique to detect the program
parts (i.e. the "slice") of the given program possibly affecting a given
property. The technique is of interest for analysing safety-critical software, since it can identify the program parts that may affect various
safety properties. Verification efforts can then be directed towards those
parts, leading to a more efficient verification process.

We have developed a novel method for static backward program
slicing. The method works for well-structured programs, as commonly
demanded by coding standards for safety-critical software. It utilises the
program structure to obtain a highly efficient slicing process, where control dependencies are inferred from the program structure, and the slicing
is done on-the-fly concurrently with the data dependence analysis.

We have evaluated our method experimentally. For applications that
require few slices to be taken, like checking for a set of safety properties, we obtain large speedups as compared with the standard method
for static backward program slicing. We have also investigated how the
speedup varies with various parameters such as code size, size of the slice
relative to the full program, and relative frequency of conditions in the
code.

Keywords: Program slicing · Dataflow analysis · Strongly live variable ·
Program dependency graph

1   Introduction

Program slicing refers to a collection of techniques to find the parts of the given
program (so-called "slices") that can affect, or be affected by, a certain property [23]. The property is often abstracted into a *slicing criterion*, which typically
consists of some program variables in some specific program points. Program
slicing was first introduced by Weiser [24] in the context of debugging and parallel processing. It has since been applied in areas like software testing, software measurement, program comprehension, program integration, and software
maintenance.

A particular slicing technique is *static backward program slicing*. For a given
slicing criterion, backwards slicing computes a slice consisting of all the statements, conditions, and inputs to the program that can possibly affect the values

© Springer International Publishing Switzerland 2015
J.A. de la Puente and T. Vardanega (Eds.): Ada-Europe 2015, LNCS 9111, pp. 50–65, 2015.
DOI:10.1007/978-3-319-19584-1_4

of the variables in the slicing criterion in the respective program points. These values can be affected in two ways: either through *data dependencies*, where data produced by some statement are being read by some other statement, or through *control dependencies* where a condition may affect the possible execution of a statement. Fig. 1 shows a piece of code, and its backward slice (in boldface) with respect to the slicing criterion $\{z\}$ located at the last line.

```
p();
read(x); read(y); read(z);
z = y;
u = x + z;
if (x > 0) then x = 5 else z = 9;
y = x/z;
```

Fig. 1. Backward slicing example

Backward program slicing can be used to identify the program parts that can possibly affect value-related safety properties, like, for instance, whether memory accesses may be out of bounds. In the example in Fig. 1, there may be a possible division by zero at the last line. The corresponding safety property can be abstracted into the aforementioned slicing criterion $\{z\}$. Thus, the slice computed w.r.t. this criterion is the part of the program that can possibly affect whether a division with zero will occur or not. From this slice we can deduce that the formation of test data to test for division of zero should focus on the inputs for x and y, since the read statement for z and the initial value of u are not included in the slice and thus cannot possibly influence the value of z at the last line.

Backward slicing can also be used to find opportunities for early testing before the software is complete. This can be valuable, since it helps catching bugs early. In the example, the call to the procedure p is not included in the slice. This means that this call cannot influence whether or not a division by zero occurs, regardless of the code for p. Consequently we can replace p with a stub, and test for division by zero before the actual code for p is written.

The standard method for static backward slicing is based on the *Program Dependence Graph* (PDG) [9,20]. The nodes of the PDG are the nodes in the control flow graph (CFG) of the program, and it is the union of the *control dependence graph* (CDG) and the *data dependence graph* (DDG). The CDG is computed from the CFG by a control dependence analysis computing the strongest post-dominators for the conditions in the CFG. The DDG is computed using some data flow analysis, typically Reaching Definitions [19], from which the def-use pairs that constitute the edges in the DDG can be built. Once the PDG is built, slicing w.r.t. some slicing criterion can be done by a simple backwards traversal of the PDG from the criterion. The PDG-based slicing is intra-procedural. It can be extended to the inter-procedural case by instead considering the *system dependence graph* (SDG) [22].

A potential problem with PDG-based slicing is that the whole PDG has to be built before the actual slicing is performed. This can be wasteful especially in situations where the resulting slice is small relative to the full program, and it may also cause problems with scalability. We have developed such a method for static backwards slicing that avoids this problem. Our experiments show that it performs considerably better than the PDG-based method when few slices are computed, and it is also more space efficient. Our method computes slices concurrently with the dependence analysis, avoiding the construction of any dependence- or flow graphs. It works for well-structured, jump-free code: such code is prescribed by coding standards for safety-critical applications such as MISRA-C and SPARC 2014.

The rest of the paper is organized as follows. Section 2 reviews some background that is needed for the reading of the rest of the paper. In Section 3 we give the distinguishing features of our algorithm, and in Section 4 we define the underlying program representation that it uses. Section 5 explains more in detail how the algorithm works. In Section 7 we give an account for our experimental evaluation, comparing our approach with the PDG-based algorithm. Section 8 gives an account for related work, and Section 9 concludes the paper.

2   Preliminaries

2.1   A Model Language

Our work considers well-structured programs. Our algorithm is defined for a minimal, well-structured model language with the following abstract syntax:

$$s \ ::= \ x := a \ \mid \ skip \ \mid \ s'; s'' \ \mid \ \text{if } c \text{ then } s' \text{ else } s'' \ \mid \ \text{while } b \text{ do } s'$$

We assume that all variables are numerical, and that arithmetic expressions a and conditions c have no side-effects.

Adding features like procedures, pointers, non-numerical data types, structured types such as arrays and records, and procedures, is straightforward. Our algorithm is interprocedural, and handles procedures with input and output parameters (see Section 6). It can be extended to deal with the other features as well.

2.2   Data Flow Analysis

Data flow analysis is used to compute data dependencies. We give a short account for it here, as our algorithm uses a particular data flow analysis. Details can be found in, e.g., [19].

Data flow analysis is often defined over a flowchart representation of the program; a flowchart is essentially a CFG where the nodes are individual statements, or conditions, rather than basic blocks. (For our model language in Section 2.1 the nodes are assignments, conditions, or *skip* statements.) The edges in the flowchart are the program points: a data flow analysis computes a set of data flow items for each program point. These data flow items vary with the analysis, but they typically represent some kind of data flows in the program.

A data flow analysis assigns a monotone *transfer function* f_n to each flowchart node n, which is used in an equation relating the sets $S_{entry}(n)$ and $S_{exit}(n)$ for ingoing and outgoing edge of the node, respectively. (For simplicity we neglect that some nodes may have more than one ingoing or outgoing edge.) For a *forward* analysis the equation has the form $S_{exit}(n) = f_n(S_{entry}(n))$, and for a *backward* analysis it has the form $S_{entry}(n) = f_n(S_{exit}(n))$. In both cases we obtain a system of equations for the sets. This system is solved by a standard fixed-point iteration. The resulting sets provide the result of the analysis.

Besides being forward or backward, data flow analyses are also classified as *may* or *must* analyses. We will only be concerned with may analyses here: these compute data flows that will never underapproximate the real data flows.

PDG-based slicing uses the Reaching Definitions (RD) analysis [19]. It is a forward may analysis that computes sets of pairs (x, n), where x is a program variable and n is a CFG node. If (x, n) belongs to the set associated with the edge p, then the value of x assigned at n may still be present in x when at p and thus, if x is possibly used at the node n' immediately succeeding p, there is a possible data flow from n to n'.

Our slicing algorithm uses another data flow analysis known as *Strongly Live Variables* (SLV) [19]. It is a backward may analysis: given some "uses" of some variables in some program points (basically a slicing criterion) it traces backwards the variables that may influence the values of the used variables. Thus it computes in each program point a set of "Strongly Live Variables", whose values in the respective program point may affect the values of the used variables. The SLV sets also represent data dependencies: if x belongs to a SLV set, and the preceding node possibly assigns x, then there may be a data flow from that node to some of the variable uses. For SLV analysis the transfer functions take the following form:

$$
\begin{aligned}
S_{entry}(n) &= (S_{exit}(n) \setminus kill(n)) \cup gen(n), \text{ if } kill(n) \subseteq S_{exit}(n) \\
S_{entry}(n) &= S_{exit}(n), \text{ otherwise}
\end{aligned}
\tag{1}
$$

where, $S_{entry}(n)$ and $S_{exit}(n)$ represents respectively the SLV set that is present before and after the CFG node n. In the original formulation of SLV analysis [19], the $kill$, and gen sets are defined as follows for assignments $x := a$, conditions c, and *skip* statements:

$$
\begin{aligned}
kill(x := a) &= \{x\} \quad kill(c) = \emptyset \quad kill(skip) = \emptyset \\
gen(x := a) &= FV(a) \ gen(c) = FV(c) \ gen(skip) = \emptyset
\end{aligned}
\tag{2}
$$

Here, $FV(a)$ denotes the set of program variables that appear in the expression a. The above definitions are according to the original formulation of SLV analysis where it is assumed that variables in the conditions are always used. The definitions can easily be modified to deal with variable uses corresponding to any possible slicing criterion in arbitrary program points [15].

3   An Overview of the Slicing Algorithm

Our algorithm has the following distinguishing features:

- It uses an internal representation of interconnected code blocks, which basically provides a representation of the syntax tree. It can be generated from the syntax tree in time linear in the size of the tree. No CFG is needed.
- For well-structured code the control dependencies are found directly from the syntax. For our model language, the control dependencies are exactly from a branch condition to the statements in the branches of a conditional statement, and from a loop condition to the statements in its loop body. This information is retained in the code blocks: thus, no further control dependence analysis is necessary.
- The data dependence analysis uses SLV rather than RD. If the SLV set succeeding an assignment $x := a$ contains x then we know that some part of the slicing criterion will be dependent on the value of x produced there, and thus $x := a$ can be immediately put into the slice already during the data flow analysis. No DDG has to be built.
- Rather than maintaining a set of SLVs in each program point, and performing a conventional fixed-point iteration where the sets grow until a fixed-point is reached, the algorithm maintains a single set of SLVs for each code block and keeps track of how far each variable has propagated within the block. This reduces the memory requirements, and it can also sometimes eliminate unnecessary iterations through statements that will not be included in the slice anyway.

Thus the algorithm performs the slicing in a dynamic fashion, without the need to build any control flow or dependence graphs.

4   Predicated Code Blocks

We use *Predicated Code Blocks* (PCB) to represent the control flow in the program. A predicated code block, $(s_0, \ldots, s_n)$, consists of a conditional predicate s_0 followed by a sequence of statements $s_1, \ldots, s_n$. Conditional statements, while loops, and procedure bodies are represented by such code blocks, and a set of interconnected blocks represents the whole program. The code blocks are derived for these kinds of statements as follows:

$$\text{if } c \text{ then } s_1; \ldots; s_m \text{ else } s'_1; \ldots; s'_n \rightarrow \{(c, s_1, \ldots, s_m), (\neg c, s'_1, \ldots, s'_n)\}$$
$$\text{while } c \text{ do } s_1; \ldots; s_n \rightarrow \{(c, s_1, \ldots, s_n)\}$$

A conditional statement is represented by two PCBs, one for each branch. A procedure with body $s_1; \ldots; s_n$ is represented by the PCB $(true, s_1 \ldots, s_n)$.

If some statement within a block B is a compound statement (if or while), then a block is recursively created for that statement. That block will be connected to the "parent" block B by *interfaces*, which are explained below. If the statement is a while, then it is removed from B. If it is a conditional, then it is

```
int Add(int a,int b){
    return a+b;
}
void F(int c){
    int p=0, n=0;
    while(c >= 0){
        if(c%2 == 0)
            p=Add(c,p);
        else
            n=Add(c,n);
        c=c-1
    } print(p);
}
```

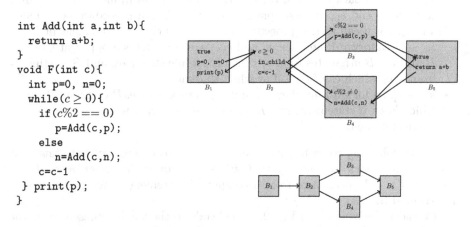

Fig. 2. Running Example (left), PCB representation (above right), immediate successor relation among PCBs (below right)

replaced by a so-called *in-child* statement that acts as a place-holder (as shown in PCB B_2 in Fig. 2). The in-child statements play a certain role in directing the flow of the slicing algorithm, see Section 5. The whole set of PCBs representing the program is generated in a single traversal of the syntax tree, generating new blocks when compound statements are encountered.

Within a PCB the program flow is represented by the sequence of statements. For blocks representing while loops the represented flow is *cyclic*, with a back-edge from the last statement to the condition, whereas the flow represented by PCBs for conditional branches and non-recursive procedure bodies is acyclic.

Program flow between PCBs can be represented by *interfaces*. These are graph edges that connect statements in different blocks: $s_i \rightarrow s'_j$ is an interface if s_i and s'_j belong to different blocks B, B', and there is a possible direct flow of execution from s_i to s'_j. Interfaces will connect blocks representing while and if statements to their "parent" blocks, and also procedure bodies to call sites. Since we consider structured code, there will always be a "forward" interface from parent to child block and a "back" interface in the reverse direction. We obtain the following possible interfaces connecting B and B' (s_0 and s'_0 are the conditions in B and B' respectively):

- $s_i \rightarrow s'_0$: a forward interface where either s_i is a simple statement or an *in_child* statement in B, and code block B' originates from s_{i+1} which is an if or while statement, or s_i is a procedure call and B' is the block for the body of the called procedure.
- $s_0 \rightarrow s'_{i+1}$: a back interface where B originates from s'_i which is a while statement, and s'_{i+1} is a simple statement in B'. (If s'_i is the last statement in the program part represented by B', then we can consider s'_{i+1} to be a dummy statement following s'_i.)

- $s_n \rightarrow s'_{i+1}$: a back interface where either B originates from s'_i, which is an if statement, and s_{i+1} is a simple statement, or B is a procedure body block and s_{i+1} is a call to this procedure in B'. (s_n is the last statement in B.)
- $s_0 \rightarrow s'_0$: a forward interface. s_i and s_{i+1} are statements in a parent block to B and B'. B originates from s_i which is a while staement, and B' originates from s_{i+1} which can be an if or while statement.
- $s_n \rightarrow s'_0$: a forward interface. s_i and s_{i+1} are as above. B originates from s_i which is an if statement, and B' originates from s_{i+1} which can be an if or while statement.

In the following we will sometimes write $B.s$ to emphasise that statement s belongs to block B. We say that B' is an *immediate successor* to B, or $succ(B, B')$, if B' originates from a compound statement in the program part represented by B.

Consider the example in Fig. 2. The C code to the left is represented by the set of interconnected PCBs to the right. Note how the connecting edges represent the inter-PCB control flow, while the intra-PCB control flow is represented by the sequences of statements within the blocks. At the bottom, to the right, the immediate successor relation between the PCBs is shown.

5   The Slicing Approach

We slice a program represented by a set of PCBs by solving local slicing problems for PCBs individually. Initially, the slicing criterion for the global slicing problem is distributed into local slicing criteria for the different PCBs. The local slicing problems are then solved. In this process, new sets of SLVs may be communicated over the backedges of interfaces connecting PCBs. The arrival of such a set will create a new local slicing problem, which subsequently is solved taking the set of SLVs as local slicing criterion. This procedure is iterated until no local problems remain: then the slice can be computed as the union of the locally sliced statements, and the algorithm terminates. A simple work list or job pool can be used to manage the computation.

Solving the local slicing problems amounts to computing both data and control dependencies to identify statements to slice. We use the SLV analysis, which is a backward data flow analysis, for computing data dependencies where the analysis of a block will proceed backwards from the statement(s) of the slicing criterion towards the condition. If the block is acyclic then the local analysis will terminate there; if it is cyclic then it will continue backwards, through the backedge towards the condition.

Our version of the SLV analysis uses the fact that the *kill* and *gen* sets of a statement are constant. This has three consequences:

- a statement s where $v \in kill(s)$ for some SLV v can be immediately sliced,
- the variables in $gen(s)$ can then be generated as SLVs once and for all, not being re-generated at subsequent visits to s, and

– an SLV that is created at statement s, in a cyclic block, need only be propagated until it comes back to s: then it can be safely removed.

Every SLV will therefore be removed sooner or later: either by being killed, or by being removed at the end of a cycle for a cyclic block or at the beginning of an acyclic block, and it can only be generated a finite number of times since the statement generating it will be sliced, and there can only be finitely many such statements. Thus, rather than doing a conventional fixedpoint iteration where SLV sets grow to reach the fixedpoint, we maintain a single set of SLVs for each block, and the iteration continues until this set is empty. To track the movement of SLVs the SLV sets contain *SLV pairs* (i, v), rather than just variables v, where s_i is the first statement in the block to start looking for the definition of the SLV v. Global slicing criteria SC are also sets of SLV pairs: if variable v at statement s_i belongs to the slicing criterion, then $(i, v) \in SC$. For each block B, its set of SLV pairs S_B is initialized to its part of the global slicing criterion before the slicing starts.

If an SLV pair (k, v) is propagated or generated by a statement s_i in B, with an incoming interface edge $s'_j \to s_i$ where s'_j is in $B' \neq B$, then (k, v) will be propagated into (j, v) at s'_j. This pair will be added to the slicing criterion $S_{B'}$ for the next local slicing problem for B' to be solved.

Control dependencies are handled in the following way. A statement in block B is control dependent on the condition of B as well as the condition of all blocks "above" it: that is, all blocks B' such that $succ^+(B', B)$ where $succ^+$ is the transitive closure of $succ$. The first time a statement is sliced in block B, the condition c of B' will be sliced for each B' where $succ^+(B', B)$, and $\{(0, v) \mid v \in gen(c)\}$ will be added to the current slicing criterion of B'.

Suppose the given program is represented by the interconnected PCBs $\langle Bs, Rs \rangle$ where Bs is the set of PCBs, and Rs is the set of interface edges connecting the PCBs. The initial set of SLV pairs S_B for all $B \in Bs$ is obtained from the global slicing criterion SC. The SLV set S_B for B is updated during the local SLV data flow analysis and slicing. This is done by repeatedly applying some of the transfer functions $f^j_{i,e,v}$ to the set S_B, visiting the statements in B in the backward direction. The transfer function $f^j_{i,e,v}$ applied to S_B models how (i, v) is successively propagated, and which effect this has on the set of SLVs. j is the current point where the set of SLV pairs is updated according to the SLV transfer function (3) based on the dependency between s_j and v, and e is an "endpoint" where the propagation of (i, v) can be safely terminated. It is defined as follows:

$$f^j_{i,e,v}(S_B) = \begin{cases} S_B \setminus \{(i, v)\} & \text{if } (j = e \wedge v \notin kill(s_j)) \\ & \vee (s_j = \text{"}in\_child\text{"}) \vee \\ & (v \in kill(s_j) \wedge s_j \in N_{slice}) \\ S_B & \text{if } j \neq e \wedge v \notin kill(s_j) \\ S_B \setminus \{(i, v)\} \cup \{(j-1, u) \mid u \in gen(s_j)\} \cup \Phi_B & \text{if } v \in kill(s_j) \wedge s_j \notin N_{slice} \end{cases}$$

$$(3)$$

Here, $\Phi_B = \{ (0, v) \mid v \in gen(s_0), s_0 \in B, s_0 \notin N_{slice} \}$ is the set of SLV pairs generated due to control dependency.

Algorithm 1. SlicingProgram($\langle B_s, R_s \rangle, SC$)

```
   /* Initialization */
 1 forall (B ∈ B_s) do  S_B := select SLV pairs from SC for B;
 2 forall (s → s' ∈ R_s) do  R_m(s → s') := ∅;
 3 N_slice := ∅;
   /* Slicing PCBs */
 4 while (∃B ∈ B_s. S_B ≠ ∅) do
 5 │   Let B = (s_0, ..., s_n) ;
 6 │   (i, v) := Select(S_B) ;
 7 │   e := i if B is cyclic and n otherwise;
 8 │   j := i;
 9 │   repeat
10 │     │  S_B := f^j_{i,e,v}(S_B);
11 │     │  if (B'.s_l → B.s_j ∈ R_s ∧ v ∉ kill(B.s_j) ∧ v ∉ R_m(B'.s_l → B.s_j)) then
12 │     │     │  S_{B'} = S_{B'} ∪ {(l, v)};
13 │     │     │  R_m(B'.s_l → B.s_j) = R_m(B'.s_l → B.s_j) ∪ {v} ;
14 │     │  if (v ∈ kill(s_j) ∧ (s_j ∉ N_slice) then
15 │     │     │  N_slice := N_slice ∪ {s_0, s_j};
16 │     │     │  forall B' such that succ^+(B', B) ∧ B'.s'_0 ∉ N_slice do
17 │     │     │     │  S_{B'} := S_{B'} ∪ { (0, v) | v ∈ gen(B'.s'_0) };
   │     │     │     │  /* s'_0 is the condition in B' */
18 │     │     │     │  N_slice := N_slice ∪ {B'.s'_0};
19 │     │     │  if (B'.s_l → B.s_j ∈ R_s ∧ v ∉ R_m(B'.s_l → B.s_j)) then
20 │     │     │     │  S_{B'} = S_{B'} ∪ { (l, v') | v' ∈ gen(B.s_j) };
21 │     │     │     │  R_m(B'.s_l → B.s_j) = R_m(B'.s_l → B.s_j) ∪ gen(B.s_j) ;
22 │     │     │  break;
23 │     │  if (s_j = "in_child") ∨ (v ∈ kill(s_j) ∧ s_j ∈ N_slice) then
24 │     │     │  break;
25 │     │  j := (j − 1) mod (n + 1);
26 │   until (j = e);
27 return N_slice;
```

Algorithm 1 describes the steps of slicing based on the SLV data dependence analysis in the given PCBs $\langle Bs, Rs \rangle$. It will, for each block B with nonempty slicing criterion S_B, repeatedly pick a SLV pair (i, v) from S_B and propagate (i, v) in the block until either killed, or the "endpoint" e is reached. If (i, v) is killed at s_j then s_j is sliced, if not already done, and new SLV pairs are generated according to $gen(s_j)$ and added to S_B: the details are found in (3), where the transfer function $f^j_{i,e,v}$ is defined. If a statement $s_j \in B$ is sliced, the condition $s_0 \in B$ is sliced also as s_j is control dependent on the condition s_0 as well as on the conditions for all blocks B' "above" it (lines 16-18).

For each interface $s \rightarrow s'$, the set $R_m(s \rightarrow s')$ contains the SLVs propagated over the interface so far. This set is used to prevent the same SLV to be propagated several times: if not done, there would be a risk of nontermination due to an SLV being propagated in a cycle through different blocks without ever being killed.

6 Interprocedural Slicing

The slicing algorithm discussed so far is intra-procedural. In this section we sketch how to extend it to an inter-procedural algorithm. We consider an extension of the model language in Section 2.1 with procedures according to the following. The arguments are both readable and writable, and actual arguments are variables. (Basically this is call-by-reference, passing pointers to the actual arguments.) For simplicity we assume that each procedure has a single return statement, at the end of the procedure body. Our approach is easily extended to deal with arguments that are call-by-value, and multiple return statements: indeed, our implementation can handle these features.

Global variables accessed in the procedure body can be considered as actual arguments with the same name as the formal argument. Thus, global variables are handled without further ado.

The PCB representation is easily extended to represent procedures and procedure calls. Each procedure body is represented by a block. Interfaces connect call sites with procedure body blocks: from each call site a "call" interface reaches the entry point of the procedure, and a "return" interface connects the return statement with the call site. This is similar to how procedure calls are represented for CFGs [19]. An example is shown in Fig. 2.

We now describe an approach to inter-procedural slicing that is context-sensitive in that it treats different call sites separately. For a call site $p(\bar{a})$ to procedure p, wich actual arguments $\bar{a}$, there are two problems to solve:

- How will the call contribute to the slice of the procedure body of p?
- What is the transfer function for the call? (I.e., given a SLV pair (i,v) where v is an actual argument to p, which actual arguments when entering p may influence the value of v at exit?

Our solution addresses both these problems. The idea is to slice the procedure body separately for each call site, and for each SLV appearing as actual argument. For each procedure p, and formal argument x of p, we define $\mu_p(x)$ as the set of formal arguments whose value at entry may affect the value of x at return. μ_p can be used to compute transfer functions for calls to p by substituting actual arguments for formal arguments. Our inter-procedural algorithm works as follows when encountering a call site $p(\bar{a})$. Assume that an SLV pair (i, v) appears at the return interface of $p(\bar{a})$:

1. If v is not an actual argument in $\bar{a}$, then the pair is just propagated to the call interface. No slicing of p takes place.

2. If v is an actual argument in $\bar{a}$, for the formal argument x, then we check whether $\mu_p(x)$ is already computed or not:
    - If it is, then $\mu_p(x)$ is used to compute new SLV pairs at the call interface by substituting actual arguments for formal arguments. No slicing is done of the body of p.
    - If it is not, then the slicing of the block holding $p(\bar{a})$ is temporarily halted. Instead the body of p is sliced, with x as slicing criterion at the return statement. During this process, $\mu_p(x)$ can be computed by adding some bookkeeping of SLVs to Algorithm 1. Then the slicing of the block holding $p(\bar{a})$ is resumed, using $\mu_p(x)$ as above.

This demand-driven approach attempts to minimise work by computing $\mu_p(x)$ only for formal arguments x holding some SLV as actual argument, and by reusing already computed sets $\mu_p(x)$ thus avoiding slicing the procedure body anew for the same slicing criterion.

When all call sites to p have been sliced, for all SLVs appearing as formal arguments, the slice of the body of p is computed as the union of the slices computed with slicing criteria formed from the different SLVs. Note that each slicing of the procedure body should be seen as a separate slicing problem, where the original body is sliced: if subsequent slicings are done on already sliced code, then dependences may be different from the original code and the computed $\mu_p(x)$ sets may be incorrect.

7 Experimental Evaluation

We have implemented both the SLV-based and the PDG-based slicing algorithms, and made an experimental evaluation of the results in order to measure the relative correctness, and compare the efficiency of both approaches. Both implementations are done in Microsoft Visual C++ 2013 (MVC), programs are parsed using the "Regular Expression" built-in library in MVC, and experiments have been performed on an Intel Core i5 3320M with 2.66GHz processor, 8 GB RAM, and 64-bit operating system. In addition to our own implementations we have also measured the running times for the CodeSurfer commercial tool[1], which uses PDG-based slicing. The execution times of CodeSurfer are not directly comparable to the execution times for our implementations, as CodeSurfer is implemented in a different framework, but it is still of interest to compare with a state-of-practice tool.

Five factors influence the time and space complexities of the slicing process: number of lines of code (LOC), number of variables, percentage of conditional predicates, size of the slice relative to the size of the sliced program, and the maximum depth of the nested loops. Our experiments study each factor individually. To do so we have used automatically generated, synthetic codes where these factors are systematically varied. These codes can be generated either in the model language of Section 2.1, or as the corresponding C code. Our implementations analyse the model language, and CodeSurfer analyses C code.

---

[1] From GrammaTech, www.grammatech.com

7.1   Experimental Results

As regards of correctness, the PDG-based and the SLV-based slicing compute the same slices in all our experiments. Otherwise the experiments compare running times and memory consumption, and we compute speedup figures. The parsing time is not included in the running times for any method. For CodeSurfer, which also performs a number of other analyses, the time is measured as the time to build the PDG plus the time to perform the backwards search to form the slice. The resolution of the time reported by CodeSurfer to build the PDG is whole seconds, which limits the precision of the computed execution time. In some experiments the reported time for building the PDG is zero: those cases are marked as "-" in the tables.

Table 1. SLV- vs PDG-based slicing: (a) code size is varied, (b) slice percentage is varied

	(a)						(b)				
	10K	20K	50K	100K	150K	200K	80%	40%	20%	10%	1.5%
SLV(sec.)	0.015	0.034	0.081	0.165	0.253	0.343	0.172	0.093	0.062	0.031	0.015
PDG(sec.)	0.676	1.5	4.028	8.183	12.86	16.945	8.158	8.127	8.128	8.128	8.112
C.Surfer(sec.)	-	2	6	15	31	53	15.45	15.25	15.155	15.07	15
SpeedupPDG	45.06	44.12	49.73	49.59	50.83	49.40	47.43	87.39	131.10	262.19	540.80
SpeedupCS	-	58.82	74.07	90.90	122.53	154.52	89.8	164.0	244.4	486.1	1000.0

Table 1(a) shows the slicing time of six different source codes varying in size from 10K to 200K. The slicing is performed with respect to a single slicing criterion, and time is measured in seconds. Each example program contains 50 variables, 18% conditional predicates, the nesting of conditionals is at most four, and the relative size of the slices is 70% of the source code. The execution time is computed as an average of the times for five different runs. The execution times of SLV-based slicing, our implementation of PDG-based slicing, and the PDG-based slicing by CodeSurfer are shown in rows 2-4. The fifth and the sixth rows show the speedups obtained by the SLV-based slicing over the PDG-based slicing implemented by our tool, and CodeSurfer respectively. The results in both rows indicate that SLV-based slicing gains a significant speedup compared to the PDG-based method when computing single slices.

The reason for this speedup is that the SLV-based slicing is a demand-driven method that avoids computing unnecessary data dependencies. As the PCB-based representation efficiently captures all control dependencies, detecting control dependencies also becomes inexpensive. PDG-based slicing, on the other hand, requires a complete dependence analysis. This method consumes most of its time in building the PDG. Therefore, for the same source code, decreasing the slice sizes (i.e., slicing w.r.t. a different slicing criterion) does not have a noticeable effect on the execution time for the PDG-based method whereas the SLV-based method runs significantly faster for smaller slices. Table 1(b) gives execution times when the relative size of the slice varies from 80% to 1.5%, with source code size 100K, containing 50 program variables, 18% conditional predicates, and nesting of conditionals at most four. As can be seen, the speedups are significantly higher for the SLV-based method when the relative size of the slice is smaller.

Increasing the number of variables will on average yield an increased number of data dependencies in the program code. This increases the execution time of both building the PDG, and the sizes of the SLV sets for the SLV-based slicing method. This is shown in Table 2(a), where the slicing time increases with the number of variables for both methods. Still, the SLV-based slicing method is consistently faster than the PDG-based method. We also compare the memory consumption of these methods in this table. The SLV-based slicing consumes considerably less memory than the PDG-based slicing, and the difference increases as the number of variables grows.

Table 2. SLV- vs PDG-based method: (a) varying number of variables, (b) varying number of control predicates. Program size 100K, 50 variables (b), 18% conditional predicates (a), nesting of conditionals at most four, relative slice size 70%.

	(a)							(b)		
	40	80	120	160	200	300	500	7%	14%	28%
SLV(sec.)	0.171	0.359	0.624	1.061	1.622	3.65	12.574	0,078	0,125	0,156
PDG(sec.)	4.321	15.881	33.181	54.288	78.655	141.961	406.5	0.671	2.698	28.267
SpeedupPDG	25.3	44.2	53.2	51.2	48.5	38.9	32.3	8,60	21,58	181,20
C.Surf(sec.)	13.47	32.5	48.59	62	84	151.56	238.6	4	10	21
SpeedupCS	78.8	90.5	77.9	58.4	51.8	41.5	19.0	51.28	80.00	134.62
SLV(Mb)	17.3	23.5	25.8	26.7	29.4	32.9	31.7	14	16	19.4
PDG(Mb)	96.7	348.5	501.8	763	912	1005	1600	49.7	122.5	506.8
Mem.Save	5.6	14.8	19.4	28.5	31.0	30.5	50.3	3.5	7.6	26.1

Table 2(b) shows the effect on slicing time and memory consumption of varying the percentage of control predicates in the code. The slicing time and memory requirements increase with the number of control predicates for both methods, however much faster for the PDG-based method. For the SLV-based method the number of PCBs will increase, which will affect the execution time some. For the PDG-based method, however, several factors affecting the execution time will increase. First, the size of the CFG will be larger since more control predicates will yield more edges. Second, the number of data dependencies will tend to increase since there will be more paths in the code, increasing the likelihood that different dependencies are carried by the same variable through different paths. This will result in a larger PDG. Third, more fixed-point iterations will be needed in the Reaching Definitions analysis due to the more complex nature of the control and data flow.

The results shown in Table 2(b) confirm that the influence of an increased percentage of control predicates is stronger for the PDG-based method than for the SLV-based method, both as regards execution time and memory consumption. Both the speedup and the relative memory savings for the SLV-based method grow quickly with the percentage of control predicates.

We also have studied briefly the effects of increasing the depths of loop nests on the slicing time. This is interesting since loops will necessitate conventional fixed-point iterations in the RD data dependency analysis used by PDG-based slicing, whereas our SLV-based method uses a different mechanism to handle loops.

We have obtained increasing speedups over the PDG-based method when the source code contains loops that are nested deeper. For example, we analyzed a program for loop nesting depths one to five, obtaining speedups 2.4, 6.3, 14.7, 27.3, 48.2. When we compared the execution times of our SLV-based method with those of CodeSurfer, we obtained the speedups -, 80.0, 96.0, 92.0, 92.5. (Here, the speedup for the first item could not be computed since the time resolution of CodeSurfer gave zero execution time.)

8   Related Work

Program slicing was first introduced by Weiser [24,25] in the context of debugging. Since then, different approaches to slicing were introduced including static [24,25], conditioned [7], dynamic [13], amorphous [10], semantic [3], and abstract slicing [11,18], of which static slicing techniques are the ones that are most comparable to our approaches.

Ottenstein et. al. [9,20] introduced the PDG, and proposed its use in program slicing. PDG-based slicing has then been the classical program slicing method that has been extended to interprocedural slicing [12,21,22], to produce executable slices [1,2,8], and to handle pointers [16].

Apart from PDG-based slicing, slicing based on data flow equations have been proposed by Weiser [24,25], Lyle [17], and Lisper [15]. Even though some of these approaches can handle unstructured control flow and low-level code, our approach is more time and memory efficient for computing single slices of source codes that does not contain arbitrary jumps. There have been several empirical studies and survey papers [5,6,23,26] that compare different slicing techniques.

Sprite [4] is a slicing approach that divides the information of the code into two levels: hard-to-demand and on-demand. The hard-to-demand information is calculated early, and on-demand information like the data and control dependencies are found during the slicing. The precision of Sprite is tunable, but the algorithm favors less precise slicing. Katana [14] is a slicing approach that uses a database-like program representation: it is fast, but less precise than PDG-based slicing.

9   Conclusions and Future Work

We have proposed a slicing approach for well-structured programs appearing in safety critical systems. The algorithm performs the slicing in a dynamic fashion, using an internal representation that is efficiently derived from the syntax tree. An experimental evaluation indicates that the algorithm outperforms the current state-of-the practice algorithm by a magnitude, both as regards execution time and memory requirements, when single slices are taken for the same slicing criterion. As future work we would like to extend the slicing approach to handle arbitrary control flow, and make an empirical evaluation for large industrial code. Furthermore we want to investigate how well a parallel job pool implementation performs: its decoupled job structure should make the algorithm very amenable to such an implementation.

Acknowledgments. The research presented in this paper is supported by the FP7 Marie Curie IAPP programme under the project 251413 APARTS, by the Swedish Foundation for Strategic Research under the SYNOPSIS project, and by the KKS Foundation under the project TOCSYC. We also thank GrammaTech for providing access to CodeSurfer.

References

1. Agrawal, H.: On slicing programs with jump statements. SIGPLAN Not. **29**(6), 302–312 (1994)
2. Ball, T., Horwitz, S.: Slicing programs with arbitrary control-flow. In: Fritzson, P.A. (ed.) Proc. First International Workshop on Automated and Algorithmic Debugging, AADEBUG 1993. LNCS, vol. 749. pp. 206–222. Springer, Heidelberg (1993)
3. Barros, J.B., da Cruz, D., Henriques, P.R., Pinto, J.S.: Assertion-based slicing and slice graphs. In: Proceedings of the 2010 8th IEEE International Conference on Software Engineering and Formal Methods, SEFM 2010, pp. 93–102. IEEE Computer Society, Washington, DC (2010)
4. Bent, L., Atkinson, D.C., Griswold, W.G.: A qualitative study of two whole-program slicers for C. University of California San Diego, Tech. rep. (2000)
5. Binkley, D., Harman, M.: A large-scale empirical study of forward and backward static slice size and context sensitivity. In: Proc. International Conference on Software Maintenance, ICSM 2003, p. 44. IEEE Computer Society, Washington, DC (2003)
6. Binkley, D., Harman, M.: A survey of empirical results on program slicing. In: Advances in Computers, Advances in Computers, vol. 62, pp. 105–178. Elsevier (2004)
7. Canfora, G.: Conditioned program slicing. Information and Software Technology **40**(11–12), 595–607 (1998)
8. Choi, J.D., Ferrante, J.: Static slicing in the presence of goto statements. ACM Trans. Program. Lang. Syst. **16**(4), 1097–1113 (1994)
9. Ferrante, J., Ottenstein, K.J., Warren, J.D.: The program dependence graph and its use in optimization. ACM Trans. Program. Lang. Syst. **9**(3), 319–349 (1987)
10. Harman, M., Binkley, D., Danicic, S.: Amorphous program slicing. In: Software Focus, pp. 70–79. IEEE Computer Society Press (1997)
11. Hong, H.S., Lee, I., Sokolsky, O.: Abstract slicing: A new approach to program slicing based on abstract interpretation and model checking. In: 2013 IEEE 13th International Working Conference on Source Code Analysis and Manipulation (SCAM), pp. 25–34 (2005)

12. Horwitz, S., Reps, T., Binkley, D.: Interprocedural slicing using dependence graphs. ACM Trans. Program. Lang. Syst. **12**(1), 26–60 (1990)
13. Korel, B.: Dynamic program slicing. Information Processing Letters 29 (October 1988)
14. Kraft, J.: Enabling Timing Analysis of Complex Embedded Software Systems. Ph.D. thesis, Mälardalen University Press (August 2010)
15. Lisper, B., Masud, A.N., Khanfar, H.: Static backward demand-driven slicing. In: Proceedings of the 2015 Workshop on Partial Evaluation and Program Manipulation, PEPM 2015, pp. 115–126. ACM, New York (2015)
16. Lyle, J.R., Binkley, D.: Program slicing in the presence of pointers (1993) (extended abstract)
17. Lyle, J.R.: Evaluating Variations on Program Slicing for Debugging (Data-flow, Ada). Ph.D. thesis, College Park, MD, USA (1984)
18. Mastroeni, I., Nikolić, D.J.: Abstract Program Slicing: From Theory towards an Implementation. In: Dong, J.S., Zhu, H. (eds.) ICFEM 2010. LNCS, vol. 6447, pp. 452–467. Springer, Heidelberg (2010)
19. Nielson, F., Nielson, H.R., Hankin, C.: Principles of Program Analysis, 2nd edn. Springer (2005). iSBN 3-540-65410-0
20. Ottenstein, K.J., Ottenstein, L.M.: The program dependence graph in a software development environment. SIGSOFT Softw. Eng. Notes **9**(3), 177–184 (1984)
21. Reps, T., Horwitz, S., Sagiv, M., Rosay, G.: Speeding up slicing. In: Proceedings of the 2Nd ACM SIGSOFT Symposium on Foundations of Software Engineering, SIGSOFT 1994, pp. 11–20. ACM, New York (1994)
22. Sinha, S., Harrold, M.J., Rothermel, G.: System-dependence-graph-based slicing of programs with arbitrary interprocedural control flow. In: Proceedings of the 21st International Conference on Software Engineering, ICSE 1999, pp. 432–441. ACM, New York (1999)
23. Tip, F.: A survey of program slicing techniques. Journal of Programming Languages **3**, 121–189 (1995)
24. Weiser, M.: Program Slicing. IEEE Transactions on Software Engineering SE-**10**(4), 352–357 (1984)
25. Weiser, M.D.: Program Slices: Formal, Psychological, and Practical Investigations of an Automatic Program Abstraction Method. Ph.D. thesis, Ann Arbor, MI, USA (1979), aAI8007856
26. Xu, B., Qian, J., Zhang, X., Wu, Z., Chen, L.: A brief survey of program slicing. SIGSOFT Softw. Eng. Notes **30**(2), 1–36 (2005)

A Novel Run-Time Monitoring Architecture for Safe and Efficient Inline Monitoring

Geoffrey Nelissen[✉], David Pereira, and Luís Miguel Pinho

CISTER/INESC TEC, ISEP, Polytechnic Institute of Porto,
Porto, Portugal
{grrpn,dmrpe,lmp}@isep.ipp.pt

Abstract. Verification and testing are two of the most costly and time consuming steps during the development of safety critical systems. The advent of complex and sometimes partially unpredictable computing architectures such as multicore commercial-of-the-shelf platforms, together with the composable development approach adopted in multiple industrial domains such as avionics and automotive, rendered the exhaustive testing of all situations that could potentially be encountered by the system once deployed on the field nearly impossible. Run-time verification (RV) is a promising solution to help accelerate the development of safety critical applications whilst maintaining the high degree of reliability required by such systems. RV adds monitors in the application, which check at run-time if the system is behaving according to predefined specifications. In case of deviations from the specifications during the runtime, safeguarding measures can be triggered in order to keep the system and its environment in a safe state, as well as potentially attempting to recover from the fault that caused the misbehaviour. Most of the state-of-the-art on RV essentially focused on the monitor generation, concentrating on the expressiveness of the specification language and its translation in correct-by-construction monitors. Few of them addressed the problem of designing an efficient and safe run-time monitoring (RM) architecture. Yet, RM is a key component for RV. The RM layer gathers information from the monitored application and transmits it to the monitors. Therefore, without an efficient and safe RM architecture, the whole RV system becomes useless, as its inputs and hence by extension its outputs cannot be trusted. In this paper, we discuss the design of a novel RM architecture suited to safety critical applications.

Keywords: Run-time monitoring · Run-time verification · Safety critical systems · Ada

1 Introduction

Run-time verification (RV) [7, 16] entails adding pieces of code called *monitors* to a running application. The *monitors* scrutinise the system behaviour and check if it respects associated specifications. The monitors can detect anomalies during the execution of the application. That information may be logged and back

© Springer International Publishing Switzerland 2015
J.A. de la Puente and T. Vardanega (Eds.): Ada-Europe 2015, LNCS 9111, pp. 66–82, 2015.
DOI:10.1007/978-3-319-19584-1_5

propagated to the system designer. It is therefore an efficient solution to detect bugs and other deficiencies when a complete static verification of the system is not possible. By keeping the monitors running in the system after its deployment, run-time verification can also be used as a tool to increase the safety and reliability of systems during their operation, triggering counter-measures when anomalies are detected and hence acting as a safety net around the monitored application.

With the advent of more and more complex computing platforms (e.g., multicore processors, many-core accelerators, networks on chip, distributed systems interconnected with various communication networks) and the adoption of new computing paradigms to exploit the power of those architectures, verifying whether a system respects its functional (e.g., order of execution and validity of results) and extra-functional (e.g., timing constraints) specifications became a big challenge. Static verification (i.e., the formal proof that the system is correct) has proven limited either because of the state space explosion problem as in the case of approaches based on model checking, or simply due to theoretical limitations related to the expressivity and decidability of approaches based on deductive verification. Furthermore, ensuring the correctness of extra-functional properties before the system deployment is usually subject to a high degree of pessimism, essentially because the data that must be manipulated (e.g., execution time, inter-arrival time or response time) are almost always available only at run-time, and depend on specificities of the underlying hardware (e.g., communication protocols on shared buses, replacement policies in caches, operation ordering in execution pipelines), interactions with the external physical environment and interference caused by concurrent applications.

Testing and simulations are often presented as solutions to improve the confidence in the final system. However, one can never ensure an exhaustive testing of all the possible situations that may be encountered after deployment. Therefore, successfully passing all the tests does not provide any guarantee that the system is bug-free or that it will always respect all its requirements.

Furthermore, today's practices in product development rely extensively on distributed development. Multiple partners and subcontractors develop different functionalities that are later integrated together to form the final product. As a result, most of the components are black-boxes and none of the partners knows exactly how they all have actually been implemented. Therefore, ensuring an exhaustive testing and fully trusted verification of the system before its deployment becomes nearly impossible. Keeping monitors running together with the applications in order to detect potential misbehaviours and trigger safe-guarding measures should therefore be considered as a promising solution to accelerate the product development cycle whilst maintaining the high safety requirements associated to such systems.

Most of the state-of-the-art on run-time verification focuses on the design of formal languages [3,15,18] for the specification of properties that must be verified at run-time. Those languages are then used to generate monitors in a correct-by-construction manner. However, run-time verification cannot work without appropriate mechanisms to actually monitor the system and extract meaningful information that can then be used by the monitors to assert the respect of the specifications. This basic infrastructure over which any run-time verification framework is built has received much less attention from the research community. Run-time monitoring is however a corner stone of an efficient and safe run-time verification framework as it plays the interface between the monitors and the monitored applications. Previous works have developed run-time monitoring solutions as a part of full run-time verification frameworks. Most of them though, put the accent on the specification language and the monitor generation process, neglecting the implementation and run-time monitoring aspect. In this paper we specifically focus on the run-time monitoring architecture and propose a new, efficient and safe solution to integrate monitors with application code. The design of the presented run-time monitoring framework is perfectly suited to safety critical systems such as avionics, space, railway or automotive applications, as well as any other embedded system.

Contribution. This paper introduces a novel reference architecture for inline run-time monitoring. The presented solution has been designed in order to fulfil the requirements of safety critical systems. The architecture has been kept simple so as to ease its implementation in various run-time environments. A prototype, written in Ada, of this new reference architecture is presented and experimental results show that the overhead caused by the instrumentation of the code is constant w.r.t. the worst-case execution time of the tasks constituting the monitored application.

Paper organisation. In Section 2, the requirements for the design of a reliable and efficient run-time monitoring framework for safety critical systems are presented. In Section 3, those requirements are compared with the solutions existing in the state-of-the-art. The strengths and limitations of each solution identified during this analysis, are used in Section 4 to design a novel reference architecture suited to the run-time monitoring of safety critical systems. Section 5 presents the implementation of the reference architecture in Ada and Section 6 provides results of experiments conducted on this first implementation.

2   Requirements

As later discussed in Section 3, most of the state-of-the-art solutions on run-time monitoring and verification rely on software engineering concepts that are not compatible with the requirements of safety critical systems. Therefore, with the objective of providing an adequate solution for run-time monitoring, in this section, we start by studying the requirements of safety critical systems. Those will serve as a basis to build the foundations of our new run-time monitoring framework presented in Section 4.

2.1   Independent and Composable Development

Distributing the development of complex systems between different partners and subcontractors became a common practice in the industry. Once delivered, the components are integrated together to form the final product. This methodology is well established in the industry and should not be reconsidered for the development of monitors. Yet, it can only be achieved in an efficient manner if both *composability* and *compositionality* are possible. Compositionality ensures that the overall application behaviour can result from the composition of its constituting subcomponents. On the other hand, composability enforces that the behaviour of individual components remain unchanged when considered in isolation and after their integration within the system.

In fact, the certification standards recommend the development and the verification of safety critical systems to be performed by different actors in order to reduce the chances of undetected anomalies. The same principle should thus be followed for the monitors generation. Indeed, if the same actor is responsible for both the application development and the monitor generation, this would increase the likelihood of common errors being introduced in the monitor specification and in the monitored application. The generated monitor would become useless as the potential system misbehaviour would remain undetected during the execution.

2.2   Time and Space Partitioning

Time and space partitioning is a way to ease the composable development of software applications, as well as to improve the overall safety of the system. Spatial partitioning ensures that a task in one partition is unable to change private data of another task in another partition. Temporal partitioning, on the other hand, guarantees that the timing characteristics of tasks, such as their worst-case execution times, are not affected by the execution of other tasks in other partitions. Consequently, time and space partitioning enforces two important features:

- the properties of different components pertaining to different partitions and integrated in the same system are not impacted by each other;
- because the tasks of different partitions are isolated, a fault in one partition cannot propagate to another partition, thereby improving the reliability of the whole system.

Therefore, it becomes evident that it should be possible to isolate monitors and monitored applications through time and space partitioning. This would ensure (i) that the newly introduced monitors do not modify the behaviour of the monitored applications and (ii) that a fault happening in the monitored application does not propagate to the monitors, which would prevent its detection and the triggering of the appropriate safe-guarding measures.

In a completely safe design, it should also be possible to isolate monitors from each other. Hence, a monitor misbehaving due, for instance, to corrupted input data or other external causes, could not affect other monitors and their own verification work.

2.3 Simplicity

Although simplicity should always be one of the main concerns in any development process, it is of special importance for safety critical systems. Indeed, a simple design eases the understanding of the overall system, the writing of detailed specifications and hence the potentially expensive and time consuming certification or qualification processes.

Moreover, one of the advantages claimed by run-time verification is the acceleration of the system development by partially removing the need of a complete verification of the system before its deployment. Indeed, correctly implemented monitors that are cleverly introduced in the system will be responsible for keeping safe the corresponding blocks of code that they observe, thereby acting as a safety net in case of the manifestation of an untested execution scenario. It would thus be contradictory to replace the complex and time consuming testing and formal verification phase by a difficult process of code instrumentation and monitor integration.

2.4 Efficiency and Responsiveness

Monitors should be able to detect misbehaviours and respond in an acceptable amount of time in order to be useful. It would be of poor interest to launch counter-measures long after some anomalies have caused irremediable consequences to the system. Therefore, an efficient implementation is required to ensure that the information needed for the verification of the system correctness reach the monitors as soon as needed.

3   Study of Existing Solutions

This section reviews the solutions for run-time monitoring that were already considered in the literature. We relate each of them to the requirements derived in Section 2 in order to extract their strengths and limitations. The results of this study will then be used in Section 4 to design a run-time monitoring architecture suited to safety critical systems.

All the works discussed in this paper, target the run-time monitoring of software systems. In that context, we formally define an *event* and *event instance* as follows:

Definition 1 (Event). *An event is a set of conditions that must be encountered during the system execution.*

Definition 2 (Event instance). *An event instance is the realisation of its associated event. An event instance is therefore characterised by a unique timestamp.*

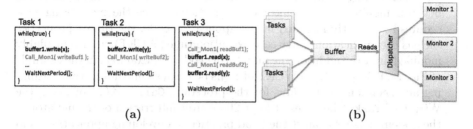

Fig. 1. State-of-the-art run-time monitoring architectures

3.1   Code Injection

The most common implementation of monitors in the state-of-the-art run-time verification frameworks consists in injecting the monitoring code directly in the application code. Fig. 1a illustrates that approach with three tasks. Two tasks write data that are read by the third task. A monitor named `Mon1` is called after each write and before each read to check properties on the data exchange. In such implementation, the monitoring procedure is executed as part of the three tasks.

Eagle [1], Hawk [6], RuleR [2], MOP [4], TemporalRover [8], Rmor [9] and RV [17] are examples of frameworks implementing that solution. Those monitoring frameworks are based on Aspect Oriented Programming [12] such as AspectJ [14], AspectC [5], or similar instrumentation mechanisms. The monitoring procedures are directly called when the monitored application passes by pre-specified positions in the source or compiled code. Whilst simple to implement, this monitoring architecture exhibits multiple drawbacks as discussed below:

- Whereas space partitioning could still be enforced with such monitoring architecture, the existing implementations of those frameworks simply do not consider it. This lack of isolation is the cause of two major issues:
  - Since the monitored application shares the same address space as the monitors, a faulty application generating memory errors due, for example, to stack overflows or wrong pointer manipulations, may corrupt the data manipulated by the monitor and alter its correct behaviour. The monitor would become unreliable, incapable to detect the fault or even worse, outputting a wrong diagnosis, which may lead to the triggering of counter-productive measures, thereby worsening the situation.
  - Monitors have direct reading and writing access to globally defined entities of the monitored application (for example, `Buffer1` and `Buffer2` in the example of Fig. 1a). A faulty monitor, wrongly implemented (voluntarily or not), could therefore modify and corrupt the content of the application variable and hence impact its execution. This generates safety and security threats for the overall system. This would be unacceptable in safety-critical applications.

– Such monitoring architecture does not allow any kind of timing isolation between monitors and monitored applications. Since the monitoring procedures are directly included in the application code, the timing properties such as the application worst-case execution time (WCET), are irremediably modified after the addition the monitoring code. For example, in the example of Fig. 1a, if `Task 1` has a WCET of 15ms before instrumentation and assuming an execution time of 5ms for the procedure `CallMon1(.)` of `Mon1`, the WCET of `Task 1` becomes at least 20ms after integration of the monitor in the system. It goes against the good practice of developing applications and monitors independently and later integrating them in a composable manner in the final system, and leads to two unwanted consequences:

  • Any timing analysis that would have been performed before the monitor integration are not valid anymore after their insertion. They should all be redone, thus generating extra work, which may be expensive and time-consuming.

  • There is no assurance that the behaviour of the application is not impacted by the addition of this extra-code. Therefore, it is impossible to predict if a well-behaving application will still respect all its specifications and thus remain correct if the monitoring code was removed.

– Since the currently adopted approaches introduce monitors as pieces of sequential code in the target application, only one thread at a time can call a given monitoring procedure, access a specific internal data, or change a state variable. A synchronisation protocol must be introduced, thereby limiting the parallelism in the monitored application. This makes this implementation particularly inefficient for multi-threaded applications such as the one presented in Fig. 1a, where events generated by different threads (i.e., tasks) may be required by a same monitor. This is a major drawback of this monitoring architecture in a context of generalisation of the use of multicore processors in embedded and general purpose systems and considering the common adoption of multi-threaded programming languages.

3.2   Independent Monitors and Buffered Communications

The alternative to the monitoring architecture presented above is to implement monitors as independent components that receive events information through buffers (see Fig. 1b). It is the approach followed in Java-MaC [13], Java PathExplorer [10] and Java MultiPathExplorer [19].

One Global Buffer. The most straightforward implementation of this solution would assume that all events are written in a shared buffer. In order to avoid the need for every monitor to read all events stored in the buffer — including those that are of no interest — an event dispatcher (see Fig. 1b) is usually attached to the output of the buffer [10,13]. The dispatcher reads the events pushed in the buffer by the monitored application and redistributes them to the monitors requiring them.

Unfortunately, the use of a unique global shared buffer causes a bottleneck in the flow of information. Indeed, only one event instance can be written in the buffer at a time. This requires the use of a synchronisation mechanism among different threads that would try to access the buffer concurrently. This may lead to unwanted blocking of the tasks of the monitored application, thereby impacting their timing properties and thus going against any sort of timing isolation as their timing behaviours now become dependent on the number of threads pushing events in the buffer. Moreover, forbidding parallel event writing slows down the transfer of information to the monitors and hence their capacity to detect anomalies in an acceptable amount of time (i.e., responsiveness).

One Private Buffer per Monitor. An alternative implementation would be to provide a private buffer for each monitor. As a consequence, there is no need for an event dispatcher anymore. Although diminishing the number of potential concurrent accesses to the same buffer, a synchronisation mechanism is still necessary when events generated by multiple threads are needed by the same monitor. Furthermore, additional issues must now be considered:

- When an event is useful for multiple monitors, the monitored application must be instrumented multiple times in order to push the event in the buffers of each relevant monitor. This means that the instrumentation code is redundant. Moreover, the same event instance might be copied in multiple buffers, thereby increasing the memory footprint of the monitoring architecture.
- The monitors using the events must be known when instrumenting the application. Adding, removing or replacing monitors require re-instrumenting the code, even if they all use the same events and data. This impacts the extensibility of the system as well as the independency between monitors and monitored applications.

4 A Novel Reference Architecture for Run-Time Monitoring

Strong from the analysis performed in the two previous sections, we propose a new reference architecture for run-time monitoring suited to safety critical as well as non-critical applications. This reference architecture could then be implemented in any language, as long as it respects the prescriptions discussed below. The proposed run-time monitoring framework is depicted in Fig. 2. It is composed of five main components: (1) the monitored application, (2) the monitors, (3) *buffers* through which events are transmitted, (4) *buffer writers* for writing events in a specific buffer and (5) *buffer readers* used by the monitors to read events stored in a buffer. This structure may look straightforward, yet multiple details discussed below, allow us to fulfil each and every requirement presented in Section 2.

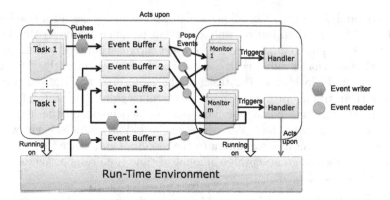

Fig. 2. Proposed reference architecture for run-time monitoring

4.1   Event transmission

Whenever an event instance is generated during the execution of the monitored application, the information must be transmitted to the monitors. However, unlike most of the run-time monitoring frameworks presented in the previous section, in the proposed reference architecture, event instances are not directly sent to the monitors using them. Instead, the timestamps of the event instances are stored in an intermediate buffer specific to that event. That is, there is one buffer per event rather than one buffer per monitor. As a consequence, the monitored application is unaware of the existence of any potential monitor using the transmitted information thanks to the buffers playing the role of an interface. Moreover, the monitored application must be instrumented only once, thereby reducing the dependency between the application instrumentation and the monitors generation. Finally, it avoids any type of data or monitoring code redundancy.

Efficient Event Reading. As shown in Fig. 2, each event (i.e., the completion of a task, the access to a data, the release of a semaphore, ...) is associated with a different buffer. Each buffer can then be accessed by any monitor that would require information about that specific event. Multiple monitors can access the same buffer using different *buffer readers*. Buffer readers are independent from each other. Indeed, each buffer reader uses its own pointer pointing to the oldest data that has not yet been accessed. Because each buffer reader uses a different pointer to read data in the buffer they are associated with, simultaneous accesses to a same buffer is possible without any blocking time. Furthermore, a data read by one buffer reader is not erased from the buffer and can thus still be accessed by any other buffer reader that did not read it yet. This mechanism allows multiple monitors to use the same events without using any synchronisation protocol nor duplicating the events data for each monitor making use of it. Consequently, there is a gain in terms of transmission time as well as required memory space.

Efficient Event Writing. One of the major design choice in the reference architecture of the proposed run-time monitoring framework is that only one task can have write accesses to a specific buffer. Those rights are granted by a *buffer writer*. Only one buffer writer can be instantiated per buffer and only one task can use that buffer writer. This added constraint avoids the need of synchronisation mechanisms since concurrent writing in the same buffer becomes impossible.

With the same objective of reducing the impact of the code instrumentation on the application performances, the buffers are circular. That is, a task writing an event in the buffer can never be blocked due to the buffer being full. In such a situation, the oldest event instance in the buffer will simply be overridden with the new data. It is therefore the role of the monitor developer to make sure that (i) the buffer is large enough and (ii) the monitors are reading events frequently enough to avoid missing any meaningful information.

4.2 Monitor Implementation

In the proposed reference run-time monitoring architecture, a monitor is a task which is periodically activated. At each activation, a monitor calls a monitoring procedure, which is provided by the monitor designer. A monitoring procedure is usually implemented as a finite state machine. It reads information about some specific events and makes its state evolve. If the state machine reaches an erroneous state, safe-guarding measures may be activated. The generation of the monitoring procedure is however out of the scope of this paper as it relates to the general run-time verification problem rather than the specific run-time monitoring issue discussed in this paper. The interested reader may consult the following (non-exhaustive) list of references for further information on that topic [2–4,11,18].

Note that, because the monitors are implemented as periodic tasks, their activation is completely independent from the execution of the monitored application. Unlike the solutions based on Aspect Oriented Programming and similar technologies, the execution of the monitored application is not delayed by the execution of the monitor whenever an event instance is generated. Instead, the monitor is periodically activated and checks all the meaningful information on events that may have been realised during its last period of inactivity. Therefore, implementing a monitor as an independent task rather than inserting code in the application, keeps the properties of the monitored application unaffected by the execution of the monitors, thereby allowing for the independent and composable development of monitors and monitored applications.

However, because the monitors are isolated in time from the monitored application (i.e., their executions are independent), there is a delay between the realisation of an event and its treatment by the monitor. This latency impacts the time needed to react to a system fault. However, because the monitors are implemented as periodic tasks, and under the assumption that the system is schedulable, this latency can be upper-bounded. Let T be the period of monitor Mon1 and let t_0 be the beginning of a period of Mon1. Mon1 can be executed at any time between t_0 and $t_0 + T$. A second execution of Mon1 will then happen between

$t_0 + T$ and $t_0 + 2 \times T$. In the worst-case scenario, Mon1 executes right at t_0 and then at the end of its next period, that is, right before $t_0 + 2 \times T$. If an event instance is generated just after the first execution of Mon1, it will be treated only during the second execution of the monitor at time $t_0 + 2 \times T$. The maximum latency can thus be upper-bounded by $2 \times T$ (i.e., twice the period of the monitor). As a consequence, the responsiveness of the monitor can be configured by modifying its period of activation.

4.3 Events Ordering

One of the major advantages of the architecture depicted on Fig. 2 is also one of its major issues. Because different events are stored in different buffers, instances of different events are not ordered (w.r.t. their timestamps). Yet, the order in which events happen is often a key property to detect faults, bugs, deficiencies or other execution anomalies. Since a monitor may need information from more than one event, it becomes its job to reorder event instances stored in different buffers before to treat them. In the proposed reference architecture, the monitor performs this task by using *synchronised buffer readers*. The synchronised buffer readers are instantiated inside the monitors. Synchronised buffer readers associated with a same monitor share a synchronisation variable. This variable stores the timestamp of the last event instance read by the monitor in any buffer. This information is used by all the synchronised event readers to determine which is the next event instance that must be considered in their buffer. The use of the synchronisation variable by the synchronised event readers is summarised in the pseudo-code provided in Algorithm 1.

When accessing its buffer, the synchronised event reader looks for the first event instance stored in the buffer with a timestamp larger than or equal to the timestamp saved into the synchronisation variable. If such an element exists, the timestamp of that event instance is saved in the synchronisation variable and the event instance information are sent back to the monitor. Otherwise, the event reader keeps the synchronisation variable unchanged and notify the monitor that the buffer is empty.

Algorithm 1. Pseudo-code of the function reading an event in a synchronised buffer reader.

Data: Synch_Variable; Current_Index; End_Buffer

```
1  while Current_Index ≠ End_Buffer do
2      if Buffer[Current_Index].timestamp ≥ Synch_Variable then
3          Synch_Variable ← Buffer[Current_Index].timestamp;
4          Current_Index ← Current_Index+1;
5          return Buffer[Current_Index−1];
6      end
7      Current_Index ← Current_Index+1;
8  end
9  return "Buffer empty";
```

Note that because a monitor is implemented as a sequential task and because all the synchronised event readers sharing the same synchronisation variable are associated with the same monitor, only one synchronised event reader is called at a time. Therefore, there cannot be concurrent accesses to the synchronisation variable and no access protection mechanism is hence required.

4.4   Isolation

The architecture described above is particularly well designed to achieve the complete isolation of the monitors from the monitored application. Indeed, each monitor is an independent task which can be restricted to its own memory address space, interacting with the application only through the unidirectional communication channels implemented by the event buffers.

Furthermore, if the system was deployed on a multicore platform, monitors could be executed on their own core(s), in parallel with the monitored application thanks to the multi-threaded approach promoted in this architecture.

4.5   Additional Remarks

As depicted on Fig. 2, the proposed architecture is quite flexible and thus allows task of the monitored application, but also the run-time environment (usually an operating system) and the monitors themselves to generate events and push them in their own buffers. Since the monitors are isolated from the rest of the system, they do not know anything about the architecture of the monitored application. Therefore, from the viewpoint of one monitor, another monitor generating events is seen as any other task pertaining to the monitored system. This paves the way to the definition of parallel and hierarchical verification frameworks, in which big monitoring procedures would be decomposed in a set of smaller monitors that would implement the overall monitoring functionality by exchanging information through event instances.

5   Library Implementation and Usage

A prototype of the monitoring architecture described in Section 4 has been implemented in Ada.

The buffer is implemented as a generic package. Each instance of that package is associated with a specific event. As shown in the example code below, it requires the definition of two generic variables; the length of the circular buffer and the type of an additional data that can be saved together with the timestamp of each event instance. This data could be the identifier of a task, the value of a counter or any other meaningful information for the monitors using it. For safety reasons, and to keep external components from altering the buffer content without using a buffer writer as prescribed in the reference architecture, the package is entirely private, leaving no interface for the external world to interact with it.

```
1  package Buffer_1 is new
2      Buffer(Event_Info_Type => Integer, Buffer_Length => 20);
```

Implementing the buffers as a generic package rather than a generic type (e.g., a record) may look unconventional. However, it allows us to implement the buffer writer as a generic child package, thereby permitting the package to check that there is only one buffer writer per buffer instance.

In order to be fully compliant with the proposed reference architecture, the event writers should be instantiated as described in the example code provided below, limiting the scope of the event writer to one task only.

```
1   task T1 with Priority => 10;
2   task body T1 is
3       package Buffer1_Writer is new Buffer_1.Writer;
4       T : Ada.Real_Time.Time;
5   begin
6       loop
7           T := Ada.Real_Time.Clock;
8           Buffer1_Writer.Write(Data => 1, TimeStamp => T);
9           (...)
10      end loop;
11  end T1;
```

The event writer interface provides only one procedure, which allows to write an event instance in the associated buffer. The Write procedure (see line 8 in the example code above) takes two parameters; the timestamp of the event instance and a data that provides extra-information for the monitors.

The skeleton of any monitor is implemented in the generic Monitor package. It implements the synchronised event readers and the periodic monitoring task as two private nested packages. This isolates the monitor from the external world, forbidding any external component to generate new monitoring tasks or synchronised event readers that could mess with the synchronisation variable of the monitor and hence with its correct behaviour.

To generate a new monitor, the system designer must first create a new child package to the Monitor package. It is in that new package that the monitoring procedure must be implemented and the periodic monitoring task calling that procedure instantiated. An example of such monitor definition is provided below.

```
1   generic
2   package Monitor.Procedure1 is
3       (...)
4   end Monitor.Procedure1;
5
6   package body Monitor.Procedure1 is
7       procedure MonProc1 is
8           Data : Integer;
9           Timestamp : Ada.Real_Time.Time;
10          IsEmpty, HasGap : Boolean;
```

```
11          package B1_Reader is
12              new Synchronized_Reader(Buffer_1);
13          (...)
14      begin
15          B1_Reader.Pop(Data, Timestamp, IsEmpty, HasGap);
16          (...)
17      end MonProc1;
18
19      package MonTask1 is
20          new Monitoring_Task(Monitoring_Procedure => MonProc1);
21  end Monitor.Procedure1;
```

The implementation of the monitoring procedure is left completely to the monitor designer. This procedure may instantiate synchronised readers — as exemplified at line 13 of the code above — to access the content of some specific event buffers. The Synchronised_Reader package takes the buffer from which it must read as a generic argument, and provides two procedures to extract information from that buffer: Pop and Get. Pop implements the basic reading procedure presented in the pseudocode of Algorithm 1. It finds the first event instance with a timestamp larger than the value saved in the synchronisation variable, updates the synchronisation variable and sends the data and timestamp associated with the found event instance back to the monitoring procedure. Get, however, also finds and sends back the information associated with the first meaningful event instance in the buffer but does not update the synchronisation variable. The monitoring procedure can use Get in order to read multiple times the same event instance or to first compare the timestamps and data of events stored in different buffers before deciding which event must actually be considered. Pop and Get may set the two booleans given as parameters in order to notify if the buffer is empty and if there is a gap in the trace stored in the buffer due to the circular nature of that buffer.

Once the monitoring procedure is implemented, the monitor designer must instantiate a monitoring task as described on line 21 of the example code provided above. This task will periodically call the monitoring procedure. Note that only one task can be instantiated per monitor. If multiple instantiations were attempted, then an exception would be raised.

Finally, the integration of the monitor in the system is done as shown below, defining the period and the priority of the monitoring task as the values of the two generic arguments of the Monitor package.

```
1  package Monitor1 is new Monitor(Period=>100, Priority=>61);
2  package Monitor1_Proc is new Monitor1.Procedure1;
```

Table 1. Experimental results (values in μs)

Tasks-Monitors-read/write	1-1-w	1-5-w	1-10-w	5-1-w	10-1-w	1-1-r	1-5-r	1-10-r	5-1-r	5-5-r
Average	0.74	0.69	0.58	0.62	0.82	0.53	0.81	0.70	0.94	0.83
Standard Deviation	0.48	0.53	0.5	0.49	0.52	0.50	0.54	0.52	0.34	0.47
Maximum	1	2	2	1	2	1	2	2	2	2

6   Experimental Results

In order to evaluate the overhead generated by our run-time monitoring architecture, we conducted a set of experiments varying the number of monitored tasks (from 1 to 10), event buffers (one per task) and monitors (from 1 to 10) reading from a same buffer. For each configuration, the time needed to read and write 100 event instances in their buffers has been monitored. The average value, maximum value and the standard deviation have been computed for each experiment. The experimental systems were implemented using the Ada prototype of the architecture presented in the previous section and compiled using the **gnat** toolchain. The experiments were performed on a quad-core Intel i7 processor cadenced at 2.3GHz with 8GB of RAM memory and a 500 GB Solid State SATA Drive. The results of the experiments are presented in Table 1. As a consequence of the absence of protection mechanisms in the reference architecture, the variation on the cost of writing and reading event instances is small and independent of the number of monitors and tasks generating events. Consequently, the maximum overhead induced by the monitoring architecture can be precisely calculated and hence included in the timing analysis of the application.

7   Conclusion

After the study of the requirements of safety critical systems and the extraction of the limitiations in the solutions implemented in the existing run-time verification frameworks, we presented a novel architecture for the implementation of a safe and reliable run-time monitoring framework. We exposed how this new design, whilst remaining simple and efficient, allows for the independent and composable development of monitors and monitored applications, and improves the safety and reliability of the overall system by making possible the complete isolation of the monitors from the rest of the system. As a consequence, a fault in the monitored application cannot propagate anymore to the monitors checking its correct behaviour. A first implementation of the proposed reference architecture together with experimental results were presented in the paper, thereby proving the feasibility of the promoted approach.

Acknowledgments. This work was partially supported by National Funds through FCT/MEC (Portuguese Foundation for Science and Technology) and when applicable, co-financed by ERDF (European Regional Development Fund) under the PT2020 Partnership, within project UID/CEC/04234/2013 (CISTER Research Centre); also by, FCT/MEC and the EU ARTEMIS JU within projects ARTEMIS/0003/2012 - JU grant nr. 333053 (CONCERTO) and ARTEMIS/0001/2013 - JU grant nr. 621429 (EMC2).

References

1. Barringer, H., Goldberg, A., Havelund, K., Sen, K.: Rule-Based Runtime Verification. In: Steffen, B., Levi, G. (eds.) VMCAI 2004. LNCS, vol. 2937, pp. 44–57. Springer, Heidelberg (2004)
2. Barringer, H., Havelund, K., Rydeheard, D., Groce, A.: Rule Systems for Runtime Verification: A Short Tutorial. In: Bensalem, S., Peled, D.A. (eds.) RV 2009. LNCS, vol. 5779, pp. 1–24. Springer, Heidelberg (2009)
3. Bauer, A., Leucker, M., Schallhart, C.: Runtime verification for ltl and tltl. ACM Trans. Softw. Eng. Methodol. **20**(4), 14:1–14:64 (2011)
4. Chen, F., Roşu, G.: Mop: An efficient and generic runtime verification framework. In: Proceedings of the 22Nd Annual ACM SIGPLAN Conference on Object-Oriented Programming Systems and Applications, OOPSLA, pp. 569–588. ACM, New York (2007)
5. Coady, Y., Kiczales, G., Feeley, M., Smolyn, G.: Using aspectc to improve the modularity of path-specific customization in operating system code. SIGSOFT Softw. Eng. Notes **26**(5), 88–98 (2001)
6. d'Amorim, M., Havelund, K.: Event-based runtime verification of java programs. SIGSOFT Softw. Eng. Notes **30**(4), 1–7 (2005)
7. Delgado, N., Gates, A.Q., Roach, S.: A taxonomy and catalog of runtime software-fault monitoring tools. IEEE Trans. Softw. Eng. **30**(12), 859–872 (2004)
8. Drusinsky, D.: The temporal rover and the atg rover. In: Havelund, K., Penix, J., Visser, W. (eds.) SPIN 2000. LNCS, vol. 1885, pp. 323–330. Springer, Heidelberg (2000)
9. Havelund, K.: Runtime Verification of C Programs. In: Suzuki, K., Higashino, T., Ulrich, A., Hasegawa, T. (eds.) TestCom/FATES 2008. LNCS, vol. 5047, pp. 7–22. Springer, Heidelberg (2008)
10. Havelund, K., Roşu, G.: An overview of the runtime verification tool java pathexplorer. Form. Methods Syst. Des. **24**(2), 189–215 (2004)
11. Havelund, K., Roşu, G.: Synthesizing Monitors for Safety Properties. In: Katoen, J.-P., Stevens, P. (eds.) TACAS 2002. LNCS, vol. 2280, pp. 342–356. Springer, Heidelberg (2002)
12. Kiczales, G.: Aspect-oriented programming. ACM Comput. Surv. 28(4es) (1996)
13. Kim, M., Viswanathan, M., Kannan, S., Lee, I., Sokolsky, O.: Java-mac: A run-time assurance approach for java programs. Form. Methods Syst. Des. **24**(2), 129–155 (2004)
14. Kiselev, I.: Aspect-Oriented Programming with Aspect J. Sams, Indianapolis, IN, USA (2002)
15. Konur, S.: A survey on temporal logics for specifying and verifying real-time systems. Front. Comput. Sci. **7**(3), 370–403 (2013)
16. Leucker, M., Schallhart, C.: A brief account of runtime verification. The Journal of Logic and Algebraic Programming **78**(5), 293–303 (2009), the 1st Workshop on Formal Languages and Analysis of Contract-Oriented Software (FLACOS 2007)

17. Meredith, P., Roşu, G.: Runtime Verification with the RV System. In: Barringer, H., Falcone, Y., Finkbeiner, B., Havelund, K., Lee, I., Pace, G., Roşu, G., Sokolsky, O., Tillmann, N. (eds.) RV 2010. LNCS, vol. 6418, pp. 136–152. Springer, Heidelberg (2010)
18. Sen, K.: Generating optimal monitors for extended regular expressions. In: Proc. of the 3rd Workshop on Runtime Verification (RV 2003). ENTCS, vol. 89 . pp. 162–181. Elsevier Science (2003)
19. Sen, K., Rosu, G., Agha, G.: Runtime safety analysis of multithreaded programs. SIGSOFT Softw. Eng. Notes **28**(5), 337–346 (2003)

Real-Time Applications

Schedulability Analysis of PWM Tasks for the UPMSat-2 ADCS

Juan Zamorano$^{(\boxtimes)}$ and Jorge Garrido

Sistemas de Tiempo Real e Ingeniería de Servicios Telemáticos (STRAST),
Universidad Politécnica de Madrid (UPM), Madrid, Spain
str@dit.upm.es

Abstract. This paper discusses the schedulability analysis of a Pulse-Width Modulation (PWM) control algorithm of an on-board spacecraft software system. The UPMSat-2 case study is used to discuss the scheduling approach of the task set of the Attitude Determination and Control System (ADCS). The Ravenscar profile is a key element of the project in order to ensure temporal predictatibilty and analysability. However, the task population must be maintained low as available computational resources are limited. As a result, the PWM task has not a single activation point, which prevents a traditional schedulability analysis. The approach used by the authors to carry out the scheduling analysis is presented in the paper.

Keywords: Real-time systems · High-integrity software · Embedded systems · Schedulability analysis · Ada · Ravenscar profile

1 Introduction

The UPMSat-2 is a project aimed at developing an experimental micro-satellite conducted by several UPM research groups. The project is leaded by the IDR institute[1], which has wide experience in this kind of systems, having led different successful projects as UPMSat-1.

The Real-Time Systems Group (STRAST)[2] is in charge of developing the software for the mission. For the flight software, the programming language used is Ada due to its suitability for real-time high-integrity systems. The software runs on top of the ORK+ kernel [15], the Open Ravenscar Kernel developed by STRAST.

The on-board software follows the ECCS-E-ST-40 [4] and ECCS-Q-ST-80 [5] standards, requiring schedulability analysis to be conducted. In order to perform this analysis, the Ravenscar profile [2] is used, among other additional

This work has been partially funded by the Spanish Government, project HI-PARTES (TIN2011-28567-C03-01), and by the European Commission FP7 programme, project MultiPARTES (IST 287702).

[1] Instituto Ignacio da Riva, www.idr.upm.es.
[2] www.dit.upm.es/str

© Springer International Publishing Switzerland 2015
J.A. de la Puente and T. Vardanega (Eds.): Ada-Europe 2015, LNCS 9111, pp. 85–99, 2015.
DOI:10.1007/978-3-319-19584-1_6

high-integrity restrictions as it is usual in this kind of systems [10,12]. These restrictions ensure temporal predictability and analysability, being therefore key elements of the project.

This paper describes the approach taken by the authors to analyse one specific system, the UPMSat-2 Attitude Determination and Control System (ADCS). The control algorithm used in this system has been designed by aeronautic engineers at IDR using a Simulink[3] engineering model. From this model, the functional code of the controller has been generated and then integrated with concurrent, real-time container code following a model-driven approach. The functional code that drives the operation of the sensors and actuators has been developed by the authors and its scheduling singularities are discussed.

The rest of the paper is organised as follows: Section 2 offers a general overview of UPMSat-2 satellite system. Section 3 presents the general characteristics and duties of the ADCS. Section 4 describes the details of the ADCS hardware. Section 5 presents the software architecture and the tasks schema that motivates the discussion. Section 6 discuses the scheduling analysis. Section 7 presents the validation approach. Finally, section 8 presents the conclusions of the analysis and some ideas for future work.

2   Overview of the Satellite System

UPMSat-2 is characterised as a micro-satellite of an approximate mass of 50 kg and an external dimensions of $0.5 \times 0.5 \times 0.6$ m. The general structure of the satellite platform is shown in figure 1. The satellite has a low Earth noon sun-synchronous polar orbit [6] with a period about 97 min. Describing this orbit, the satellite will have two visibility periods from the ground station every 24 hours, each of them up to 10 minutes.

During the visibility periods, the communications with the spacecraft will be carried out by means of a dual radio link in the VHF 400 MHz band, with a raw transfer rate of 9600 bit/s. For the rest of the orbit, the satellite will maintain a periodic downlink stream in an amateur band also in the range of the 400 MHz.

The UPMSat-2 is conceived as a technology demonstrator. In consequence, its payload consists on several experiments proposed by both research groups and industry. These experiment are mainly focused on testing equipment on the space environment.

The architecture of the software controlling this system is as depicted in figure 2:

- *Platform monitoring*: this subsystem is in charge of monitoring the satellite physical integrity by periodically reading housekeeping sensor data. This includes data from battery and electric buses, temperatures, etc.
- *Telemetry and telecommand (TMTC)*: this subsystem is in charge of maintaining the communications with the ground station during the visibility periods by means of the telecommunications hardware (TMC). This hardware is also used to transmit in the amateur band.

---

[3] *Simulink* is a registered trade mark of The MathWorks Inc.

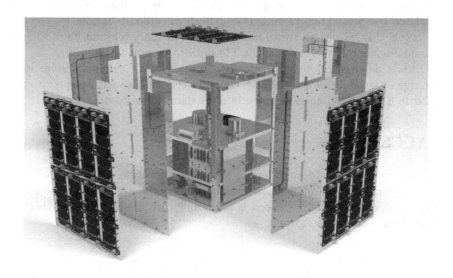

Fig. 1. General view of the satellite platform

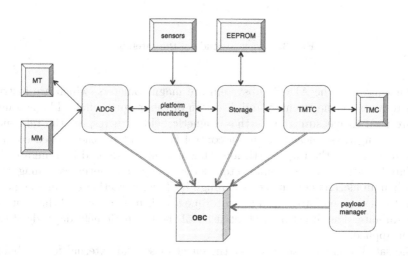

Fig. 2. UPMSat-2 software architecture

- *Payload manager*: this subsystem operates the payload experiments as ordered by specific telecommands sent from the ground station.
- *Storage*: this subsystem stores in non-volatile memory relevant data, such as configuration parameter values or TM data to be sent to ground.
- *Attitude determination and control system (ADCS)*: this subsystem is in charge of keeping the proper orientation of the satellite with respect to the Earth. The subsystem is describe in more detail in section 3.

3   ADCS System

The ADCS is in charge of maintaining the satellite attitude within its orbit, in such a way that the communication antenna is properly orientated to the Earth as well as a constant angular speed is maintained to provide a better thermal control. This is shown in figure 3.

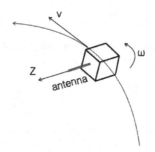

Fig. 3. Target attitude of the satellite

The sensors of the ADCS subsystem are magnetometers, which are instruments to measure the strength and direction of the magnetic field. Magnetometers are used to measure the Earth's magnetic field with respect the reference axis. By using these measurements a control law calculates the needed control action to maintain the target attitude. Magnetorquers are used to generate the calculated control torque. A magnetorquer is a coil that develops a magnetic field when an electric current flows through it. The interaction of this magnetic field with that of the Earth produces a torque that is used to control the attitude of the satellite. The direction and intensity of the magnetic field depends of the current applied.

The satellite is constantly under the effect of several external forces, being the most relevant the Earth's magnetic field, but also the drag of the residual atmosphere, the solar radiation pressure and the gravity gradient. As a result, the ADCS has to be executed periodically.

It is important to note, as it will be discussed in following sections, that, as both sensors and actuators rely on magnetic fields to operate, they cannot be used at the same time. Any measurement from magnetometers would be influenced by the magnetic field generated by any active magnetorquer.

The control algorithm has been designed by aerospace engineers using a closed-loop simulation model of the spacecraft dynamics as shown in figure 4. The model has been design using Simulink, which also allows to test its innovative B-dot derived control law and study the effects of its parameters.

The left side variables on the simulation model are those influencing the spacecraft dynamics, including the red-shaped controller block which represents the control algorithm. The controller block has as inputs the magnetic field measurements read by magnetometers ($\mathbf{B}_{b\_T}$) and its derivatives ($\mathbf{B}_{dot}$). The outputs of the controller block are the magnetorquer actuation, influencing the spacecraft dynamics.

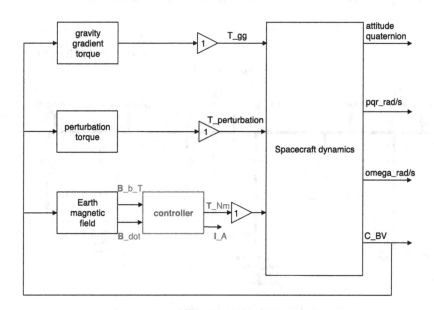

Fig. 4. ADCS simulation model

From the simulation model, the functional code for the controller block is automatically generated by Simulink. The generated code is about 500 lines of C code with several conditional paths, as the controller can adapt its output in the event that any magnetorquer or magnetometer is out of service. This code is embedded in an Ada task, being part of the software architecture of the ADCS subsystem described in the following section 5.

4   Hardware Architecture of ADCS

The ADCS subsystem follows the classical embedded system hardware structure with sensors, actuators and the control computer. The sensors of the ADCS

subsystem are three sets of magnetometers located in different positions of the
satellite, each of them providing a magnetic field measurement for each of the
three axis of the satellite. As a result, up to nine measurements (three for each
axis) can be acquired at any given time. The actuators of the ADCS subsystem
are three magnetorquers, one for each axis.

The control computer is the UPMSat-2 On-Board Computer (OBC) itself.
It is composed by a System On Chip (SOC) based on an Actel FPGA with 4
MB of SRAM memory and 2 MB of EEPROM, along with Analog to Digital
Converters (ADC) and other hardware devices. The SOC has been developed
from the GPL version of the IP Core library GRLIB[4], it includes a LEON3 [7]
processor with data and instruction caches, one AMBA bus hierarchy together
with serial interfaces including RS-232, RS-422, SPI, I2C and 112 digital I/O
signals. Figure 5 shows the hardware structure of the on-board computer.

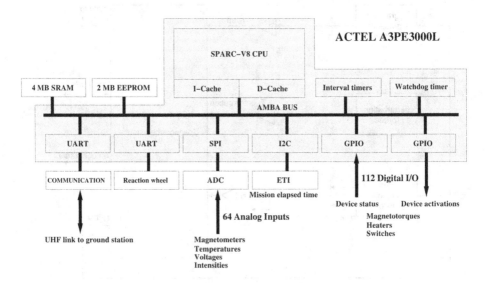

Fig. 5. UPMSat-2 OBC hardware structure

Floating-point arithmetic needed in the control algorithm is not available in
hardware, due to limitations in the GPL version of GRLIB used in the project,
and is thus emulated by software.

Magnetometers are read through analog input channels. The actuating signals to magnetorquers are the only analog outputs of the OBC. In order to
simplify the hardware design and avoid the inclusion of Digital to Analog Converters (DAC) and amplifiers, digital outputs and H-bridges are used to produce
the required currents. As is common practice in embedded systems, the energy
supplied to each magnetorquer is controlled by means of Pulse-Width Modulation (PWM) waveforms.

---

[4] http://www.gaisler.com/index.php/products/ipcores/soclibrary

5 Software Architecture of ADCS

The ADCS control algorithm has been designed for a period of 2 s. This includes acquiring magnetometer inputs, calculating the control action and actuating on magnetorquers. The high level architecture of the ADCS subsystem is depicted in figure 6. This design is intended to decouple data acquisition, control and actuation. As above stated, magnetorquers can not be activated when magnetometers are being read. Therefore, there are three tasks that communicate and synchronise by means of two protected objects.

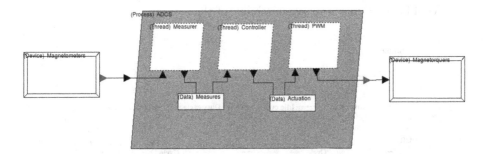

Fig. 6. Software architecture of the ADCS Subsystem

The Measurer task is in charge of acquiring the magnetic field measurements from the magnetometers and elaborating the data to be provided to the control algorithm. This process consists on acquiring measurements from each magnetometer and calculating the average for each axis each 200 milliseconds during the first second of the cycle. Then, these values are passed to the Controller task by means of the Measures protected object.

The Controller task receives each 2 seconds (with an offset of 1 second) these values through the Measures protected object. Then, the imported control algorithm described in section 3 is executed taking the measurements as inputs. The outputs of the control algorithm are the required actuation on each axis to keep the proper attitude. These outputs are signed integers in which the sign represents the direction in which the torque has to be applied, and the absolute value represents how long the current shall be applied to the magnetorquer in milliseconds, that is the PWM duty cycle. The longer the duty cycle, the more energy is applied. The Controller task interacts with the PWM task by means of the Actuation protected object.

Finally the PWM task takes the outputs from the Actuation protected object and activates the magnetorquers accordingly. Figure 7 shows the chronogram for the actuation on the magnetorquers. The duration of the cycle is equal to the sampling period of the control system (2 seconds). The duration of the duty cycle for the UPMSat-2 ADCS can be 0 and a range of values between 200 ms and 500 ms.

This waveform can be generated with hardware support, that is programming a timer, or by software with a periodic task. It must be noticed that there are three magnetorquers and then three hardware timers would be needed. UPMSat-2 uses the software solution in order to maintain hardware complexity low and because this implementation has been shown appropriate for systems with slow dynamics [16]. Moreover, in order to keep the population of tasks low, only one PWM task is in charge of the actuation on the three magnetorquers. This PWM task has a period equal to the PWM cycle, but the task has to be suspended for the duration of duty and idle cycles in order not to monopolise the processor, which could compromise the schedulability of the system.

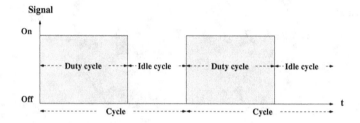

Fig. 7. Chronogram for PWM control of magnetorquers

Listing 6.1 details the PWM task code. As stated before, the Controller task sets the parameters of a duty cycle in the PO, and the PWM task retrieves the parameters by calling the PO entry, as in a typical sporadic pattern. The task then switches on the magnetorquers on the required direction and delays until the closest end of duty cycles. At this time the magnetorquer of the axis with the shortest duty cycle is switched off. The task can be delayed up to three times to switch off the three magnetorquers. Then the task blocks in the entry until the start of the next cycle.

The PWM task has not a single activation point but up to four. It should be noted that, although the single activation point condition is normally assumed to be part of the Ravenscar profile, it is not included in the standard definition [11, ap.D], and it is not detected at compilation time.

6   Schedulability Analysis of ADCS

The Ravenscar Profile includes pragma Task_Dispaching_Policy (FIFO_Within_Priorities) and pragma Locking_Policy (Ceiling_Locking) and thus an analysis based on fixed-priority scheduling theory [1] can be carried out. However, the Measurer and PWM tasks have neither a periodic nor a sporadic activation pattern. Therefore, it is needed to model them with an equivalent task set of periodic and sporadic tasks in order to perform the schedulability analysis.

Listing 6.1. PWM task

```
task body PWM is
   ...
begin
   loop
      Actuation.Get_Duty_Cycle (These_Duty_Cycles);
      Set_Digital_Outputs (These_Duty_Cycles);
      while Magnetorquer_On loop
         delay until End_Of_Next_Duty_Cycle (These_Duty_Cycles);
         Reset_Digital_Outputs (These_Duty_Cycles);
      end loop;
   end loop;
end task;
```

6.1 Equivalent Task Set

The Measurer task can be trivially modelled with a periodic task with a 200 ms period. However, this simplification introduces pessimism as the Measurer task is only activated during the first second of the 2 s period of the ADCS. As a result, the analysis will yield more interference on low priority tasks than the actual values.

An exact way of modelling the Measurer task is by five periodic tasks with 2 s periods, 200 ms deadline and activation offsets of 0, 200 ms, 400 ms, 600 ms and 800 ms. Offsets add difficulty to the computations but the resulting interference values on low priority tasks are the actual ones.

The Control task has a periodic activation pattern as it is activated each 2 s. However, it has a 1 s offset because it is executed at the beginning of the last second of the ADCS period. In order to set the deadline of this task it must be taken into account that there is a 1 s interval to execute the Control and the PWM tasks. Otherwise magnetorquers could be active when magnetometers are been read. Therefore, one second is the end-to-end deadline of the transaction built with the set of activities that must be executed during the last second of the ADCS period. Fortunately, deadlines are not required in response time analysis in order to compute the worst-case global response time.

The PWM task has up to four activation points and therefore it cannot be analysed using basic RTA techniques. It must be noticed that this task handles actually up to four events, it switches on magnetorquers after its first activation and there are up to three additional activations to switch off the corresponding magnetorquer. Implementing the four tasks in this way would be unpractical as it leads to a high resource consumption, but this scheme can be used as an equivalent task model for analysing the PWM task. Again, the equivalent task set must include offsets in the activations as well as release jitters, which adds difficulty to the analysis.

Let PWM_{On} be the task that switches on the magnetorquers, and $R_{Control}$ the worst case response time of the Control task. Let us also assume that the best case response time of any task is 0. The PWM_{On} task is a sporadic task activated by a periodic task (Control task). Therefore it can be modelled as a periodic task with an activation jitter equal to $R_{Control}$. Moreover, the PWM$_{On}$ task has a 1 second offset like the Control task. The computation of its deadline is avoided too.

Duty cycles for the UPMSat-2 ADCS can range from 200 ms to 500 ms. Therefore, tasks that are in charge of switching off magnetorquers (PWM$_{Off}$) have jitters of 300 ms. Moreover, the PWM$_{Off}$ tasks are activated by the PWM$_{On}$ task and thus the response time of the PWM$_{On}$ task ($R_{PWM_{On}}$) must be included in these task jitters. As a result, the jitter of these tasks is 300 ms plus $R_{PWM_{On}}$. They also have offsets of 1200 ms because they are activated in the last second of the ADCS cycle and the minimum valid duty cycle is 200 ms. The PWM$_{Off}$ tasks perform the last activities of the transaction and therefore their deadlines are equal to the end-to-end deadline minus their offsets, that is 800 ms.

Table 1 shows the summary of the equivalent task set with the Worst Case Execution Times (WCET) of task activities. It must be said that the flight version of the OBC is not available yet. Therefore, WCETs have been obtained by using RapiTime[5] in a preliminary version of the OBC [8] and have been adjusted to the flight version by taking into account processor clock frequency and memory access time.

Table 1. Equivalent task set for ADCS tasks

Task	Period	Offset	Release jitter	Deadline	WCET
Measurer_1	2 s	0	0	200 ms	2.73 ms
Measurer_2	2 s	200 ms	0	200 ms	2.73 ms
Measurer_3	2 s	400 ms	0	200 ms	2.73 ms
Measurer_4	2 s	600 ms	0	200 ms	2.73 ms
Measurer_5	2 s	800 ms	0	200 ms	2.73 ms
Control	2 s	1 s	0		4.02 ms
PWM$_{On}$	2 s	1 s	$R_{Control}$		2.41 ms
PWM$_{Off}$_1	2 s	1200 ms	300 ms + $R_{PWM_{On}}$	800 ms	0.8 ms
PWM$_{Off}$_2	2 s	1200 ms	300 ms + $R_{PWM_{On}}$	800 ms	0.8 ms
PWM$_{Off}$_3	2 s	1200 ms	300 ms + $R_{PWM_{On}}$	800 ms	0.8 ms

The processor utilization is fairly low and could be anticipated that the ADCS alone is schedulable. However, the aim of the analysis is to evaluate the deviation of the PWM software actuation against an ideal hardware driven one. It is also interesting the interaction with other UPMSat-2 subsystems and therefore two other significant tasks are included in the analysis.

6.2   Task Priorities

The ADCS has a paramount importance and thus its tasks are the highest priority tasks in the UPMSat-2 software. In this way, actual release jitters and

---

[5] http://www.rapitasystems.com/rapitime

response times are minimised so that the attitude control behaves as close as possible to the Simulink model. It must be noticed that the PWM tasks should have the highest priority in order to mimic waveforms as they are generated by hardware timers. Highest priority tasks suffer minimum interference and therefore they produce duty cycle durations with the highest software accuracy.

However, the response time equations for these high priority tasks include blocking because there is an activity that must be executed at Interrupt_Priority'Last. Messages to be send to ground are stored in EEPROM until visibility periods start. Due to EEPROM characteristics, write accesses to EEPROM must be separated by 15 ms. Therefore, individual word writing would provide a poor bandwidth. The solution is to use the EEPROM block mode that allows up to 128 consecutive word write accesses and then wait 15 ms. This mode provides largely the required bandwidth but block writings must be atomic. Therefore, block writings are implemented in a protected procedure with the highest interrupt priority as its ceiling priority. Fortunately, the WCET of this protected action is 48μs, which is fairly low. The EEPROM task has a period of 200 ms and provided that it must elapse 15 ms between consecutive executions, the deadline is 185 ms.

As is customary in non-accessible embedded systems, UPMSat-2 incorporates a WatchDog Timer (WDT) to achieve fault recovery. That is a hardware timer that must be periodically recharged by software, otherwise it provokes a hardware reset. Taking into account the stability property of fixed-priority scheduling, the task that restarts the WDT has been assigned the lowest priority. Therefore, in case of an infinite loop in any task or transient overload, the WDT task will overrun its deadline and the on-board computer will be restarted. The hardware timer is programmed for a 15 s time interval and the WDT task has a period of 10 s. As a result, the deadline of this task is 5 s.

Table 2 shows the task set to be analysed ordered by priorities.

Table 2. Task set of UPMSat-2

Task	Period	Offset	Release jitter	Deadline	Blocking	WCET
PWM$_{Off\_1}$	2 s	1200 ms	300 ms + R$_{PWM_{On}}$	800 ms	0.048 ms	0.8 ms
PWM$_{Off\_2}$	2 s	1200 ms	300 ms + R$_{PWM_{On}}$	800 ms	0.048 ms	0.8 ms
PWM$_{Off\_3}$	2 s	1200 ms	300 ms + R$_{PWM_{On}}$	800 ms	0.048 ms	0.8 ms
PWM$_{On}$	2 s	1 s	R$_{Control}$		0.048 ms	2.41 ms
Control	2 s	1 s	0		0.048 ms	4.02 ms
Measurer_1	2 s	0	0	200 ms	0.048 ms	2.73 ms
Measurer_2	2 s	200 ms	0	200 ms	0.048 ms	2.73 ms
Measurer_3	2 s	400 ms	0	200 ms	0.048 ms	2.73 ms
Measurer_4	2 s	600 ms	0	200 ms	0.048 ms	2.73 ms
Measurer_5	2 s	800 ms	0	200 ms	0.048 ms	2.73 ms
EEPROM	200 ms	0	0	185 ms	0	0.87 ms
WDT	10 s	0	0	5 s	0	1 ms

6.3   Response Time Analysis

The task set of table 2 can be analysed by using fixed priority analysis theory as described in e.g. [13] or [3]. It can be argued that some task have unknown jitters. However, tasks with unknown release jitters are released after tasks whose response times are needed. Therefore, a priori unknown response times can be calculated and the analysis can be performed in an iterative way. The MAST [6] (Modeling and Analysis Suite for Real-Time Applications) tool has been used to perform the analysis as it includes the needed analysis techniques.

MAST [9] is based on the concept of transactions, which are modelled as trees of events and activities released by the events. In particular, the PWM task can be modelled as a multi-path transaction with four events that have offsets and release jitters as specified in table 2. MAST also includes offset-based optimised RTA for fixed priority scheduling [14] that provides an exact response time analysis of task sets with offsets.

Table 3 shows the response times calculated by MAST. The task set is schedulable as it was foreseen because the processor utilization is quite low, 1.18%.

Table 3. Task set of UPMSat-2

Task	Period	Offset	Release jitter	Deadline	Blocking	WCET	Response
PWM_{Off}_1	2 s	1200 ms	313.916 ms	800 ms	0.048 ms	0.8 ms	314.584 ms
PWM_{Off}_2	2 s	1200 ms	313.916 ms	800 ms	0.048 ms	0.8 ms	315.384 ms
PWM_{Off}_3	2 s	1200 ms	313.916 ms	800 ms	0.048 ms	0.8 ms	316.184 ms
PWM_{On}	2 s	1 s	9.058 ms		0.048 ms	2.41 ms	13.736 ms
Control	2 s	1 s	0		0.048 ms	4.02 ms	8.878 ms
Measurer_1	2 s	0	0	200 ms	0.048 ms	2.73 ms	11.608 ms
Measurer_2	2 s	200 ms	0	200 ms	0.048 ms	2.73 ms	14.338 ms
Measurer_3	2 s	400 ms	0	200 ms	0.048 ms	2.73 ms	17.068 ms
Measurer_4	2 s	600 ms	0	200 ms	0.048 ms	2.73 ms	19.798 ms
Measurer_5	2 s	800 ms	0	200 ms	0.048 ms	2.73 ms	22.528 ms
EEPROM	200 ms	0	0	185 ms	0	0.87 ms	22.528 ms
WDT	10 s	0	0	5 s	0	1 ms	23.567 ms

The worst case response time of PWM_{Off} tasks is 316.184 ms for PWM_{Off}_3, which has the lowest priority among them. That is only 16.184 ms apart from the ideal and supposes an error of 8% for the shorter duty cycle of 200 ms. This actuation error could be fed back to the Simulink model in order to adjust accordingly the control algorithm.

At last, it must be said that timing events could be used to switch off magnetorquers. In this way the PWM task could switch on magnetorquers and one timing event could be set to switch off the magnetorquer with the shortest duty cycle. Then the handler could set itself to switch off the next one and so on. It

---

[6] http://mast.unican.es

must be noted that the schedulability analysis will also be valid for this implementation. However, response times could vary with a precise analysis that takes into account context switch and interrupt latency times.

7   Verification of ADCS

An engineering model of the satellite based on a Virtex-5 LXT FPGA ML505 development board is being used for software validation purposes. The board implements a LEON3 CPU at 50 MHz and 1 GB of RAM memory. This engineering version of the OBC allows the early testing of mature parts of the software, as the working version of the ADCS subsystem.

A Software Validation Facility (SVF) overcomes the impossibility of testing the ADCS in its real environment. Based on a Hardware-in-the-Loop (HIL) approach, the SVF allows the execution of the application software with a simulated environment. Following this approach, the ADCS software executes on the embedded computer, while the system sensors, actuators and the spacecraft dynamics are simulated on a development computer using the Simulink model discussed in section 3.

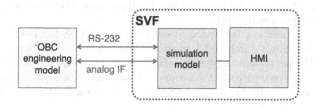

Fig. 8. Architecture of software verification facility

This configuration has been used not only to prove the correct behaviour of the system, but also to measure execution times using Rapitime [8], as was said in section 6.

8   Conclusions and Future Plans

The UPMSat-2 satellite project has proven to be a relevant demonstrator for many kind of experiments and technology. Several research groups and industry proposed a wide number of experiments in different fields. With regard to the Real-Time Systems Group, the project has given several scenarios in which to exercise our knowledge and tools in real-time embedded for a real project.

The Ravenscar profile provides a timing-predictable subset of Ada, widely used in the real-time industry. The restriction of single-point activated tasks is not in the definition of the profile but it is considered necessary for schedulability analysis. However, there are common task patterns in real-time embedded systems such as the PWM ones that does not verify such restriction. It can be argued that PWM waveforms can be generated wit a set of single-point activated tasks and a corresponding set of protected objects. However, it could be unpractical if the computational resources are limited. It must be noticed that not only memory is wasted but also the response and activation times of PWM tasks would be worse if run-time overhead is included in the analysis. The UPMSat-2 ADCS has shown that non-Ravenscar task patterns can be used and analysed.

The following steps in the development of the system are, among others: to include in the current ADCS model the rest of the system in order to perform a response time analysis of the whole system, to include the run-time overhead in the analysis as described in [17], and to include the flight version of the OBC into the testing facility.

References

1. Audsley, N., Burns, A., Davis, R., Tindell, K., Wellings, A.J.: Fixed priority preemptive scheduling: An historical perspective. Real-Time Systems 8(3), 173–198 (1995)
2. Burns, A., Dobbing, B., Vardanega, T.: Guide for the use of the Ada Ravenscar profile in high integrity systems. Ada Letters XXIV, 1–74 (June 2004)
3. Burns, A., Wellings, A.J.: Real-Time Systems and Programming Languages. Addison-Wesley, 2 edn. (1996)
4. European Cooperation for Space Standardization: ECSS-E-ST-40C Space engineering – Software (March 2009), available from ESA
5. European Cooperation for Space Standardization: ECSS-Q-ST-80C Space Product Assurance – Software Product Assurance (March 2009), available from ESA
6. Fortescue, P., Swinerd, G., Stark, J.: Spacecraft Systems Engineering, 4 edn. Wiley (2011)
7. LEON3 - High-performance SPARC V8 32-bit Processor. GRLIB IP Core User's Manual (2012)
8. Garrido, J., Brosnan, D., de la Puente, J.A., Alonso, A., Zamorano, J.: Analysis of WCET in an experimental satellite software development. In: Vardanega, T. (ed.) 12th International Workshop on Worst-Case Execution Time Analysis. OpenAccess Series in Informatics (OASIcs), vol. 23, pp. 81–90. Schloss Dagstuhl-Leibniz-Zentrum fuer Informatik (2012)
9. González Harbour, M., Gutiérrez, J.J., Palencia, J.C., Drake, J.M.: MAST modeling and analysis suite for real time applications. In: Proceedings of 13th Euromicro Conference on Real-Time Systems, pp. 125–134. IEEE Computer Society Press, Delft, June 2001
10. ISO: ISO/IEC TR 24718:2005 – Guide for the use of the Ada Ravenscar Profile in high integrity systems (2005), based on the University of York Technical Report YCS-2003-348 (2003)
11. ISO: ISO/IEC 8652:1995(E)/TC1(2000)/AMD1(2007): Information Technology – Programming Languages – Ada (2007)
12. ISO/IEC TR 15942:2000 – Guide for the use of the Ada programming language in high integrity systems (2000)
13. Klein, M.H., Ralya, T., Pollack, B., Obenza, R., González Harbour, M.: A Practitioner's Handbook for Real-Time Analysis. Guide to Rate Monotonic Analysis for Real-Time Systems. Kluwer Academic Publishers, Boston (1993)

14. Palencia, J.C., Harbour, M.G.: Schedulability analysis for tasks with static and dynamic offsets. In: RTSS 1998: Proceedings of the IEEE Real-Time Systems Symposium, p. 26. IEEE Computer Society, Washington, DC (1998)

15. de la Puente, J.A., Ruiz, J.F., Zamorano, J.: An open Ravenscar real-time kernel for GNAT. In: Keller, H.B., Plödereder, E. (eds.) Ada-Europe 2000. LNCS, vol. 1845, pp. 5–15. Springer, Heidelberg (2000)

16. Sánchez, F.M., Zamorano, J.: A low cost laboratory for teaching embedded real-time systems. In: Real-Time Programming 2003. Proceedings of the IFAC/IFIP Workshop, pp. 195–200. Elsevier Science Ltda (2003)

17. Vardanega, T., Zamorano, J., de la Puente, J.A.: On the dynamic semantics and the timing behaviour of Ravenscar kernels. Real-Time Systems **29**(1), 1–31 (2005)

Guaranteeing Timing Requirements
in the IXV On-Board Software

Santiago Urueña[1]([⊠]), Nuria Pérez[1], Bruno N. Calvo[1],
Carlos Flores[1], and Andreas Jung[2]

[1] GMV Aerospace and Defense, Tres Cantos, Madrid, Spain
{suruena,nuperez,bncalvo,cflores}@gmv.com
[2] ESA ESTEC, Noordwijk, The Netherlands
andreas.jung@esa.int

Abstract. Ensuring the correct timing behavior of the control software of a spacecraft is a complex endeavor. This paper describes the real-time aspects of the Intermediate eXperimental Vehicle's (IXV) On-Board Software (OBSW), including the schedulability analysis performed for the validation of this safety-critical, hard real-time system of the European Space Agency (ESA). We then give details of how the Ravenscar profile has been used to obtain predictability over RTEMS, and quantify the overhead of different mechanisms for measuring computation times. We provide the timing measurements of each task during the different modes of the mission, including the Guidance, Navigation, and Control (GNC) tasks, to aid in the development of future OBSW projects.

Keywords: IXV OBSW · SVF · Ravenscar · RTEMS · Schedulability analysis

1 Introduction

The European Space Agency's (ESA) Intermediate eXperimental Vehicle (IXV) project [1] is developing and flight-testing the technologies and critical systems for Europe's future autonomous, controlled, atmospheric re-entry, from low Earth orbit. Based on the knowledge gained from the IXV technology demonstrator, which was successfully launched on February 11th 2015, ESA's may build an affordable and reusable spacecraft, capable of operating modular payloads for multiple applications in various orbits before it returns to Earth to touch down on a conventional runway.

Inside the IXV spacecraft, the On-Board Software (OBSW) plays an important role. The OBSW manages the IXV elements that are necessary to perform all mission modes, including Launch, Orbital, Re-Entry and Descent-Flight. The IXV needs the OBSW to control the vehicle, perform experiments, monitor data, and provide data storage and telemetry. A number of constraints affect the OBSW: it is embedded software, with hard real-time, dependability and safety constraints; it must operate autonomously over extended periods of time; it faces important hardware limitations; and it has to cope with a hostile environment (radiation, large temperature changes).

Since the OBSW is in charge of the safety of the whole IXV spacecraft (and thus the success of this mission), this software is assigned a high Design Assurance Level

© Springer International Publishing Switzerland 2015
J.A. de la Puente and T. Vardanega (Eds.): Ada-Europe 2015, LNCS 9111, pp. 100–115, 2015.
DOI: 10.1007/978-3-319-19584-1_7

(DAL-B), and it is developed following the best practices in industry and with the most strict validation requirements from the beginning of the project [2]. To ensure the OBSW never violates any of its hard software deadlines, schedulability analysis must be performed even before the software has been written. This entails specific challenges, such as obtaining adequate estimations on the execution time during the software design phase (based on the known computation times of similar algorithms from previous missions); achieving the proper level of predictability during execution; and ensuring the timing measurements taken during the test campaign are representative of an actual mission.

After a short review of the related work and an overview of the different subsystems of the spacecraft and testing environments, this paper will describe the design decisions taken during the design phase to avoid unpredictability as much as possible (mainly through the use of the Ravenscar profile), as well as a discussion of the different techniques used to measure the execution time, including the actual timing values and schedulability results obtained so they can be reused in future missions.

2   Contributions and Related Work

Previous papers about the IXV are available, including an overview of the whole avionics [1] or the testing environment for the Guidance, Navigation and Control (GNC) algorithms [3]. This paper is focused instead on the IXV OBSW, specifically on the timing behavior. The process used for obtaining the computation time of another on-board spacecraft software has been already studied by Rodríguez et al. [4] using static analysis, but the final timing results had not yet been published. Finally, the Ravenscar profile, originally defined and standardized for the Ada language [5], has been also proposed for its use within Java [6], but as far as we know this is the first publication about its use with the C language over RTEMS.

3   IXV Avionics

The OBSW executes inside the On-Board Computer (OBC), and commands and controls the various equipment through the different I/O lines, synchronous/asynchronous RS-422 serial cable, and MIL-STD-1553 bus. The OBC, provided by QinetiQ Space, hosts a 50 MHz LEON2-FT processor, as well as 64 MB SDRAM, 128 KB PROM, and 4 MB Flash memory to hold both the OBSW and configuration tables.

The LEON2-FT processor (Atmel AT697E) implements the 32-bit SPARC V8 architecture. It includes a 5-stage instruction pipeline, an IEEE 754 Floating point unit, two 24-bit timers, watchdog, external memory controller, and triple modular redundancy on flip-flops. All internal and external memories are protected by EDAC or parity bits. It also includes separate 32 KB instruction and 16 KB data caches (LRU, write-through, no-write-allocate). Write operations to RAM are preformed asynchronously using an internal write buffer. The OBSW configures the instruction cache to load instructions in bursts to increase performance, but cache freezing on interrupt (i.e. do not modify the caches during interrupts) was not used due to a hardware bug.

The equipment connected to the OBC includes:

IXV Control devices:
- **FpCS** (**Flaps Control System**): Controls the vehicle's flight by acting on the flaps.
- **RCS** (**Reaction Control System**): Group of actuators consisting on pyrotechnical valves, latching valves and flow control valves.

IXV Navigation devices:
- **IMU** (**Inertial Measurement Unit**): Provides the velocity increments and orientation of the vehicle to the navigation and control application.
- **GPS** (**Global Positioning System**): Provides the position and velocity of the vehicle in phases where GPS satellites are sufficiently visible.

Communication devices:
- **RF**: Radio frequency transmitter to downlink telemetry data to ground.

Power devices:
- **PPDU** (**Power Protection and Distribution Unit**): Management and distribution of the electrical power and to provide commands for actuators and other devices.

Data acquisition and recording devices:
- **Vital Layer data recorders**: Devices to store the received data at the synchronous RS-422, a continuous CCSDS bit-stream coming from the OBC Telemetry Board.
- **Flight DAU** (**Data Acquisition Unit**): To acquire information from pressure, temperature, and thermocouple sensors.
- **EDAR** (**Experiment Data Acquisition and Recording**): In charge of collecting, recording, formatting, and sending all the experiment telemetry data.

4   OBSW Description

The IXV OBSW is written in the C language (C89 plus some compiler-specific extensions, mainly for adding assembly code), following MISRA-C:2004. Unlike other critical software, its code is optimized (using -O2 compilation flags with GCC 4.2.1), due to the tight timing requirements and that object code traceability was not required.

It runs over RTEMS (Real-Time Executive for Multiprocessor Systems), an open source, real-time operating system, which provides event-driven multitasking, priority-based, pre-emptive scheduling, and priority inheritance/ceiling synchronization protocols. All the software executes in privileged mode, with all the threads sharing the memory space. RTEMS is internally designed as a set of managers, which can be independently disabled if the functionality of any of those managers is not needed. The IXV uses a tailored and qualified version: Edisoft's RTEMS Improvement V10 (based on RTEMS 4.8.0).

4.1   OBSW Tasks

The OBSW is composed of 15 different tasks (threads of control), to fulfil specific time and functionality constraints. They are divided in four main groups based on their frequency, leading to the following distribution:

— Tasks Running at 100 Hz:
  - **MilBus handling (MILB):** Handles communication with remote devices through the MIL-STD-1553 bus.
  - **Reaction Control System manager (RCS):** This task performs the high frequency communication with the RCS subsystem.

— Tasks Running at 20 Hz:
  - **Supervisor (SUP):** This task checks the status of the rest of OBSW tasks and resets the OBC Watchdog.
  - **Acquisitor (ACQ):** Performs the acquisition of data from the hardware components and makes them available to the rest of the software, including the GNC.
  - **GNC Control:** Computes the required outputs to thrusters and flaps in order to control the attitude of the vehicle as specified by the Guidance block. Includes its own attitude estimation function to work at the high frequency needed by the vehicle attitude dynamics.
  - **Event Handler (EH):** This task is responsible for implementing ECSS-E-70-41A scheduling, monitoring and event-action services.
  - **Mode Manager (MVM):** This task is in charge of managing all MVM mode operations not controlled by the scheduling service.
  - **Command Executor (CMD):** Calls each device periodically in order to perform the devices' pending actions in small pieces, so that timing is not compromised.
  - **Global Positioning System receiver (GPS):** This task is in charge of management and control of the GPS device.
  - **Housekeeping Service (HK):** This task collects information and builds the corresponding telemetry packets.
  - **Telemetry Manager (TTM):** This task transmits to ground the packets it receives from other tasks and maintains a buffer for storing packets during non-visibility periods.
  - **Telecommand (TC):** Reads telecommands from the EGSE (Electrical Ground Support Equipment) through a serial connection and executes them.

  These 20 Hz tasks form the core of the IXV OBSW, and are executed in a specific order since the outputs from one task are used as inputs for the following ones.

— Tasks Running at 2 Hz:
  - **GNC Navigation:** Responsible for estimating the current state of the vehicle based on measures provided by sensors and actuators. It also computes derived air data and aerodynamics parameters required by Guidance and Control.
  - **GNC Guidance:** Keeps the vehicle on track during the flight to reach the desired location. It gets the actual location from the Navigation algorithm and provides the reference attitude to the control subsystem that assures its objective.

— Sporadic Tasks:
  - **Flash Memory Writer:** This sporadic task is activated when data must be read from or written to the flash. It is the task with the lowest priority, so these time consuming operations do not block any critical task.

These tasks have also been created and scheduled to guarantee that the chain including data acquisition, processing and conversion to actuator's commands does not exceed 50 ms.

The following table shows the size details, including the effective number of lines of source code (LOC) for each software component, and the size of the executable:

OBSW Application layer:		OBSW image:	3060 KB
- OBSW MVM:	55 kLOC	- Code (.text section):	480 KB
- OBSW GNC:	22 kLOC	- Global data (.data):	40 KB
OBSW Basic layer:		- Global data (.bss):	2550 KB
- BSW (drivers):	7 kLOC		
- RTEMS (subset):	16 kLOC		

Each task has 12 KB of memory reserved for its stack, but the measured maximum usage of the stack is between 1 and 5 KB, depending on the task.

4.2   Ravenscar Profile

To allow the usage of simple algorithms and available tools for analyzing the schedulability of the system, it was decided to base the design on the Ravenscar profile [4]. This subset of the Ada programming language has been successfully used in safety-critical software with hard real-time requirements [7]. Ravenscar is rich enough to program typical embedded systems, while requiring a small, high-performance and certifiable run-time system.

For IXV OBSW, a subset of Edisoft's RTEMS was selected to replicate functionality and restrictions defined by the Ravenscar profile, defining a set of wrapper routines to ensure only the adequate RTEMS functionality is used. Specifically:

- **Periodic Tasks:** The rtems_rate_monotonic_period directive is called in an infinite loop to block the task execution until the adequate clock tick arrives (statically configured for each task), ensuring two activations of the same task are always separated by the configured relative period (equivalent to No_Relative_Delay restriction).
- **Sporadic Tasks:** These tasks call rtems_message_queue_receive (with flags RTEMS_WAIT and RTEMS_NO_TIMEOUT) inside an infinite loop. This blocks the task until another task sends to that RTEMS queue (always created with RTEMS_FIFO policy) a signaling dummy byte with rtems_message_queue_send.
- **Critical Sections:** Implemented via semaphores with priority ceiling protocol.

The following list details how each constraint of the Ravenscar profile has been translated to RTEMS, with a reference to the related Ada pragma or restriction:

- **Static Number of Tasks:**
  - The rtems_task_create and rtems_task_start routines are just called during initialization (No_Task_Allocators).
  - Each task body is a function, which is called by the task wrapper within an infinite loop (No_Task_Termination). The routine rtems_task_delete is never used (No_Abort_Statements)

- **Static number of interrupt service routines**: The routine rtems_interrupt_catch is only used during initialisation (No_Dynamic_Attachment).
- **Static number of protected objects**: The routines rtems_semaphore_create and rtems_message_queue_create are only called during the initialisation (equivalent to No_Protected_Type_Allocators), and there are no calls to rtems_semaphore_delete or rtems_message_queue_delete (No_Local_Protected_Objects).
- **Fixed Priority preemptive scheduling**: Every OBSW task is created with the mode flags RTEMS_PREEMPT and RTEMS_NO_TIMESLICE (and a 0 interrupt level), and with a statically defined priority (FIFO_Within_Priorities). There are no calls to rtems_task_mode or rtems_task_set_priority (No_Dynamic_Priorities).
- **Priority ceiling protocol**: Semaphores are created with flags RTEMS_PRIORITY and RTEMS_PRIORITY_CEILING (Ceiling_Locking). It is not possible to change the semaphore ceiling after creation (No_Dynamic_Priorities).
- **No task attributes**: The rtems_task_variable_add routine is never used (No_Dependence => Ada.Task_Attributes). In addition, all tasks are created with attribute RTEMS_FLOATING_POINT, even if floating point instructions are not used, so the context switch time is as similar as possible for all tasks.
- **No implicit heap allocation**:
  - During the mission, there are no calls to RTEMS primitives that allocate dynamic memory. In particular, rtems_rate_monotonic_create, rtems_task_create, rtems_semaphore_create, rtems_extension_create are called only during initialisation and rtems_timer_create is never called (No_Implicit_Heap_Allocations).
  - There are neither RTEMS calls deallocating memory (rtems_task_delete, rtems_timer_delete, rtems_semaphore_delete, rtems_rate_monotonic_delete, rtems_extension_delete).

The rest of the Ravenscar restrictions have no equivalency in RTEMS (e.g. pragma Detect_Blocking), as far as we know. It is worth noting that the device drivers (BSW module), made by a third party, use instead different semaphores without any priority policy (due to the problems to specify the adequate priority ceiling for each one). Therefore, dedicated semaphores are created with the adequate priority ceiling in the application layer to wrap every call to a driver routine, so they are protected with the priority ceiling protocol too.

5   Test Environments

Like in other space projects, different test environments exist for the development and validation of the OBSW. These range from a pure software emulator (which provides great flexibility, like full introspection, fault injection, and debugging capabilities) to the actual flight hardware with additional components to simulate the environment (providing the maximum possible representativity). Examples are:

1. The IXV **Software Validation Facility (SVF)** is a software product running on a standard Linux host whose aim is to validate the OBSW against its Technical Specification requirements. The SVF is formed by different components: an OBC

emulator, containing the Gaisler's LEON2 TSIM 1.3.2c simulator (with the same memory configuration as the AT697E), and an emulator of the OBC I/O boards developed by QinetiQ Space; simulation of the Vehicle and the IXV avionics devices (GPS, IMU, FPCS and RCS); and the Real-World simulator, to provide the IXV FES (Functional Engineering Simulator) vehicle model (Dynamics and Kinematics Environment, sensors and actuators).

2. The **Avionics/GNC test bench (AGTB)** is a hardware/software product whose aim is to validate the OBSW against the Requirements Baseline Specification. It is composed of (*i*) the hardware IXV Avionics (EM/QM/EQM unit under test and the flight representative harness) including Power, Radiofrequency, TM, tracking and command, data handling, and an OBC FuMo (Functional Model) containing an FPGA with the AT697E model instead of the ASIC of the Flight OBC; and (*ii*) the ATB GSE (Avionics Test Bench Ground Support Equipment), a hardware and software system including all the devices necessary to stimulate and measure the avionics system.

3. The **Proto-Flight Model (PFM)**, including GNC & EGSE checkout equipment (Avionics, TM/TC, RF Spacecraft Check-Out Equipment, GPS RX stimulator…), and Master Test Processors (MTP).

All the tests described in this paper have been performed on the SVF, because it provides the maximum observability and it is the only available environment to the authors. With SVF, it is of uttermost importance to configure the adequate number of wait-cycles for each memory type, so that the timing of load and store instructions is accurate with respect to the actual hardware. Using the same flight executable, we compared the timestamps of the telemetry sent in a mission simulated with SVF and the timestamps of the same packets sent when executing within the AGTB. The differences were almost always under 1 millisecond (furthermore, the AT697E of the AGTB was usually a bit faster than TSIM), so the temporal results obtained with SVF can initially be considered representative enough.

6   Timing Results

Since the beginning of the project, we have been obtaining the OBSW's Worst-Case Execution Time (WCET) together with a schedulability analysis, even before the source code or the detailed design was written. A computational model was created based on the real-time constraints of the system, including: timing constraints based on OBSW processing deadlines, design constraints such as the selected real-time policy, and dimensioning constraints based on the available resources (CPU, RAM, buses). This model was continuously refined as the requirements evolved, like additional constraints on initialization time, sum of data acquisition, GNC Control processing, actuator commands time lower than a specified value, CPU load peak, etc.

The computational model was then filled with an estimated WCET (during early phases) or measured WCET (once the source code was available) for each task and critical section, task priorities and ceilings, providing a schedule table with priority (P), time consumed (C), task period (T), deadline (D) and maximum blocking time (B) per task. This data was processed by the UPM's RTA tool [8] to obtain the response time per task and total CPU utilization.

6.1 Obtaining Timing Measurements

The first approach to observe the timing behavior of the OBSW was to record the following absolute timestamps of every task i for each activation k:

1. **Arrival time** (a_i^k): The task is ready (i.e. for cyclic tasks, when the periodic timer expires, and for sporadic tasks, when the activating event occurs).
2. **Activation time** (s_i^k): When the task starts executing.
3. **Deactivation time** (d_i^k): When the task finishes its execution.

Note the arrival time is different from the activation time because there is always a jitter due to the RTOS overhead, blocking times (B_i^k) of lower-priority tasks locking a shared resource, and interference (I_i^k) of higher-priority tasks.

The execution time of Interrupt Service Routines (ISR) is not recorded, however just the interrupt for the RTEMS clock tick is enabled (configured to 100 Hz). All the other nominal interrupts are masked to reduce unpredictability (device polling is always used). Furthermore, every time the clock tick is received the MILB task is scheduled, so this ISR overhead is finally attributed to this task, which has the highest priority. In addition, the predictability impact of not being able to use freeze-on-interrupt in the caches is greatly reduced as every time an interrupt arrives a context switch will be performed anyway.

Since every single activation of each task for the complete test is recorded, it is possible to automatically compute the interference time of each task activation by subtracting the execution time of the different time spans where a thread preempts it (set of tasks directly preempting task i during the activation k, denoted by $dp(i,k)$, but not those tasks indirectly preempting task i). This time value is approximate because it does not take into account the context switch, but is close enough for our schedulability analysis.

4. **Activation Jitter** $(J_i^k) = s_i^k - a_i^k$
5. **Response Time** $(R_i^k) = d_i^k - a_i^k$
6. **Interference Time** $(I_i^k) = \sum_{\{j,l\}\in dp(i,k)}(d_j^l - s_j^l)$
7. **Execution Time** $(C_i^k) = (d_i^k - s_i^k) - I_i^k$

The computation of C_i^k does not need to take into account the blocking time because, since the Ravenscar profile is used, blocking is guaranteed to occur at most just once, at the beginning of the task activation.

To obtain the maximum blocking time for each task, additional timestamps have been recorded for each lock and unlock operation of every semaphore in the system.

Besides semaphore operations, there are additional critical sections consisting in disabling all the interrupts to avoid pre-emption (used just in device drivers and RTEMS routines). But as these are meant to be used for very short operations, and they cannot be instrumented (due both to the overhead and the fact that is not application code), it is appropriate to consider just the worst-case blocking produced by the application locks. Finally, the analysis of these traces proved very useful, revealing different bugs in lock usage.

To measure the abovementioned timestamps, two techniques were considered:

Traces. LEON2 provides a UART, normally used to show a trace of messages (e.g. the BIOS information) for debugging purposes. However, writing each character to the serial cable is very slow, and often can cause a deadline violation of a task just printing a couple of debug messages in the same activation. Even if a specific background task can be created to write every message logged by any thread, the number of characters per second is very limited. To allow a high number of tracing messages during the debug phase, an ad-hoc mechanism was implemented for the IXV OBSW: we used a printf-like function (taking a severity level, the format string, and a variable number of arguments), where the body of this function was just a single invalid SPARC instruction. This invalid instruction, when interpreted by the SVF, is passed to an ad-hoc TSIM plugin that we implemented to recognize this instruction as a log trace, gathering all the parameters and the backtrace from the CPU register windows and task stack, and then writing a string to a log file (in the simulator's host) with the complete debug message including a precise timestamp with the simulated clock. All these operations execute inside the plugin and do not affect the simulated time, since this invalid instruction is configured to take zero CPU cycles from a TSIM point of view. So the only overhead is caused by the additional instructions to save the logged parameters in registers (and maybe in the stack) and to call this function. The overhead includes not only the extra cycles for executing these additional instructions, but also the extra code that must be loaded in caches, and the fact that the compiler will apply a different set of optimizations when the software is compiled without traces. These traces are just for the debug images. By using conditional compilation, the tracing capability is not built into the flight images. The option to write debug traces to the serial cable is retained as a build flag for those cases were the OBSW must be debugged in the AGTB instead of the SVF, but with the capability to filter traces of a specific severity and module.

Breakpoints. Since a simulator is used, it is possible to stop the execution at any time and inspect the whole software state externally from the host (e.g. the simulated timestamp), without instrumenting the OBSW and with a very low overhead on the simulated environment or even no overhead at all. Particularly, it is possible to also instruct the simulator to stop the execution when a specific instruction is reached (e.g. using a breakpoint of the debugger or even an internal simulator breakpoint), for example when a task finishes each activation. This technique is thus less intrusive than the use of traces (it can be used with the flight OBSW version, which is not instrumented), allowing more flexibility in the information gathered (e.g. also breakpointing in the RTOS or ISRs, which are more difficult to instrument). This functionality, however, is not designed to obtain timing measurements, and it requires specific support on the host, so it will be more difficult to qualify as an acceptable method for performing schedulability analysis; besides, it is much more difficult to obtain information like the status of specific variables than with traces, due to the optimizations performed by the compiler. Finally, it is usually more costly to use for monitoring non-global variables, and it is fragile in the sense that it is usually easy to break at the first instruction of a function, but is more difficult to do it at an arbitrary instruction because when the software evolves the addresses change. All in all, it is a very specific technique for timing analysis, but not adequate as a general logging mechanism for debugging purposes.

One of the goals of this paper was thus to check the overhead of these different approaches and find out whether breakpointing must always be used, given the higher overhead introduced by the traces (and thus a higher interference in the executions); or it is better to use traces during the development phase and breakpointing only for the final OBSW flight version, given its complexity and fragility.

6.2   Response Time Results

At the end of this paper, Table 4 shows, for each task, the maximum recorded execution time (in milliseconds) of a single activation in the complete nominal scenario (full mission without fault injection). The SVF is deterministic, so there is no need to repeat the test runs to obtain a statistical result. Since the behavior of the software depends on the operating mode (e.g. Guidance algorithms are in an idle state until Reentry), specific columns are provided depending on the mission mode. The diagrams in Fig. 1 show two 50-ms plots with the execution of each task (ordered by priority), comparing the estimated schedule at design time (left) with the schedule derived from the timing measures (right). Fig. 2 shows the evolution of the WCET of the GNC tasks depending on the mission mode.

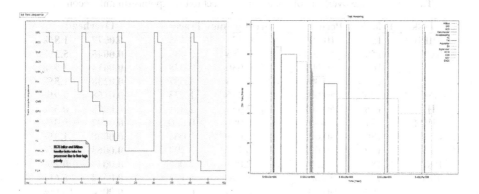

Fig. 1. Time diagrams of estimated (left) vs. measured (right) task execution.

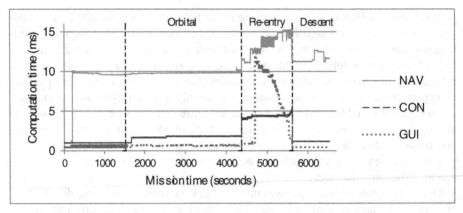

Fig. 2. Computation times of the GNC tasks during the whole mission

Note that both caches are always enabled (TSIM emulates caches, and is considered to offer an 80% timing accuracy [9]), as well as instruction burst. Both when using traces and breakpoints, the timestamp is not obtained within the OBSW execution but from the simulator, by reading the current CPU cycle counter from TSIM, with a clock resolution of 20 ns. Hence the operation to get the current time does not affect the simulated time.

Table 1 compares the timing results of both techniques (note that in RTEMS threads with a lower numeric priority preempt threads with a higher numeric priority). It can be seen that the traces introduce a small overhead in the average computation time of each task, a mean of 9 microseconds for each task activation (mean 3% overhead of average task time), increasing the 50-ms frame to about 62 microseconds. Note that this overhead is not accumulative; given that the CPU usage is less than 100%, the overhead of traces is absorbed in the idle time at the end of the frame, and so the next frame will not be delayed by this overhead.

Table 1. Average overhead of traces with respect to breakpoints (in milliseconds)

Task	Priority	Period	Breakpoints	Traces	Overhead	
MILB	150	10.00	0.427	0.435	**0.0077**	**1.8%**
RCS	155	10.00	0.085	0.089	**0.0045**	**5.3%**
SUP	160	50.00	0.036	0.038	**0.0014**	**3.9%**
ACQ	165	50.00	1.634	1.657	**0.0238**	**1.5%**
GNC_C	170	50.00	1.956	1.973	**0.0168**	**0.9%**
EH	175	50.00	2.353	2.361	**0.0078**	**0.3%**
MVM	177	50.00	0.059	0.060	**0.0002**	**0.3%**
CMD	180	50.00	0.063	0.064	**0.0008**	**1.3%**
GPS	182	50.00	0.188	0.194	**0.0063**	**3.4%**
HK	185	50.00	2.061	2.066	**0.0049**	**0.2%**
TTM	190	50.00	1.190	1.124	**−0.0662**	**−5.6%**
TC	195	50.00	0.034	0.039	**0.0054**	**16.0%**
GNC_N	200	500.00	10.655	10.458	**−0.1977**	**−1.9%**
GNC_G	210	500.00	1.574	1.601	**0.0267**	**1.7%**

Surprisingly, the execution time of a few tasks (TTM and GNC Navigation) is lower when instrumented with traces than when measuring the flight image with breakpoints. This may be caused by timing anomalies due to the caches [9] because for these tasks, the instrumented version places some frequently accessed code/data in a more favorable location from the point of view of the caches; or it may be due to changes in the pre-emption pattern. But it is not possible to sustain this assumption because the caches statistics were not available.

Table 2. Comparison example of event generation time

Event	Task	Reference	Breakpoints	Traces
EV_MOS_ACTION_TRIGGERED	EH	4316.97509 s	+0.00 ms	+424.32 ms
EV_ACTION_SUCCESSFUL_EXEC	CMD	4316.97686 s	+0.00 ms	+424.38 ms
EV_MOS_TRANS_TO_REENTRY	MVM	4371.97497 s	+0.06 ms	−75.68 ms
EV_ACTION_SUCCESSFUL_EXEC	CMD	4371.97552 s	+0.06 ms	−75.62 ms

Table 2 shows a comparison example of the absolute timestamps for the generation of some telemetry packets sent by different OBSW tasks, with a reference test run not measuring the execution time. For example, the event for the transition to Re-entry was generated by the MVM task at second 4371.97497, according to the OBC clock (the task raising the event directly reads the clock to obtain a precise generation time, which is later sent in the message header to ground) with the flight image with no execution time measurements; that event was generated at second 4371.97503 (60 µs later) with the flight image using breakpointing; whereas it was generated at second 4371.89929 when running the instrumented executable (75.68 ms earlier).

So breakpointing introduces some changes in the simulated behavior, as the event messages are sent at not exactly the same time (the resolution of the timestamp in the telemetry packets is 15 microseconds, so when the number of breakpoints per frame is low, the timestamp difference is unnoticeable). In the execution with traces the packets are generated at considerably different times, usually having a nearly constant delay depending on the mode of the mission. The initialization of an OBSW instrumented with traces takes longer, so the first task frame starts at second 2.842613 instead of 2.418330. But events may also be generated a little earlier, as shown in Table 2. This depends on the slight differences of the mission due to small overheads (e.g. in the simulated closed-loop environment).

Regarding the running time of the test suite with the SVF, it is worth mentioning that the time to execute a test increases as expected when taking timing measurements. The SVF takes a bit longer to execute a test with traces (due to the extra processing in the host machine) than when not obtaining timing values, but this extra time is nearly negligible (19 minutes more in a 9-hour SVF test, including post-processing in the host time, for a 2-hour mission in simulated time). In our environment the overhead in the host is considerably higher with breakpoints (42 more minutes instead of 19 minutes in the 9-hour test).

These measured execution times are not the actual worst-case execution times, because those worst-case paths may have never been exercised in the tests run. Six different scenarios for the mission are executed with nominal and non-nominal situations in closed-loop, with the hope to ensure the OBSW behaves properly in as many situations as possible, taking timing measurements and performing specific schedulability analyses for each of them. In addition, several functional and robustness system tests in the simulator are run for testing specific situations, but no timing results are analyzed in these tests.

Finally, it is worth noting that each task has dedicated code to monitor its own timing behavior, sending an error event in case of deadline miss (an event we never received in any execution, except when we specifically injected this timing fault).

6.3   Final Schedulability Analysis

Table 3 shows the schedulability analysis of the OBSW for the Re-entry mode (the one with the highest CPU load), using the maximum execution times recorded during that mode for tasks and locks, measured with the use of breakpoints. It can be seen that all the tasks are schedulable in the worst-case scenario (the response times of all tasks are always lower than their deadlines). The total processor utilization is 63.05% during that mode, as reported by the RTA tool, giving a 36.95% slack of unused CPU time (the software developer standard mandates a 35% margin for the CPU at the final phase of the project, which could for example absorb the 20% difference in TSIM timing accuracy).

Table 3. Response Time Analysis for Re-entry mode (in milliseconds)

Task	Period	Offset	Jitter	WCET	Block	Deadline	Response
MILB	10.000	0.000	0.000	0.670	0.933	5.000	**1.603**
RCS	10.000	0.000	0.000	0.147	0.933	5.000	**1.750**
SUP	50.000	0.000	0.000	0.044	0.933	50.000	**1.794**
ACQ	50.000	0.000	0.000	1.993	0.941	50.000	**3.795**
GNC_C	50.000	0.000	0.000	5.250	1.299	20.000	**9.403**
EH	50.000	0.000	0.000	5.115	1.299	50.000	**15.335**
MVM	50.000	0.000	0.000	0.312	1.299	50.000	**15.647**
CMD	50.000	0.000	0.000	3.853	1.299	50.000	**19.500**
GPS	50.000	0.000	0.000	0.974	1.299	50.000	**21.291**
HK	50.000	0.000	0.000	2.985	1.299	50.000	**24.276**
TTM	50.000	0.000	0.000	4.163	1.299	50.000	**28.439**
TC	50.000	0.000	0.000	0.025	1.805	50.000	**29.970**
GNC_N	500.000	0.000	0.000	15.456	1.805	50.000	**47.060**
GNC_G	500.000	0.000	0.000	11.791	0.001	100.000	**84.029**

A separate schedulability analysis is performed for each mission mode, and in all cases the OBSW was schedulable and granted the required CPU margin. However, no specific schedulability analysis was performed for the mode changes (the duration of mode transitions is lower than 100 ms), nor any of the mode change protocols found in the literature [10] was used. In any case, the mode changes in the IXV OBSW are much simpler than these more general approaches: Our tasks are never aborted or created; the priority, period and deadline of tasks is never modified (nor the priority of semaphores); and no delay is introduced for any task during a mode change. The only difference between modes is the change in the WCET due to the different activities

Table 4. Computation time of tasks per mission mode (in milliseconds)

Task	Start		Prelaunch		Launch		Orbital		Re-entry		Pre-release		Descent	
	max	avg	max	avg	max	avg	max	avg	max	avg	max	avg	max	avg
MILB	0.398	0.173	0.473	0.374	0.473	0.376	0.573	0.385	0.670	0.571	0.670	0.573	0.669	0.489
RCS	0.043	0.038	0.043	0.039	0.043	0.039	0.321	0.109	0.147	0.115	0.146	0.115	0.143	0.047
SUP	0.042	0.035	0.042	0.035	0.043	0.036	0.043	0.036	0.044	0.037	0.043	0.037	0.043	0.037
ACQ	1.593	1.203	1.712	1.570	1.739	1.597	1.966	1.583	1.993	1.836	1.992	1.838	1.994	1.662
GNC_C	1.036	0.968	1.004	0.977	1.004	0.978	1.894	1.707	5.250	4.280	5.603	5.294	5.706	1.171
EH	1.596	1.394	3.671	2.244	3.199	2.254	4.212	2.270	5.115	2.775	4.478	2.820	5.188	2.363
MVM	0.036	0.035	0.036	0.035	0.221	0.049	0.379	0.070	0.312	0.065	0.237	0.042	0.043	0.041
CMD	2.565	0.061	2.261	0.067	0.697	0.061	2.446	0.063	3.853	0.066	1.051	0.068	2.415	0.063
GPS	0.577	0.155	0.662	0.176	0.671	0.177	0.894	0.196	0.974	0.182	0.806	0.184	0.876	0.193
HK	2.474	1.075	2.681	1.877	2.867	2.083	3.338	1.988	2.985	2.343	2.866	2.337	3.168	2.107
TTM	0.707	0.197	0.616	0.267	0.803	0.271	3.800	1.094	4.163	0.900	3.751	3.155	4.511	3.425
TC	0.411	0.065	0.648	0.067	0.306	0.065	0.274	0.024	0.025	0.024	0.025	0.024	0.025	0.024
GNC_N	0.967	0.964	10.235	7.063	10.269	9.846	10.682	9.955	15.456	13.758	12.166	12.090	12.850	11.985
GNC_G	0.680	0.429	0.675	0.486	0.680	0.514	0.745	0.639	11.791	5.891	0.805	0.803	0.804	0.430

performed by each task. Finally, as a pessimistic scenario, the schedulability analysis was also performed for the whole mission instead of for each mode separately and still all the tasks were schedulable, so we consider that the schedulability of the mode changes is also guaranteed (although in this case the CPU utilization is 67.19%, a bit higher than the one allowed by the required margin).

7   Future Work

Besides the use of the two described techniques for recording the execution time of every task and critical section, the RapiTime tool was also used to obtain the actual worst-case execution times. This hybrid tool is based on collecting timestamps of functional blocks during test runs, and then using static analysis to compute the worst-case path of each task or critical section, even if it has never been exercised during the tests. To obtain these execution timestamps from the IXV OBSW test suite, each functional block was instrumented with an invalid SPARC instruction interpreted by the SVF (similar approach to the SVF traces but with even less overhead), as well as inside the RTEMS context switch hook to separate the timestamps per task.

However, even if this approach was adequate for obtaining the needed timestamps for RapiTime, it was not possible to complete the WCET analysis of all tasks, but just the most critical ones, mainly due to project constraints. In any case, the use of Rapi-Time was very helpful to give further confidence on the schedulability of the OBSW, and also to perform many code optimizations and even to detect code that should not be called from specific tasks. We expect in future projects to be able to perform a full WCET analysis with RapiTime, starting at the same time as the code is being written.

In addition, since the breakpointing technique provides complete observability of any instruction of the OBSW without noticeable overhead, we intend to perform a more detailed timing analysis in the future [11], e.g. monitoring every interrupt execution, and other sources of blocking like context switch routines or those fine-grain critical sections just briefly disabling interrupts, to confirm that they are as short as expected.

Finally, in future projects, we also hope to leverage the new real-time timing mechanisms developed under the ESA GTSP program 'RTEMS LEON Upgrade', e.g. the deadline verification mechanism, automatic report of execution times (maximum and minimum), or improvements to the semaphore policies and checks. We also want to add a validation housekeeping package with activation and deactivation times of tasks, without jeopardizing the available telemetry bandwidth, to consistently compare the timing behavior of a flight executable against an instrumented executable, and the same executable in the SVF and AGTB environments, to improve the limited approach of comparing the timestamps of the telemetry packets.

8   Conclusions

This paper provided an overview of the whole IXV OBSW, listing all the tasks defined for performing the required functionality, with a focus on the timing behavior. We have also described the subset of Edisoft's Improved RTEMS that has been used, which follows the Ravenscar profile defined for the Ada programming language, to allow the use of sound schedulability analysis techniques.

Two different techniques have been compared for obtaining timing measurements during a test execution of every task activation and critical section occurrence, namely the use of low-overhead traces and simulator breakpoints. Even if the use of breakpoints introduces a reduced overhead on the simulation, its usage is very fragile and may be more difficult to qualify as the breakpointing functionality has not been designed for this purpose. Therefore, simulators for safety-critical software must be improved to provide robust and usable mechanisms for measuring the timing behavior without altering the simulated environment. Meanwhile, we recommend to normally use instrumented executables with traces during the development phase, to obtain the timing measurements in a robust way, and to just employ breakpointing for the final schedulability analysis of the flight executables, comparing the three types of executions (breakpointing vs. traces vs. no timing measurements) to ensure the approach followed gives correct results.

Finally, the results show that the IXV OBSW is schedulable, even with the unpredictability introduced by the use of caches; and the published executions times are expected to be useful estimations for future space projects.

References

1. Malucchi, G., Dussy S., Camuffo, F.: Intermediate experimental vehicle (IXV): avionics and software of the ESA reentry demonstrator. In: Data Systems in Aerospace (2012)
2. ECSS-Q-ST-80C — Software product assurance (2009)
3. Rodríguez, E., Giménez, P., Vicente Fernández, I, de M.: SCOE for IXV GNC. In: SESP 2012 – Simulation & EGSE Facilities for Space Programmes (2012)

4. Rodríguez, M., Silva, N., Esteves, J., Henriques, L., Costa, D., Holsti, N., Hjortnaes, K.: Challenges in calculating the WCET of a complex on-board satellite application. In: Gustafsson, J. (ed.) WCET 2003 (2003)
5. Burns, A., Dobbing, B., Vardanega, T.: Guide for the use of the Ada Ravenscar Profile in high integrity systems. ISO/IEC TR **24718**, 2005 (2005)
6. Kwon, J., Wellings, A., King, S.: Ravenscar-Java: A high-integrity profile for real-time Java. Concurrency and Computation: Practice and Experience **17**(5–6) (2005)
7. Vardanega, T., Caspersen, G.: Using the Ravenscar Profile for space applications: The OBOSS case. ACM SIGAda Ada Letters **21**(1), 96–104 (2001)
8. Alonso, A., de la Puente, J.A., Zamorano, J.: A test environment for high integrity software development. In: Rosen, J.-P., Strohmeier, A. (eds.) Ada-Europe 2003. LNCS, vol. 2655, pp. 359–367. Springer, Heidelberg (2003)
9. Bernat, G., Colin, A., Esteves, J., Garcia, G., Moreno, C., Holsti, N., Hernek, M.: Considerations on the LEON cache effects on the timing analysis of on-board applications. In: DASIA (2007)
10. Real, J., Crespo, A.: Mode change protocols for real-time systems: A survey and a new proposal. Real-Time Systems **26**(2), 161–197 (2004)
11. Vardanega, T., Zamorano, J., de la Puente, J.A.: On the dynamic semantics and the timing behavior of Ravenscar kernels. Real-Time Systems **29**(1), 59–89 (2005)

Maintenance of Reliable Distributed Applications with Open-Source Middleware: Fifteen Years Later

Manuel Díaz and Daniel Garrido[✉]

Departamento de Lenguajes y Ciencias de la Computación,
Universidad de Málaga, Málaga, Spain
{mdr,dgarrido}@lcc.uma.es

Abstract. Open-source middleware started to be used several years ago for the development of complex applications. When these applications were developed, no real data were available about how maintenance activities could be affected over time. This is especially important for critical applications expected to be maintained over several years. This paper presents maintenance experiences with applications using open-source middleware (TAO and JacORB). These applications are developed using a component model for real-time applications implemented on top of the middleware. Improvements for software reliability have been detected during this time. We present them and how they can be applied to applications using TAO.

Keywords: Middleware · Open-source · CORBA · TAO · JacORB · Maintenance

1   Introduction

At the beginning of the last decade, middleware approaches seemed the best alternative for the development of distributed complex applications. Middleware helped to hide the complexity of the communications and developers could focus on the functionality of their applications.

This benefit, however, comes at a cost: the developer loses part of the control over the application, which starts to depend on third-party software. If we consider software expected to be in use for years, this can be a handicap in terms of maintenance. Changes in operating systems, programming languages, libraries or simply the discontinuation of the chosen middleware can have a critical impact on complex systems.

For years, the software developer's community had no actual data about how middleware maintenance could affect complex applications, because middleware was a novelty in the software world. This was especially important in systems expected to be safe and reliable with applications working 24/7.

Very common middleware alternatives were CORBA [1], Java-RMI [2] or DCOM [3]. Within these alternatives, CORBA was platform and language independent. Java-RMI was platform-independent and DCOM was used mainly in Microsoft platforms.

© Springer International Publishing Switzerland 2015
J.A. de la Puente and T. Vardanega (Eds.): Ada-Europe 2015, LNCS 9111, pp. 116–128, 2015.
DOI: 10.1007/978-3-319-19584-1_8

In addition to middleware, an important paradigm used from those days until now, is the component-based paradigm [4]. In this paradigm, software applications are organized in components. Software components provide the basis for reuse and adaptability. A component is a basic composition unit, with a set of interfaces, which has (probably) been developed independently of the application (in time and space). These components can be configured and connected to other components.

The importance of software components for middleware is due to the fact that frequently, components are the basis for middleware implementation. From a historic perspective, the first commercial component models were COM [5] (from Microsoft) and JavaBeans [6]. These models evolved to .NET [7] and newer versions of Enterprise Java Beans (EJB) [8]. Some of the aforementioned middleware even included newer component-based extensions such as the CORBA Component Model (CCM) [9] in the case of CORBA.

How has middleware technology evolved over the years? One of the most promising technologies was CORBA from OMG [10]. CORBA had all the features necessary to develop robust and efficient applications in different languages (e.g. C++, Java, Ada, …) or platforms. It had many different implementations available, including open-source and commercial versions, from many different vendors. However, CORBA was not adopted by the majority of developers for a myriad of reasons. For instance, the huge growth of the Internet, where it was difficult to use CORBA easily, the creation of new languages and platforms (e.g. C# [11] and .NET) which did not support CORBA and finally, newer, easier technologies. In this case, the rise of web services [12] that worked in a very simple way, even in different languages was one of the most important factors preventing the popularization of CORBA. The last factor could be its steep learning curve. As CORBA is language independent, OMG provided mappings to all these languages. The developers had to thoroughly know the details of these mappings [13] to avoid problems such as, for instance, memory leaks, crashing, etc. The mapping was not the only factor. Sometimes, the deployment of the applications was not an easy task and external factors such as, for example, the network configuration, could be a nightmare for the developer. In short, technology has evolved toward the Internet where new technologies such as web services, REST [14] and so on control most of the market.

Nevertheless, CORBA has improved greatly with respect to other middleware implementations. Several of these CORBA improvements or extensions have enabled the reliability of the applications to be bettered. For instance, Real-time CORBA or RT-CORBA [15] is the CORBA extension for real-time systems. It included features for control processor resources, communication resources and memory resources in distributed real-time applications. Minimum CORBA [16] aims to use CORBA in embedded systems reducing the memory and code footprint. Finally, FT CORBA or Fault Tolerance CORBA [17] is an OMG specification for building fault-tolerant distributed real-time and embedded applications

For one reason or another, CORBA has not been accepted in the way it should have been. However, CORBA is not dead. In fact, many of the ideas of CORBA are present in these new platforms. Another reason to say that CORBA is alive and well is that it has many different applications in fields such as telecommunications, defense, simulation, etc. In fact, Java itself includes a CORBA implementation, although, probably many programmers are oblivious to this fact. Many of the most popular CORBA implementations are still active nowadays. For instance, implementations such as Orbix [18], Orbacus [19], JacORB [20] or TAO [21] are currently active, which could be an indicator that the current health of CORBA is not as bad as could be expected. There are even CORBA implementations using C++11 [22], Python [23] or Ruby [24].

What about existent CORBA-based applications? Many applications based on CORBA were developed in days gone. Some of them were changed to other technologies (e.g. web services) and are not considered in this paper. Other applications followed using CORBA as middleware and they are the basis for this paper where we present some examples of how these applications have evolved together with CORBA.

In [25], UM-RTCOM was presented. UM-RTCOM is a real-time component model for the development of distributed real-time applications. UM-RTCOM itself is platform independent (as is CORBA), but its use has several advantages. Standard CORBA implementations are not suitable for use in real-time systems. They have many different problems that have discouraged its use for the development of reliable or critical systems. Typically, they provide best-effort implementations. It could be argued that RT-CORBA could be used for this purpose and this argument is acceptable. However, UM-RTCOM is a component model on top of RT-CORBA, trying to hide the complexity of using RT-CORBA or other middleware for the development of real-time applications. UM-RTCOM developers only have to think in terms of components and real-time requirements that can be easily expressed. Later, UM-RTCOM components are mapped to a specific middleware or language implementation (e.g. RT-CORBA or Java). Finally, some analysis techniques can be applied to analyze the real-time behavior of the application.

Two very different fields were used to test UM-RTCOM: simulation and embedded systems. In the field of simulation, several papers [26] using UM-RTCOM were presented. These simulators are very complex systems where many different factors have to be considered. They are composed by many different applications with different real-time requirements. In the case of embedded systems, UM-RTCOM was used as the basis for the implementation of the communication platform in the European project SMEPP [27], where a secure middleware for embedded P2P systems was developed.

The simulators presented in these papers have been used since then and they have suffered the evolution of technologies, programming languages, operating systems, changing requirements, etc. but they still maintain the core of CORBA for the communications. This paper presents the experience gained in the maintenance of these kinds of systems with the perspective of time (15 years) and what improvements have been made since then.

The paper is organized as follows: Section 2 presents maintenance experiences in our model using TAO and JacORB. Section 3 presents some points where existing middleware could be improved in order to better support reliable software. Section 4 applies these improvements to TAO. The paper ends with some conclusions.

2   Maintenance Experiences

As stated, UM-RTCOM is a platform-agnostic component model. Complex systems can be described in terms of UM-RTCOM components and how these components interact with each other. In the following stages, UM-RTCOM definitions are mapped to a specific implementation. Two implementations have been developed:

— C++ implementation. This implementation uses CORBA and RT-CORBA. Specifically, it is based on TAO, a very popular open-source implementation of CORBA.
— Java implementation. Where interaction is needed with the C++ implementation, we have used the CORBA implementations included in the Java SE [28] or JacORB, which is another open-source implementation of CORBA in the Java programming language.

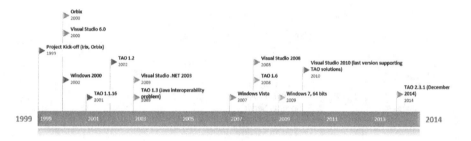

Fig. 1. TAO Timeline

Figure 1 shows a timeline with the evolution of our software and main milestones. The first versions of our software were based on Orbix (C++) on Irix, Solaris and Windows NT 4. Orbix is a commercial product and does not provide any way to customize it. Due to this, we ported our software to TAO 1.1.16 (2001). The development environment used on Windows was Microsoft Visual Studio 6.0.

These versions were maintained with no major problems until the launching of Windows Vista. We updated TAO 1.2 and made a new change to TAO 1.3 when some interoperability problems with Java appeared. All the changes at this time were related to testing, changes in requirements or deployment problems. None of these changes were specifically related to problems with middleware maintenance.

Things changed when Windows Vista was launched. From this version on, warnings about compatibility issues from the development environment were received. This motivated us to update to a new version of TAO (1.6) and development environment (Visual Studio 2008). The last milestone was related to 64 bits version of operating systems. This seems to be an importance difference with respect to previous versions and we carried out preventive maintenance.

The latest version of TAO (2.3.1) was launched in December 2014. The activity in TAO has significantly reduced but newer versions are periodically released.

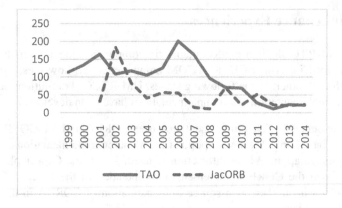

Fig. 2. Number of bugs fixed in TAO and JacORB

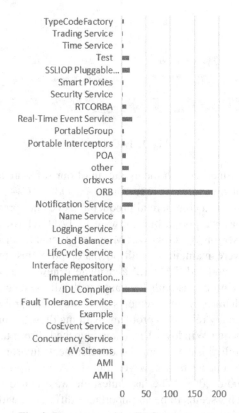

Fig. 3. Bugs grouped by TAO component

Figure 2 shows the number of bugs fixed in TAO and JacORB (obtained from their respective Bugzilla servers [29, 30]) grouped by year. In the case of TAO, the total number of bugs fixed from 1999 to 2014 was 1548. The highest activity levels can be found in 2001 and over the period 2005-2007. From this year onwards the number of bugs fixed quickly decreases, which can be interpreted in two different ways: higher software maturity or activity decreasing. In the case of JacORB, it has a total amount of 686 bugs fixed over the period 2001-2014. This time, the highest activity is registered in 2002. From this year onwards, the number of bugs fixed per year is more or less stable. In the last two years, the number of bugs fixed in TAO and JacORB has been practically the same.

Although TAO is a product, which is around 15 years old, currently there is a total number of 417 unfixed bugs in different categories. Figure 3 shows bugs grouped by component (Notification, Name, RealTime Event), ORB or IDL compiler. This is a huge number of bugs considering the rhythm of bugs fixed per year, especially in categories such as ORB or IDL Compiler. This is can be compensated with the lower number of bugs reported every year.

TAO users can send their bugs through a distribution list and they can also use a bug track system. Although it is a free product, there are several companies providing commercial support such as OCI [31] and Remedy IT [32].

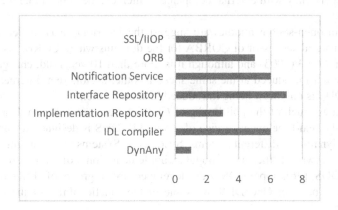

Fig. 4. Bugs grouped by JacORB component

Table 1. Code metrics

	Files	Lines	Statements	Class Defs
ACE+TAO	22,915	1,859,251	616,530	8,078
JacORB	2,138	300,129	115,547	2,532

Figure 4 shows the current active bugs of JacORB grouped by component. There are a total of 30 active bugs. JacORB is also commercially supported by users and private companies such as OCI and Remedy IT.

The philosophy of the TAO and JacORB projects aims for the developer communities to provide solutions to detected problems in these products. This is an alternative to commercial support but it is not always easy depending on the error class detected. Table 1 shows some code metrics taken from the latest ACE+TAO distribution (6.3.1) (TAO is distributed together with ACE, an object oriented framework).

This distribution has more than 20,000 files encompassing more than 1.8 million lines of code, 616,530 statements and 8,078 class definitions. With these numbers it is not an easy task to make a change in the source code. In the case of JacORB (3.5), these quantities are lower.

ACE+TAO provides the possibility of automatic testing. More than 1,000 tests are included in different categories such as ACE, TAO core tests, ORB services and others. When a change is made to the ACE+TAO code, there is the possibility (not conclusive) to compare the results before and after changes to the source code are applied. JacORB has also several tests but in a very small number compared with TAO.

The application of new technologies is a critical election for companies, especially in systems expected to have a long cycle of life of several years. Changes in operating system, programming languages or developing environments can have a critical impact on the maintenance of a system.

From our perspective, the use of open-source middleware has not been a bad alternative. For over fifteen years we have been using these technologies and we have been able to adapt to the times. Alternatives based on commercial products could increase dependency with external companies which can be undesirable for long term products.

Trends in open-source middleware suggest the Distribution Data Service (DDS) [33] is the natural successor of CORBA for the domains where CORBA is applied. It is also from OMG (2003) and although it is more than 10 years old, changes in these markets are not introduced at the same speed as other sectors (e.g. Internet technologies) and DDS is only now being introduced in some of them.

DDS shares much of the philosophy of CORBA but is centered on data. In fact, it resembles the real-time event service of TAO [34]. DDS is designed to support heterogeneity, dynamism, different systems: Systems-of-Systems programming.

Currently, two of the most popular implementations of DDS are RTI [35] and OpenDDS [36]. OpenDDS was developed by a group of TAO developers. In fact, some parts of OpenDDS use some of the functionalities of the ACE+TAO distribution.

3 Improving Communication

From our experience in developing distributed software for critical systems, we have detected some areas where implementation could be improved and where perfective maintenance could be applied to our solutions. In this section we describe, in a generic way, some of these areas in the context of open-source middleware.

- **Service Orientation.** Distributed software has evolved for the concept of services. Service oriented applications [37] are nowadays widely used for the development of distributed applications. In this approach, system components provide and require services. This is the same philosophy as CORBA: loosely coupled systems where interfaces of elements are not known a priori.
- **Different Client Types (heterogeneity).** We allow different client types in terms of operating system, programming language, etc. This feature is supported by

CORBA. However, because of our experience, we consider a unique communication technology is not enough for the highly wide-ranging requirements in a complex application. Desktop applications could use a chosen technology such as CORBA, WCF [38] or web services. However other specialized elements (for instance, those interacting with hardware) could require a higher performance not provided by these technologies or possibly they cannot use these "heavy" technologies. Thus, in our approach we consider different communication technologies.

- **Non-intrusive Communications**. The communication engine does not have to interference with other layers of applications. CORBA provides mapping for all the programming languages it supports, but sometimes this mapping badly affects other parts of applications. Communication should be isolated in such a way that later changes will not affect the rest of applications.

- **Dynamism**. This feature is related to service-orientation and non-intrusive communications. These in turn are related to the dynamic functionalities of CORBA which imply not having a priori knowledge of other parts of a system. For instance, changes in the communications should not imply a new compilation of other parts. Thus, we require a higher flexibility where we can change communication technology cleanly.

- **Performance.** Depending on the application, the data flow between applications may vary from the need to transmit tens of messages per second to the need to transmit a large amount of data several times per second. In cases like these, performance is an important factor that has to be considered, since the refresh data rate must be adequate to allow the correct running of the applications. The communication technology must be flexible enough to allow a fine degree of configuration. Second, if we do not obtain the desirable performance we could use other technologies as we have said in the previous points.

- **Reliability.** The communication system must provide mechanisms to control erroneous situations.

- **Scalability.** Should the number of connections increase, communications must still work correctly. Service-oriented applications should be able to increase the number of connections with a graceful degradation.

4   Improvement Experiences with TAO

In this section we describe overall experiences with TAO, applying some of the points described in Section 3. TAO itself is described [39] as extensible in several categories such as connection management, concurrency, pluggable protocols, etc. With this purpose, several patterns are used including: *Reactor*, *Acceptor-Connector*, *Leaders/Followers* and *Strategies*. However, an in-depth knowledge of TAO is required to be able to extend or modify some of these patterns.

It is easier trying to find one of the multiple configuration options provided by TAO. In this section we describe how to use or configure some TAO mechanisms in such a way that some of the points described in Section 3 can be applied.

4.1   Networking Improvements

Networking can be improved in terms of performance, reliability or fault-tolerance. Multicast can be used to improve performance and fault-tolerance by replication. TAO allows multicast in several ways: real-time event service, protocol configuration, etc. An efficient way of using multicasting in TAO is through the pair of MIOP/UIPMC protocols [40]. MIOP and UIPMC are the acronyms of Multicast Inter-ORB Protocol and Unreliable IP Multicast respectively. With this combination, MIOP packets are used to transmit GIOP requests (CORBA requests) over UDP/IP. Then, TAO servants are able to receive requests sent to multicast groups where they are subscribed.

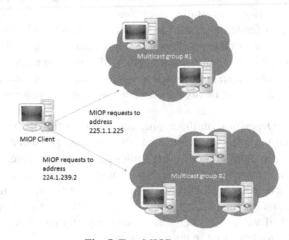

Fig. 5. Two MIOP groups

Figure 5 shows two multicast groups in TAO using MIOP/UIPMC. CORBA servants (objects able to receive invocations) are subscribed to a multicast address and the clients send requests to multicast groups. Each servant in a group is able to receive the requests. Some limitations are related to the packet size (currently, they are limited to 5-6 Kbytes), the fact that only one-way operations (no results can be returned) are supported and the unreliable nature of the communication. But the latter can be reduced by redundancy. We can obtain a very good performance by using this protocol combination.

An additional mechanism we can use to control scalability at network level is controlling the network interfaces. We can easily specify (at configuration time) which addresses can be listened on each network interface.

```
dynamic UIPMC_Factory Service_Object *
TAO_PortableGroup:_make_TAO_UIPMC_Protocol_Factory()
  "-ORBListenOnAll 0
  -ORBListenerInterfaces 224.1.239.2=192.168.20.135"
```

The code above shows how multicast address 224.1.239.2 is only listed on the network interface with IP address 192.168.20.135. This kind of code is included in TAO configuration files read during initialization.

4.2   Controlling Concurrency

TAO provides several ways of controlling concurrency on both client and server sides. Controlling concurrency is a way of improving scalability. For instance, on the server side we can use at the POA level (Portable Object Adapter):

— ORB controlled model: requests are attended to in the order specified by the ORB (Object Request Broker) where the servant (more specifically, the POA) is running.
— Single thread model.

In addition, a server can use three different concurrency models: reactive, thread-per-connection and thread-pool.
We can also use different strategies on the client side. More specifically:

— Leader-follower: in this strategy, the client uses the leader-follower pattern of TAO [41]. The client joins the leader-follower group and while waiting for the connection to be completed, the thread may eventually be chosen as leader and may be used to process other requests.
— Reactive: similar to the previous one except that the connection thread uses the thread provided by the TAO Reactor (another TAO pattern).
— Blocking: when using this strategy, the client is blocked until the connection finishes.

By using these combinations we can have a high degree of concurrency control. Some experiences we have obtained are related to CORBA upcalls while waiting for requests to be completed. The behavior of the client is determined by the so called *wait strategy*. When an application acts as client and server, *nested upcalls* are possible and then we can have deadlock problems when the ORB "steals" threads of clients waiting for invocations.

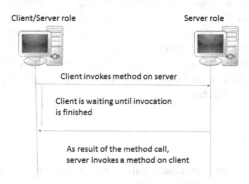

Fig. 6. Nested upcall example

Figure 6 shows a situation where nested upcalls are possible and deadlock could be present. Client playing the role of client and server invokes a method on server. As a result of the invocation, the server applies a nested upcall to the client. In some situations, the ORB could "steal the client thread to attend this request. This problem has now supposedly been solved in the latest versions of TAO by using the MT_NOUPCALL strategy, but it was certainly present until recently. Alternatives for solving this problem are the use of the Wait-on-Leader-Follower-No-Upcall Wait Strategy (but this is an experimental strategy [42]) or a blocking strategy:

```
static Client_Strategy_Factory "-ORBWaitStrategy rw -
ORBTransportMuxStrategy exclusive -ORBConnectStrategy
blocked"
static Resource_Factory "-ORBFlushingStrategy blocking"
```

As stated, concurrency control is a way of improving scalability. For instance, we can have a fine degree of how many invocations can be attended to in a server.

4.3   Other Issues

In this section we describe some other TAO features which can be used to improve the reliability of applications:

— Valuetypes: CORBA valuetypes are a little known mechanism inside CORBA. They allow information of objects with a large amount of data to be transmitted. They can be used to replace CORBA local interfaces. When an invocation over a value type is received, the receiving process only receives the state of the object and it has to provide an implementation of the value type. Operations on value types are not transmitted by the ORB, which improves efficiency. In addition, some difficult points of the C++ mapping of CORBA such as reference types (e.g. _var classes) are not needed (pointers are the most typical option). Other advantages are related to memory overhead. As value types do not derive from CORBA::Object, some compilation and memory overheads are avoided. The main disadvantage of using value types is due to the fact they are little explored area in TAO, so many problems and bugs could appear.
— Portable interceptors: portable interceptors are an excellent way of controlling CORBA requests. They can be used in many different ways. For instance, they can be used to improve security, inject dynamic code or change the behavior of methods at runtime. TAO supports interceptors at different points on both client-server sides including requests, responses and exceptions. When some of these "points" are reached in an invocation, the code of the interceptor is launched and we can manipulate the request.

5   Conclusions

Open-source middleware has reached its maturity. In this paper we have analyzed experiences using UM-RTCOM, a real-time component model built on top of TAO, a very popular open-source implementation of CORBA and RT-CORBA. For more than 15 years we have maintained simulation software for critical systems using these technologies and we have adapted our implementations to changes in technologies such as the operating system, development environment or languages. Experience has proved these choices were good. The metrics presented here show the current situation of TAO and JacORB.

Currently, we are working on several ways of improving our implementation in terms of network, concurrency and memory. Some techniques such as multicast or portable interceptors could be used to improve software reliability. Future work will include the study of new possibilities such as the use of DDS from OMG which includes features for QoS, real-time or high performance.

References

1. Object Management Group: The Common Object Request Broker: Architecture and Specification, Version 3.3 (November 2012). http://www.omg.org/spec/CORBA/3.3
2. Java.rmi: The Remote Method Invocation Guide. Addison-Wesley Longman Publishing Co., Inc. Boston (2001). ISBN:0201700433
3. Horstmann, M., Kirtland, M.: DCOM architecture. Microsoft Corporation (July 1997)
4. Szyperski, C.: Component Software: Beyond Object-Oriented Programming. Addison-Wesley Longman (1999)
5. Box, D.: Essential COM. Addison-Wesley, Reading (1997)
6. Englander, R.: Developing Java Beans. O'Reilly Media, Inc. (1997)
7. Platt, D.S.: Introducing Microsoft. Net. Microsoft press (2002)
8. Enterprise JavaBeans Specification 2.1, Sun Microsystems (2005). http://java.sun.com/products/ejb/
9. Object Management Group: CORBA Component Model Joint Revised Submission (1999)
10. Object Management Group. http://www.omg.org
11. Hejlsberg, A., Wiltamuth, S., Golde, P.: The C# programming language. Adobe Press (2006)
12. W3C Working Group: Web Services Architecture (2007). http://www.w3.org/TR/ws-arch/
13. Henning, M., Vinoski, S.: Advanced CORBA Programming with C++. Addison-Wesley Longman (1999)
14. Windley, P.J.: REST: Representational State Transfer, Chapter 11, pp. 237–261
15. Schmidt, D.C., Kuhns, F.: An overview of the real-time CORBA specification. In: IEEE Computer special issue on Object-Oriented Real-time Distributed Computing (June 2000)
16. Object Management Group: Minimum CORBA Update (2004). realtime/2004-06-01
17. Natarajan, B., Gokhale, A., Yajnik, S., Schmidt, D.C.: DOORS: Towards high-performance fault tolerant CORBA. In: Proceedings of the International Symposium on Distributed Objects and Applications. DOA 2000, pp. 39–48. IEEE (2000)
18. Orbix – Micro Focus. http://www.microfocus.com/products/corba/orbix/
19. Orbacus - Micro Focus. http://microfocus.com/products/corba/orbacus/index.aspx
20. JacORB. http://jacorb.org/
21. Levine, D.L., Mungee, S., Schmidt, D.C.: The Design of the TAO Real-Time Object Request Broker. Computer Communications 21, 294–324 (1998)
22. C++11 Language Mapping Version 1.1. http://www.omg.org/spec/CPP11/1.1/PDF/

23. Van Rossum, G.: Python Programming Language (2007). USENIX Annual Technical Conference
24. Flanagan, D., Matsumoto, Y.: The ruby programming language. O'Reilly Media, Inc. (2008)
25. Díaz, M., Garrido, D., Llopis, L., Rus, F., Troya, J.M.: UM-RTCOM: An analyzable component model for real-time distributed systems. Journal of Systems and Software **81**(5), 709–726 (2008)
26. Díaz, M., Garrido, D., Troya, J.M.: Development of Distributed Real-Time Simulators Based on CORBA. Simulation Modelling Practice and Theory. **15**(6), 716–733 (2007)
27. Caro-Benito, R.J., Garrido-Márquez, D., Plaza-Tron, P., Román-Castro, R., Sanz-Martín, N., Serrano-Martín, J.L.: SMEPP: a secure middleware for embedded P2P. In: Proceedings of the 2009 ICT Mobile Summit, pp. 1–8 (2009)
28. Java SE. http://www.oracle.com/technetwork/java/javase/downloads/index.html
29. TAO Bugzilla server. http://bugzilla.dre.vanderbilt.edu/
30. JacORB Bugzilla server. http://jacorb.org/bugzilla/
31. Object Computing, Inc. https://www.ociweb.com/
32. Remedy IT. http://www.remedy.nl/
33. Pardo-Castellote, G.: Omg data-distribution service: architectural overview. In: Proceedings of the 23rd International Conference on Distributed Computing Systems Workshops, pp. 200–206. IEEE (May 2003)
34. Harrison, T.H., Levine, D.L., Schmidt, D.C.: The design and performance of a real-time CORBA event service. In: Proceedings of the OOPSLA 1997 conference, Atlanta, Georgia, October 1997
35. RTI web page. https://www.rti.com/
36. Busch, D.: Introduction to OpenDDS (2012)
37. Erl, T.: Service-Oriented Architecture: Concepts, Technology, and Design. Prentice Hall PTR, Upper Saddle River (2005)
38. McMurtry, C., Mercuri, M., Watling, N., Winkler, M.: Windows Communication Foundation Unleashed (Wcf)(Unleashed). Sams (2007)
39. Schmidt, D.C., Cleeland, C.: Applying a pattern language to develop extensible ORB middleware. Design Patterns in Communications (2000)
40. Bessani, A.N., Fraga, J.S., Lung, L.C.: Implementing the multicast inter-ORB protocol. In: Sixth IEEE International Symposium on Object-Oriented Real-Time Distributed Computing, pp. 135–138. IEEE (May 2003)
41. Schmidt, D.C., O'Ryan, C., Kircher, M., Pyarali, I.: Leader/followers-a design pattern for efficient multi-threaded event demultiplexing and dispatching. In: University of Washington (2000). http://www.cs.wustl.edu/~schmidt/PDF/lf.pdf
42. GUIDE: TAO Developers. Object Computing. Inc. (2010). www. opendds. org

Critical Systems

The CONCERTO Methodology for Model-Based Development of Avionics Software

Andrea Baldovin[1], Alessandro Zovi[1]([⊠]), Geoffrey Nelissen[2],
and Stefano Puri[3]

[1] Department of Mathematics, University of Padua,
via Trieste, 63, 35121 Padua, Italy
{baldovin,azovi}@math.unipd.it
[2] CISTER/INESC-TEC, ISEP, Polytechnic Institute of Porto,
Rua Dr. António Bernardino de Almeida 431, 4249-015 Porto, Portugal
grrpn@isep.ipp.pt
[3] INTECS, via Umberto Forti, 5, 56121 Pisa, Italy
stefano.puri@intecs.it

Abstract. The development of high-integrity real-time systems, including their certification, is a demanding endeavour in terms of time, skills
and effort involved. This is particularly true in application domains
such as the avionics, where composable design is to be had to allow
subdividing monolithic systems into components of smaller complexity,
to be outsourced to developers subcontracted down the supply chain.
Moreover, the increasing demand for computational power and the consequent interest in multicore HW architectures complicates system deployment. For these reasons, appropriate methodologies and tools need to
be devised to help the industrial stakeholders master the overall system design complexity, while keeping manufacturing costs affordable. In
this paper we present some elements of the CONCERTO platform, a
toolset to support the end-to-end system development process from system modelling to analysis and validation, prior to code generation and
deployment. The approach taken by CONCERTO is demonstrated for an
illustrative avionics setup, however it is general enough to be applied to
a number of industrial domains including the space, telecom and automotive. We finally reason about the benefits to an industrial user by
comparing to similar initiatives in the research landscape.

Keywords: Model-based engineering · CONCERTO · IMA ·
ARINC 653 · Partitioned multicore

1 Introduction

The behaviour of real-time software must be proved correct not only in the functional dimension, as it is the case for any software system, but also in the time
dimension to ensure proper interaction with the physical world. The requirements that need to be met by those systems extend much beyond *functional*

© Springer International Publishing Switzerland 2015
J.A. de la Puente and T. Vardanega (Eds.): Ada-Europe 2015, LNCS 9111, pp. 131–145, 2015.
DOI:10.1007/978-3-319-19584-1_9

behaviour, to include timeliness, energy consumption, robustness. Those additional requirements are globally understood to designate *extra-functional properties*. Interestingly, while functional behaviour embodies the logic required to solve a specific problem and lends itself to *reuse*, extra-functional properties are usually strictly contingent on the specific deployment platform and the stipulated execution conditions.

Because of their inherent complexity, the delivery of high-integrity real-time systems is seldom the result of a single player following a strictly sequential development process from requirements to deployment. Rather, it is the result of the collective effort of numerous subcontractors, which eventually needs to be *incrementally* integrated into a coherent system and ascertained to satisfy the applicable certification requirements. To enable the involvement of multiple development parties, the system needs to be designed in a way that favours its decomposition into elementary parts. This buys into the principle of *compositionality*, which considers the system top-down to describe it as a function of its constituting components. Compositionality at system level is facilitated by *composability* at lower levels of the system stack, to guarantee that the behaviour of individual components as determined in isolation stays the same upon composition in the final system.

Unfortunately, while compositionality and composability of functional properties are comparatively easy to achieve, ensuring composable behaviour in the extra-functional dimension is a more challenging problem. This is because of the complexity of precisely characterising the interactions among different entities executing in the HW/SW stack. Consequently, designing and assessing extra-functional properties becomes harder and the resulting systems tend to represent very specific solutions tailored to the problem they address, often based on specific industrial practices. In this situation, dimensioning a system very precisely becomes impractical and over-provisioning emerges as the only solution to meet the wished integrity levels at the expense of manufacturing and operation costs.

Model-Driven Engineering. Research conducted in the context of the CHESS project[1] suggested that resorting to a *reference software architecture* in combination with a model-based component-oriented development process can be a very effective strategy for the industrial development of real-time embedded software [11]. A reference software architecture can be thought of as a template architectural blueprint defining the methodology and architectural practices that form a common baseline solution for software systems of a specific domain. A reference architecture exhibits at least the following traits, as defined in [10].

1. A component model, to define software building blocks encapsulating pure functional and reusable logic.
2. A computational model, to map the entities in the component model to a framework of analysis techniques.

---

[1] http://www.chess-project.org/

3. A programming model, to define a limited subset of programming language constructs that can be automatically generated from the component model.
4. An execution platform capable of preserving the properties ascertained at the analysis stage and monitoring their possible violation.
5. A development process inspired by Model-Driven Engineering (MDE)[14], to promote a disciplined approach capable of mastering complexity by enforcing separation of concerns[5].
6. The provisioning of domain-specific views on the system to satisfy different stakeholders.

The methodology developed by CONCERTO builds on the foundation of the CHESS research, embracing a model-based component-oriented approach to system design, a model-based analysis framework with back propagation and automatic generation of application code.

The Avionics Use Case. Modern avionics systems are designed around an integrated system architecture known as Integrated Modular Avionics (IMA)[12], where several software subsystems are allowed to share the available physical resources, provided that some constraints on space and time isolation are respected. This is imposed mainly for safety reasons, i.e., to avoid faults in any executing application, called partition, to propagate to the whole system. IMA architectures are hierarchically organised into two layers: at the top level, execution requirements for partitions are considered to determine the schedule of the whole system. That schedule allocates time slots to partitions, within the boundaries of which every partition is guaranteed to execute in isolation from others. Within any partition a local scheduler is in charge of executing application tasks with no knowledge needed about the system-level schedule.

Interestingly, partitioned design naturally promotes composability, which in turn enables incremental development and verification of the system. However, when a reference architecture is considered, some specific requirements from the avionics domain need to be supported.

1. *Hybrid design approach.* The system design process usually proceeds top-down, starting from the definition of higher-level requirements and subsystems and mapping them down to cohesive functional components of finer granularity. However, designing a hierarchical system demands additional support bottom-up to define partitions as aggregates of individual components. The component model needs therefore to support multiple levels of abstraction and aggregation.
2. *Semi-automated schedule design.* As a matter of practice, the generation of the system level schedule is performed by the system integrator taking into consideration the execution requirements of the individual partitions. This risks to be a time-consuming and error-prone activity in the absence of appropriate supporting tools. For example, if the timing requirements of one partition were to change, this potentially affects the whole schedule. However, as discussed later in Section 3.2, this job need not be carried out

by hand: rather, a number of execution constraints may be inferred from the execution needs of the individual tasks, and a valid system-level schedule can be semi-automatically built.

3. *Multicore HW architectures.* Although the IMA architecture addresses single-core systems only, the avionics industry has shown some interest for the recent advances in HW architectures and the potential of multicores in particular. Among the possible multiprocessor configurations, the partitioned approach seems to be the most interesting in this context, since inter-processor interference can be contained and controlled to some extent by the system designer. A partitioned system therefore lends itself more easily to incremental verification and certification. However, little industrial experience is available from real-world systems running on multicore processors, which motivates the need for support tools.

4. *Model analysis.* Assessing the behaviour of partitioned systems after their deployment may reveal itself a hard job in the absence of suitable techniques. Analysing the system model and verifying its validity early at design time with automated tools brings the advantage of promptly detecting any inconsistencies and identifying the parts of the architecture to be revised.

In the remainder of this paper we present the solutions devised within CONCERTO to meet the challenges above. The paper is organised as follows: Section 2 gives an insight on existing research on modelling tools and execution platforms for partitioned systems supporting the ARINC 653 standard for the avionics[1]. Section 3 presents our methodology and toolset, starting from the CONCERTO component model, then illustrating the added-value tools provided for system configuration, analysis and code generation. Finally in Section 4 our approach is compared to MultiPARTES, a similar research initiative.

2   Background

This section introduces recent research dealing with model-driven methodologies and platforms for avionics software. In a first time we look at MultiPARTES, a research project that addresses model-driven development in the context of partitioned architectures. Then, we discuss an execution platform for IMA that proved to foster time composability in avionics applications.

MultiPARTES. The MultiPARTES research project[2] addressed the development of mixed-criticality embedded systems on heterogeneous multicore platforms. Its approach was developing a model-based software development methodology and the related toolset for building partitioned applications on top of the XtratuM hypervisor[7].

According to the MultiPARTES methodology[13], a system model is first created, later elaborated by a partitioning tool and finally validated by a number

---

[2] http://www.multipartes.eu/

of tools. Those tools check the correctness with respect to different criteria, for example response time. The output of the partitioning tool is a deployment model which is amenable to code generation and can be deployed to a dedicated platform. The main component of the platform is the XtratuM hypervisor which stands in between the multicore hardware and the partitions. Each of them contains a subsystem which comprises a real-time operating system and the software applications.

The system model consists of three different models: (i) the application model represents the functional description of the system, enriched with non-functional attributes related to criticality, timing and partition configuration; (ii) the platform model represents the hardware description and the OS available for deployment; (iii) the partitioning restriction model represents the relations between the application and platform models and specifies partitioning constraints to be taken into account by the partitioning tool to generate the deployment model. Only the application model conforms to the UML2 metamodel and the MARTE profile[17], whereas the others are defined by non-standard domain-specific languages.

The XtratuM hypervisor uses paravirtualization, which means that its operations are as close to the target hardware as possible. Any OS to be deployed on top of this kind of hypervisor needs to be modified to replace some privileged part of the Hardware Abstraction Layer with the corresponding calls to the hypervisor. The design of XtratuM borrows the concept of partition from IMA, and the cyclic scheduling of partitions and the inter-partition communication mechanisms from ARINC 653. However while an IMA partition is in charge of managing the processes inside it, an Xtratum partition – which is a virtual computer – delegates such management to the virtualised operating system.

PROARTIS_sim and TiCOS. The avionics case study considered in CONCERTO needs to be deployed on a PowerPC (PPC) architecture, which is widely adopted by leading manufacturers in that domain[8]. To this end we consider the execution platform developed within the scope of the EU-FP7 PROARTIS project[3]. This includes (i) PROARTIS_sim, a highly configurable and timely accurate PPC-750 simulator developed by Barcelona Supercomputing Center, and (ii) TiCOS [3], developed at the University of Padova and providing basic OS services and implementing the ARINC 653 API on top of it. PROARTIS_sim can be deployed to build a partitioned multicore configuration as a number of identical single-core replicas executed side-by-side, with no direct communication allowed between applications running on different nodes. TiCOS meets the usual time and space partitioning requirements of IMA systems by implementing a significant part of the ARINC 653 API. At the same time it shows reduced execution jitter and enforces time composability. When running on a partitioned multicore HW configuration, one TiCOS replica is deployed on each core. Those multiple instances are completely unaware of each other and all provided API services have only local effects.

---

[3] http://www.proartis-project.eu/

Considering the sources of unpredictability present in typical HW and SW used for embedded systems, [18,19] showed that the execution stack made up of PROARTIS_sim processor and TiCOS causes much reduced interference on the execution of user-level applications and further makes them amenable to probabilistic analysis of worst-case execution time. Those results come in handy in our context to prove that it is possible in fact to preserve the extra-functional properties defined at the modelling level, and execution time guarantees in particular, down to the execution stack, so long as the latter is well-behaved versus the applications running on top of it.

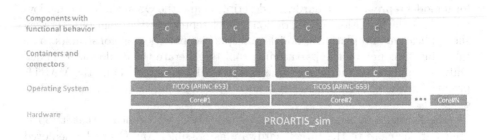

Fig. 1. Decomposition of an avionics system developed with CONCERTO

3   The CONCERTO Methodology

In this section we describe how it is possible to model an avionics use case like the one shown in Figure 1 with CONCERTO. In doing this we introduce the constituting parts of the platform starting from the component model (Section 3.1) and the additional plugins assisting system deployment (Section 3.2). We then present the analysis we are able to carry on the system model (Section 3.3) and the technology enabling automatic code generation (Section 3.4).

3.1   Modelling

MARTE is the language chosen by CONCERTO for modelling extra-functional properties, and timing in particular. Although MARTE does not provide explicit guidelines or stereotypes for modelling ARINC 653 partitions, it defines a number of fine-grained stereotypes that can be collectively used to model partitions and their properties. CONCERTO uses those artifacts to model the spatial and temporal isolation requirements of partitions.

Partition Modelling. In CONCERTO the spatial isolation property of a partition is modelled by using the «MemoryPartition» MARTE stereotype. The stereotype is defined as a virtual address space ensuring that only resources associated to it can access and modify it. This is compliant with the definition given by ARINC 653. Concerning temporal isolation, the runtime of each

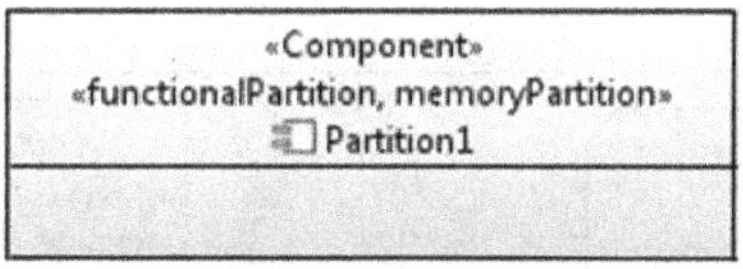

Fig. 2. Functional Partition in CONCERTO

partition, i.e. its virtual processor, is modelled by using both the MARTE «SwSchedulableResource» and «ProcessingResource» stereotypes. The former makes it possible to represent the virtual processor as a schedulable resource executing in parallel with others. The latter is used to represent the logical entity capable of scheduling and executing the tasks within the partition running on the virtual processor. The virtual processor must then be mapped to a physical processor, annotated by the «HWProcessor» MARTE stereotype.

Beside temporal and spatial isolation, we are also interested in modelling the functional behaviour of partitions. This requires support for modelling hierarchical components, which is provided by UML through composite structure diagrams. The user of CONCERTO is given the possibility to define partitions either prior or after the definition of their owned sub-components, in a top-down or a bottom-up fashion respectively. In practice however, application design influences the partitioning decisions taken at system level. Therefore, from the methodological point of view, partition modelling builds upon the functional specification of applications. For this reason, partitions are initially modelled as empty composite components, acting as wrappers of application-specific sub-components that implement the required functionality. Partitions further segregate the behaviour of child components that should not be visible to others deployed in different partitions. Instead, the behaviour to be provided to or required from the external world is exposed by the partition through specific interaction points, i.e. UML provided and required ports respectively. Thus, a partition does not provide any behaviour on its own, but rather delegates all the exposed and required functionality to its internal components. All the constraints above are enforced at model level by means of a dedicated UML Component stereotype called «FunctionalPartition», which represents the functional concern of CONCERTO partitions (Figure 2).

In our solution the «MemoryPartition» and «FunctionalPartition» stereotypes are applied together on the same component to induce the spatial isolation property. A possible alternative would be to use the «MemoryPartition» stereotype for the hardware modelling, as a distinct entity associated to the virtual processor. In our current implementation, however we have discarded that choice to keep hardware modelling simpler. Finally, the partition is allocated to a virtual processor through the «Assign» MARTE stereotype (Figure 3).

Partition Decoration. For each virtual processor timing information can be specified to enable timing analysis. A table-driven schedule can be associated to

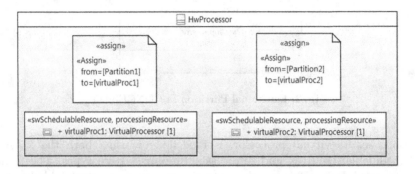

Fig. 3. Virtual Processor in CONCERTO

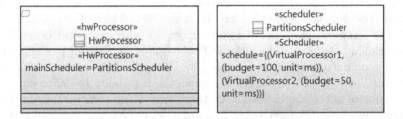

Fig. 4. Partition timing decoration in CONCERTO

a MARTE «HWProcessor» stereotype by attaching a «Scheduler» entity to it. The latter is equipped with (i) a schedule parameter that describes the absolute ordering of the referenced virtual processors, and consequently of the partitions; (ii) the budget assigned to each virtual processor, computed as a measure of the processing resource utilisation (Figure 4). The utilisation can be either provided top-down by the system designer or alternatively computed bottom-up by the schedule generation tool described in Section 3.2.

3.2   Deployment

Deployment is of paramount importance to ensure system feasibility and correctness. At this stage the software architecture, as designed in the modelling phase, meets the constraints and the limitations imposed by real target platforms. Moreover, opportunities for optimisation may emerge at this stage, which is fundamental to limit over-provisioning of system resources and contain costs. When considering partitioned multiprocessor avionics systems, decisions have to be taken about where and when partitions should execute. The former is the problem of finding an allocation of partitions to cores, the latter requires to draw a top-level schedule for partitions.

Allocation to Cores. By definition, task migration across cores is not allowed on a partitioned multicore system. In our understanding partition migration should be avoided as well, since this would have severe implications on the achievable time and space isolation. In fact task migration is the most notable drawback of global scheduling approaches because of the HW state pollution caused and the consequent additional execution time overheads introduced. Those undesired effects would be even amplified in a scenario where partitions, as collections of tasks, were allowed to migrate across processors.

Creating the partitioning, i.e. deciding where each task or partition will execute, is known to be a NP-hard problem as an instance of the general graph partitioning problem[6]. In fact, sub-optimal choices at this stage may easily impair system performance and in the worst case even its feasibility. CONCERTO provides the technology to semi-automate this step by proposing a partitioning for the system based on the execution requirements of the partitions defined in the modelling step. This is achieved by implementing a modified version of the worst-fit bin packing heuristic[4]. Modifications to the base heuristic need to be considered to account for the inter-partition communication protocol allowed by ARINC 653[1]. More precisely, we need to take care of the following implicit constraint emanating from the component model: when two partitions are meant to communicate via sampling or queuing ports, then they must be allocated for execution on the same physical processor. This is enough to generate a valid partitioning, whereas its efficiency, expressed as the minimal number of processing units needed to schedule the system, directly depends on the bin packing technique used and the specific task set. Alternative partitioning choices might have been considered to execute a partition on more than one processor. However such configurations, while promising better theoretical performance, allow concurrent execution of tasks within a partition. Consequently additional contention on shared hardware resources and interference are introduced, eventually breaking the time composability property enforced between the layers of our execution stack. This would make it harder – if not impossible at all – to precisely characterize the execution time of user applications, i.e. partitions, hampering their assembly into the final system. For this reason those setups are not considered in this discussion. Similarly, inter-partition communication across different processors is not considered, as this mandates a careful assessment of how shared memory affects the time analysability of the system. Communication between partitions residing in the same node instead is dealt with as prescribed by IMA for single-core platforms.

Schedule Generation. ARINC 653 prescribes a round-robin policy with flexible quanta for the top-level scheduling of partitions, which substantially corresponds to drawing a table-driven schedule offline. This is a critical step, since (i) the number of partitions may grow considerably in a real-world system, (ii) a wrong schedule may easily lead to violations of process deadlines and (iii) any change in the requirements of any partition may potentially impair the validity

---

[4] Any user-defined heuristic may be implemented with little impact on the platform.

of a previously computed schedule. CONCERTO provides a plugin to semi-automate the schedule generation process by computing a base schedule for the system, that can be later modified and refined by the system designer according to her specific needs. In fact, the deadline/period and worst-case execution time (WCET) parameters of the individual tasks indirectly constrain the top-level schedule of the system and restrict the search space of the problem. The tool assumes the mapping between tasks and partitions is known: this is not unrealistic in fact, since partitions are designed to encapsulate cohesive functional logic and are treated as atomic blocks when their development is outsourced. In case the individual utilisation of partitions has not been specified explicitly by the system designer as explained in Section 3.1, an initial schedule for the system is built as follows. Initially the Major Frame (MAF), i.e. the system hyperperiod in ARINC speak, and the total slack available in the system are computed. Then the execution demand of each partition is calculated at any time instant of the MAF, by considering the request bound function (rbf) of the tasks in the partition. We then look for a couple of values (budget, period) such that their ratio, corresponding to the utilisation of the partition, is minimised. After repeating this process for all partitions, the earliest schedule for the system can be easily drawn by sorting partitions according to the earliest-deadline-first (EDF) policy. However, unless the system is fully utilised, some slack is available in the system and has not been assigned by the algorithm so far. This reserve of computation resources is very useful in practice, to serve as a buffer to accommodate overruns of modest magnitude. Our plugin redistributes the remaining slack uniformly across those partitions for which utilisation was not specified by design. This process starts from the end of the MAF and proceeds backwards until either there is no remaining slack in the system or assigning more slack would make it unfeasible as a consequence of violating some deadlines.

In the case of communication between partitions with blocking semantics, the ARINC 653 specification does not prescribe any specific execution ordering of producer and consumer partitions. Rather, in the event of writes on a full buffer or reads from an empty buffer, execution is blocked and the blocking condition is re-checked on the next scheduling slot. Although inverting the execution ordering of reader and writer would be a more efficient solution, one must be careful to not compromise system feasibility. For this reason this kind of optimisation is left to the user at the moment. More generally, the user is given the chance to modify the proposed schedule to meet any specific need that an automated process can hardly capture. Also, slack distribution can be optimised to allocate extra-time for any special needs, e.g. to partitions performing the most critical operations. Validation of the new schedule is performed in the later step of analysis and back propagation of results to the user model.

3.3   Analysis and Back-Propagation

Once the deployment of the partitions done and their schedule generated in a semi-automated manner, a timing analysis of the processes mapped on each partition is performed. The timing analysis computes the worst-case response time (WCRT) of each process, which can then be compared against the process deadlines in order to assert their schedulability. If a deadline should not be met, that result is back propagated to the component model. The system integrator can then use this information to revise the component model or tailor the partition deployment in a way that would increase the partition supply and hence allow all the processes to eventually respect their deadlines. The timing analysis of the system model is thus a critical step in the design of embedded software with timing requirements as its results may initiate multiple iterations on the description of the application model.

The timing analysis is performed using an augmented version of MAST[5], a schedulability and timing analysis tool developed and maintained by the University of Cantabria. CONCERTO extended MAST to model IMA architectures and compute the worst-case response time of processes running in partitions. To that end, the input model of MAST has been improved in order to represent multicore processors as well as partitions, their mapping and their generated schedule. Those inputs are provided to the extended version of MAST directly from the result of the deployment phase by means of a model-to-text transformation based on Acceleo[6], an engine implementing the MOFM2T specification[16] defined by the Object Management Group (OMG).

From an analysis viewpoint, MAST did not support the analysis of processes running in IMA partitions. MAST was thus extended using results of a similar problem, namely the hierarchical scheduling problem, which has been extensively studied in the literature [2,4]. The state-of-the-art on hierarchical scheduling provides techniques to compute the WCRT of periodic or sporadic tasks to be scheduled using a fixed priority scheduling algorithm within a partition characterised by a given budget and replenishment period. Note however that none of the related works considers periodic tasks with release offsets. Yet, CONCERTO's component model is generic enough to model both periodic and sporadic processes and, in conformity with the ARINC 653 specification, periodic processes can be associated a release offset. Due to the lack of existing timing analysis for IMA systems composed of periodic tasks with offsets, the timing analysis implemented in the extended version of MAST is based on [4] thus assuming all the tasks to be sporadic. Although restrictive and pessimistic, this assumption provides a safe upper bound on the worst-case response times, even for systems that are partially or completely composed of periodic tasks. Yet, in an attempt to improve the accuracy of the results, researches are currently pursued in the CONCERTO project to extend the analysis to IMA partitions composed of a mix of sporadic and periodic processes with or without offsets.

3.4   Code Generation and Execution

After the user has performed all desired analyses and the model-based description of the system has been validated, most of the conceptual work has been

---

[5] http://mast.unican.es
[6] http://eclipse.org/acceleo/

already performed to shape the system and the effort shifts to implementation and deployment on a real target. At this point a number of heterogeneous technologies come into play to take the system blueprint and implement it in the form of human-readable code as a first approximation, then translating it into machine code for execution on a HW platform. Unfortunately, the abstraction gap existing between those architectural layers risks to invalidate the guarantees so hardly obtained on the modelling side and eventually undermines the whole development process. Additionally, another serious obstacle to system development comes from execution on top of unpredictable HW and OS layers, i.e., in the presence of components whose behaviour and interference are hard to characterise and consequently make it difficult to preserve extra-functional properties such as execution timing. Neglecting these considerations early in the development process may inflate the verification process and manufacturing costs consequently, or in the worst case lead to malfunctioning of the delivered system. The methodology defined by CONCERTO suggests how to mitigate both problems, i.e. the preservation of extra-functional properties at lower layers of the architecture and execution on a predictable platform.

For the preservation of timing properties ascertained at the model level our toolset includes an automated code generation facility, following the approach successfully implemented in CHESS and illustrated in [9]. That work demonstrated that it is possible to preserve the semantics of constructs defined at the modelling level, i.e., by the component model, down to implementation and deployment by resorting to a programming model, that is a limited set of code archetypes in the programming language of choice . The automatic code generation approach is useful not only to retain the guarantees obtained at the model level, but it also helps reduce the development effort required in the event of multiple deployments or even of re-targeting to different HW architectures. This is because from one single model of the system any implementation can be automatically generated, provided that the mapping from the component model to a programming model has been specified. Automatic code generation is realised in CONCERTO by means of model-to-text transformations run with the support of Acceleo.

For what concerns predictability of the execution platform, CONCERTO decided to adopt PROARTIS_sim and TiCOS in its execution stack, that proved to cause reduced interference to user applications as explained in Section 2.

4   Discussion

The methods and tools presented in Section 3 address the avionics-specific requirements presented in Section 1. Specifically, hierarchical components enable hybrid top-down and bottom-up design, the schedule generation and partitioning tools support deployment on complex hardware, and timing analysis of the model is made possible by modifications to MAST. We now compare our approach to MultiPARTES, since the latter addresses similar concerns although starting from slightly different premises, i.e. the intent of supporting mixed-criticality systems and heterogeneous multicore architectures.

Methodology and Modelling. Not surprisingly the methodologies defined by CONCERTO and MultiPARTES present significant similarities, as a consequence of sharing the common background of CHESS. The approach taken by MultiPARTES requires an additional step to model in detail the HW configuration of choice via a platform view. In return, support is given to asymmetric multiprocessor (AMP) architectures, although their adoption in real-world avionics systems is still to come. Conversely, in CONCERTO there is no need for this facility since execution on a symmetric multiprocessor (SMP) is assumed. One advantage of CONCERTO is certainly its metamodel, which is fully compliant with MARTE and UML2, whereas MultiPARTES makes use of proprietary entities that may hardly fit together with standard specifications and tools.

Execution Stack. Although both define a partitioned architecture, the execution stacks of CONCERTO and MultiPARTES differ significantly because of their different goals. While both are capable of ensuring the required degree of space and time isolation, whether to enforce it by means of a hypervisor or a partitioning kernel needs to be carefully evaluated. One advantage of the hypervisor approach over a standard OS is its capability of encapsulating large subsystems – including user applications and the OS running them – as black boxes, and to make the interactions with the HW platform transparent. Nonetheless, the paravirtualization implementation of XtratuM requires some effort to port the guest OS to a different execution environment, by transforming system calls into hypercalls and redirect them to the hypervisor. Moreover, the introduction of an additional layer in the execution stack is very likely to introduce new overheads and cause more interference to applications at the user level. On the other hand, if a partitioning kernel is deployed, full control can be retained on the deployed HW and system SW, whose interactions are known to highly affect time composability and system analysability in turn.

The XTratuM architecture silently tries to enforce time composability by providing low-jitter hypercalls and allocating partitions to virtual processors statically, thus limiting interference by creating isolated HW/SW silos. These are similar principles to those inspiring the development of TiCOS. However, one may argue that if the design of the guest OS has negative effects on the application side, the introduction of a hypervisor alone is not sufficient to solve those problems but rather moves them one layer below in the architecture. In fact, existing studies [15] confirmed by our research on TiCOS have shown how tight coupling between applications and the OS hopelessly complicates timing analysis. For these reasons putting TiCOS at the centre of the execution stack is a better solution, since it makes it possible to achieve true time composable execution.

Similarly, the possibility of assigning more than one virtual processor to one partition in XtratuM poses no limits on the kind of scheduling policy chosen within partitions. In particular, if global scheduling is chosen, the open issues related to the amount of interference generated by task migrations are still present and moved one step above in the architecture, from the hypervisor layer

Table 1. Distinguishing elements of CONCERTO and MultiPARTES

	Target system	Metamodel	Execution stack		
			Architecure	Scheduling	Effects on time composability
CONCERTO	SMP	MARTE/ UML2- compliant	partitioning OS	strictly partitioned (1 partition on 1 core)	time-composable execution stack (TiCOS + PROARTIS_sim)
MultiPARTES	AMP	proprietary	hypervisor	any (1 partition on ≥ 1 vitual cores)	coupling between app and OS + hypervisor overheads

to the partition internals. The choice of pinning partitions to cores as in TiCOS instead enforces partitioned scheduling of applications, providing a realistic setup for multicore execution with guarantees.

In conclusion, the approach to modelling partitioned systems advocated by CONCERTO and MultiPARTES is very similar, as summarized in Table 1. However, the reasons to prefer a virtualisation architecture need to be justified by specific needs, such as the execution on AMPs or the integration of systems with different criticality levels on the same machine. It is questionable whether these trends will dominate future avionics systems. Yet the known issues concerning time composability and scheduling of applications encountered in traditional OS design need to be addressed in both scenarios.

Acknowledgments. The authors are grateful to the people at Barcelona Supercomputing Center for their supply of PROARTIS_sim. The research leading to these results has received funding from the EU ARTEMIS JU, within the CONCERTO project [ARTEMIS/0003/2012], under Grant Agreement 333053.

References

1. Aeronautical Radio Inc: ARINC Specification 653–1: Avionics Applicaiton Software Standard Interface (2003)
2. Almeida, L., Pedreiras, P.: Scheduling within temporal partitions: Response-time analysis and server design. In: Proc. of the 4th ACM International Conference on Embedded Software (2004)
3. Baldovin, A., Mezzetti, E., Vardanega, T.: A time-composable Operating System. In: 12th WCET Workshop. OpenAccess Series in Informatics (OASIcs), vol. 23, pp. 69–80. Schloss Dagstuhl-Leibniz-Zentrum fuer Informatik (2012)
4. Davis, R., Burns, A.: Hierarchical fixed priority pre-emptive scheduling. In: Proc. of the 26th IEEE Real-Time System Symposium (2005)

5. Dijkstra, E.: On the role of scientific thought. In: Selected Writings on Computing: A personal Perspective. Texts and Monographs in Computer Science, pp. 60–66. Springer, New York (1982)
6. Garey, M., Johnson, D.: Computers and Intractability: A Guide to the Theory of NP-Completeness. Freeman, W. H (1979)
7. Masmano, M., Ripoll, I., Crespo, A., Metge, J.: Xtratum: a hypervisor for safety critical embedded systems. In: Proc. of the 11th Real-Time Linux Workshop (2009)
8. Moir, I., Seabridge, A., Jukes, M.: Civil avionics systems. Wiley-Blackwell (2013)
9. Panunzio, M., Vardanega, T.: Ada ravenscar code archetypes for component-based development. In: Brorsson, M., Pinho, L.M. (eds.) Ada-Europe 2012. LNCS, vol. 7308, pp. 1–17. Springer, Heidelberg (2012)
10. Panunzio, M., Vardanega, T.: An architectural approach with separation of concerns to address extra-functional requirements in the development of embedded real-time software systems. Journal of Systems Architecture $60(9)$, 770–781 (2014)
11. Panunzio, M., Vardanega, T.: A component-based process with separation of concerns for the development of embedded real-time software systems. Journal of Systems and Software 96, 105–121 (2014)
12. Radio Technical Commission for Aeronautics: Integrated Modular Avionics (IMA) Development Guidance and Certification Considerations (2005)
13. Salazar, E., Alonso, A., Garrido, J.: Mixed-criticality design of a satellite software system. In: Proc. of the 19th IFAC World Congress (2014)
14. Schmidt, D.: Guest editor's introduction: Model-driven engineering. Computer $39(2)$, 25–31 (2006)
15. Schneider, J.: Why you can't analyze RTOSs without considering applications and vice versa. In: Proc. of the 2nd WCET Workshop (2002)
16. The Object Management Group: MOF Model to Text Transformation Language, v1.0 (2008). http://www.omg.org/spec/MOFM2T/1.0/
17. The Object Management Group: UML Profile for MARTE: Modeling and Analysis of Real-time Embedded Systems (2011). http://www.omg.org/spec/MARTE/1.1/
18. Wartel, F. et al.: Measurement-based probabilistic timing analysis: Lessons from an integrated-modular avionics case study. In: Proc. of the 8th IEEE International Symposium on Industrial Embedded Systems (SIES), pp. 241–248 (2013)
19. Wartel, F. et al.: Timing analysis of an avionics case study on complex hardware-/software platforms. In: Proc. of the 18th Design, Automation & Test in Europe Conference and Exhibition (DATE) (2015)

From AADL Model to LNT Specification

Hana Mkaouar[1]([✉]), Bechir Zalila[1], Jérôme Hugues[2], and Mohamed Jmaiel[1,3]

[1] ReDCAD Laboratory, University of Sfax, National School of Engineers of Sfax,
BP 1173, 3038 Sfax, Tunisia
hana.mkaouar@redcad.org, {bechir.zalila,mohamed.jmaiel}@enis.rnu.tn
[2] Institut Supérieur de L'Aéronautique Et de L'Espace, Université de Toulouse,
BP 54032, 31055 Toulouse Cedex 4, France
jerome.hugues@isae.fr
[3] Research Center for Computer Science Multimedia and Digital Data
Processing of Sfax, BP 275, 3021 Sakiet Ezzit, Sfax, Tunisia

Abstract. The verification of distributed real-time systems designed by architectural languages such as AADL (Architecture Analysis and Design Language) is a research challenge. These systems are often used in safety-critical domains where one mistake can result in physical damages and even life loss. In such domains, formal methods are a suitable solution for rigorous analysis. This paper studies the formal verification of distributed real-time systems modelled with AADL. We transform AADL model to another specification formalism enabling the verification. We choose LNT language which is an input to CADP toolbox for formal analysis. Then, we illustrate our approach with the "Flight Control System" case study.

Keywords: AADL · LNT · Distributed real-time systems · Architecture description languages · Model transformation · Specification languages · Formal verification

1 Introduction

Building distributed real-time systems is a tedious task. They are usually complex systems, often used in safety-critical domains like avionics and aerospace. Such systems must satisfy both real-time constraints and other constraints imposed by the distribution of nodes. Several solutions have been introduced to simplify the development process through modeling and code generation thanks to Architecture Description Languages (ADLs). These languages allow the description of structure, behaviour and configuration offering an abstract view of the entire system.

The development process of distributed real-time systems requires verification in earlier phases to ensure the correctness of the produced system. For this purpose, designers have joined verification and validation formalisms with ADLs which are considered like a pivot language.

Formal methods are widely used to check rigorously a critical system. They are used to confirm if the system satisfies the user needs (validation) and if it

© Springer International Publishing Switzerland 2015
J.A. de la Puente and T. Vardanega (Eds.): Ada-Europe 2015, LNCS 9111, pp. 146–161, 2015.
DOI:10.1007/978-3-319-19584-1_10

complies with its specification (verification). However, a system modelled with an ADL cannot be directly formally verified. The use of such methods requires a formal specification of the checked system. Several formalisms are considered in the formal world for example Petri net, automata and process algebra. In this context, researches are directed towards the transformation of the architectural models into other models in order to connect with formal verification tools.

AADL [3] (Architecture Analysis and Design Language) is a rich and complete ADL for embedded real-time systems, with an emphasis on critical avionics systems. Many work in the literature apply the transformation model alternative for AADL formal verification: they transform various AADL subsets into different specification formalisms and they focus on behavioral analysis by checking general properties like deadlock with model-checking.

In our proposed approach, we include formal verification in development process of systems modelled with AADL. Our work is integrated in the Ocarina [11] tool set which is a development environment for AADL modeling and code generation. We adapt process algebra formalism for the transformation which concerns an interesting AADL subset for communication and scheduling semantics.

We choose LNT [5] as target specification language which derives from two standards Lotos [1] and E-Lotos [2]. This choice is justified by the expressiveness and richness of LNT. It provides expressive enough operators for data and behaviour description and it has a user-friendly notations to simplify the specification writing. Indeed, LNT is a CADP [6] (Construction and Analysis of Distributed Processes) input language. It is a popular formal verification toolbox that implements many formal methods.

In this paper, we report our proposed transformation AADL/LNT and we prove its effectiveness with the "Flight Control System" case study. The remainder of this paper is organized as follows: Section 2 gives an overview of AADL then presents LNT language. In section 3, we detail the translation of AADL model into LNT specification. In section 4, we present tools used in our work. Section 5 applies transformation rules on our case study. In section 6, we discuss related work. Finally, conclusions and future work end the article in section 7.

2 Preliminaries

In this section, we briefly introduce AADL with the considered subset. Then, we present our target specification language LNT.

2.1 AADL

AADL [3] is an industrial ADL for critical domains like avionics, aerospace and automotive. It is standardized by the SAE (Society of Automotive Engineers), the last version (version 2) was published in 2009. AADL is a rich language with a textual syntax and graphical representation. It allows the modeling of the structure, behaviour and configuration of distributed real-time embedded systems. Like most of ADLs, AADL consists of three basic elements: components (software, hardware and system), connections (to link components) and the description of the architecture configuration with AADL properties.

Components. An AADL component is defined through a type (it declares the component interface elements called features) and zero or more implementations (they present the component internal structure). AADL defines three categories of components: software components (data, thread, thread group, subprogram, subprogram group and process), hardware components (memory, bus, virtual bus, processor, virtual processor and device) and system component. We briefly describe the subset of AADL components considered in our work.

Software components present the applicative part of the system. In our approach, we consider these components: `data` represents a data type within the system; `subprogram` represents sequentially executed source text which can be coded in programming languages like C and Ada language; `thread` is a concurrent schedulability unit of sequential execution through source code. A thread always executes within a process; `process` represents a virtual address space which contains thread and data associated with the process and with its subcomponents.

Hardware components present the computing hardware and the physical environment. In our work, we consider the following components: `bus` represents hardware and associated communication protocols to exchange control/data among other execution platform components; `processor` is an abstraction of hardware and software for scheduling and execution of threads.

System component represents a composite of software and hardware components or system components.

Connections. AADL connection is a linkage established between component features to exchange data and control. There are four categories of features: port, subprogram, parameters, and subcomponent access. They enable three types of connections: port connection, parameter connection and access connection. In our work, we are interested in the port connection type.

Port connection presents the transfer of data and/or control between two components, explicitly declared between two ports. There are three types of ports in AADL: data, event and event data. Ports are typed with a data component (the type of transferred data) and they are directional.

Properties. AADL properties provide additional information about AADL elements (component types/implementations, connections, etc). We distinguish: properties specifying constraints for hardware binding for example `Actual_Proce ssor_Binding` property to bind thread with the processor and `Actual_Connectio` n_Binding to bind connections to the bus; properties specifying temporal information like Period and Dispatch_Protocol for threads and Scheduling_Pro tocol for processor; and properties specifying information for ports such as Dequeue_Protocol, Input_Time and Output_Time to model event processing policies and their time of arrival.

2.2   LNT

LNT [5] is a specification language for safety-critical systems developed by the Vasy team in INRIA. The latest version (Version 6.1) was published in 2014. It is a heir of Lotos [1] language and a simplified variant of E-Lotos [2]. It combines strong theoretical foundations of process algebra with features from imperative and functional programming languages. LNT is supported by the CADP toolbox which offers a rich formal verification like simulation and model checking.

LNT is similar to CSP and CCS process algebra, it represents a system by a set of processes communicating through channels. An LNT specification consists of two parts: the data part defines types and functions; and the control part defines the behaviour (process). The control part is a super-set of data part. It includes all data part instructions and adds the non-determinism, the asynchronous parallelism and communications. In the rest of this section, we present the essential elements of the LNT language. We include some definitions to make the comprehension easier. In the rest of this paper, we adopt the following notations: B for behaviour; G for gate identifier and P for process identifier.

Module. In LNT, the system is modelled by a set of parallel process in communication through communication ports. It is defined in a module, with the same name as the file in which it is contained. It can import others modules. A process called "MAIN" defines the entry point of the specification.

Process. An LNT process, whose the definition is included in listing 1.1, is an object that describe a behaviour, it can be parameterized by a list of formal gates, a list of formal variables and a list of formal exceptions. LNT allows to describe several behaviours such as sequential composition, non-deterministic assignment, conditional behaviour, non-deterministic choice and parallel composition.

Listing 1.1. LNT process definition

```
process_definition ::= process P
    [[ gate_declaration_0 ,.. , gate_declaration_m ]]
    [( formal_parameters_0 ,.. , formal_parameters_n )]
    [ raises exception_declaration_0 ,.. , exception_declaration_k ]
is
    B
end process
```

Parallel Composition. LNT processes can be combined in parallel and synchronized on gates with the par instruction. Parallel processes start execution

and terminate in the same time without preemption. **par** instruction, given in
the listing 1.2, allows two types of synchronization: the global synchronization
(defined with $G_0...G_n$), this communication can happen only if all processes
can make it simultaneously; and the interface synchronization, in this case, if a
process is waiting for a communication in a gate belongs to its synchronization
interface $(G_{(i,0)}, ..., G_{(i,n_i)})$, this communication can happen only if all process
that contain this gate in their synchronization interface can make this communication simultaneously.

Listing 1.2. LNT parallel composition

```
par  [G_0 ,..., G_0 in]
     [G_(0,0) ,..., G_(0,n_0) -> ] B_0
     || ... ||
     [G_(m,0) ,..., G_(m,n_m) -> ] B_m
end par
```

Communication. In LNT, processes communicate by rendezvous on gates.
LNT gate can be typed with channel. A channel defines a set of gate profiles.
With the same gate, process can send and receive messages. The communication
is blocked in sending or receiving. In effect, the process waiting for a communication is suspended and terminates after the rendezvous takes place.

3   Transformation Rules

Model transformation plays an essential role in model-driven engineering for
various purposes such as modeling, optimization and analysis. It defines a mechanism for generating a target model based on information extracted from a
source model. One important issue in this domain is the semantic preservation
that should be considered while defining the transformation description. In our
approach, we provide a model transformation description with a set of model
transformation rules from AADL to LNT for formal verification. We abstract
AADL model as a set of communicating execution units in real-time context.
Precisely, we consider port communication between AADL threads enriched with
scheduling properties. We find LNT language suitable and expressive enough to
specify AADL semantic in different aspects such as hierarchy of components,
parallel execution and connection types.

Basically, we translate every AADL component (type/implementation) into
an LNT process. We present AADL port connections with LNT gates and we
implement AADL properties with LNT programming structures. With this strategy, we extract the three ADL basic elements (seen in section 2.1) from AADL
model. So we obtain a specification with the same structure of the initial model.

3.1   Scheduling Mapping

In our approach, we consider periodic thread scheduling and execution mechanism without sharing resources. Our mapping considers the schedulability test like a primary condition before checking other constraints. It concerns AADL thread and processor components detailed in below sections.

Periodic Thread. First rule (table 1) in our transformation description concerns AADL thread. Every implementation of thread component is presented with an LNT process `<Thread_*>`. It has a set of gate declarations corresponding to AADL ports with a set of parameters corresponding to AADL temporal properties like execution time, input/output time, period and priority.

Table 1. Transformation rule for AADL Thread

Rule 1	

Thread
 	
- Features
  • data/event/event data port
- Properties
  • `Period`;
  • `Compute_Execution_Time`;
  • `Deadline`;
  • `Input_Time`;
  • `Output_Time`;
  • `Priority`.
	process <Thread_AADLIdentifier>
	[OutR : Request,
	 InR : Response,
	 — AADL gate declarations
	]
	(LCM : Nat,
	 priority : Nat,
	 Destination : Connections,
	 Idt : Identifier,
	 Execution_Time : Time,
	 Input_Time : IO_Time_Spec,
	 Output_Time : IO_Time_Spec,
	 Period : Nat,
	 Deadline : Nat)

Initially, all `<Thread_*>` processes are considered in the ready state. To start the execution and enter the running state, every `<Thread_*>` contacts the processor, it requests time corresponding to its `Activate_Execution_Time` parameter. Depending on processor scheduling, `<Thread_*>` can be in three behaviours:

- Starting execution and remaining in the running state until the completion of execution in the current dispatch;
- In the case of a completion, `<Thread_*>` enters the awaiting dispatch state for the next dispatch;
- In the case of a preemption, `<Thread_*>` returns to the ready state to request the needed time to complete execution;
- In the case of exceeding its deadline, `<Thread_*>` declares (with specific gate) the failure of schedulability test and stop its execution.

LNT language is not a specific process algebra for real-time systems, it has no time operators and no preemptions. So we use counters to present time. We perform calculation, based on AADL property values, to deduct needed values like dispatching and communication times.

Processor. For Rule 2 (table 2), we extract the scheduler of AADL processor providing thread scheduling functionality. It becomes an LNT process `<Processor_*>` with two gates: the first one for receiving `<Thread_*>` requests and the second for sending the response. This process complete the scheduling mapping by computing start and completion execution time for each bounded thread.

Table 2. Transformation rule for AADL Processor

Rule 2	

Processor
 	
- Features
   • requires bus access
- Properties
   • `Scheduling_Protocol`
	`process <Processor_AADLIdentifier>`
	`[Input    : Request,`
	`Output  : Response_List] is`
	`  -- code`
	`end process`

When starting, `<Processor_*>` receives requests from all ready threads which are queued and sorted by priority. After all calculations, it sends a response to enable the execution. Thus, each bounded thread gets its execution time and then starts the running state.

Thanks to its programming ability, we can implement many scheduling algorithms with LNT. We developed the Rate-monotonic scheduler for periodic threads: threads can be preempted; they share no resources; their deadlines are equal to their periods; and they have static priorities.

3.2 Communication

Port feature and port connection semantic are well detailed in AADL standard. We are interested in port communication between threads and processes. Port declarations are transformed in gate declarations in LNT processes. However, port connections cannot be transformed directly in gate synchronizations. LNT provides a rendezvous communication that cannot present AADL semantic port connection in which inputs and outputs are frozen. For example, incoming data, event or event data are not available to the receiving thread until the next dispatch (the default input time). So, we do not synchronize `<Thread_*>`s directly on gates. In addition, LNT language does not provide queues with its gates. To obtain the closest behaviour, we add an auxiliary LNT process (table 3) to present connections and handle queues. Thus, `<Thread_*>` is never blocked in a communication and ports can stack inputs in the case of exchanging events. The additional generic process `<*Port_*>` has two gates: the first one for inputs (can be from Bus, Thread or Process) and the second one for outputs (can be data or a list of event/event data). `<*Port_*>` implements connection properties: type of communication: **data**, **event**, **event data**; queue size; overflow handling protocol: drop oldest, newest drop, error; queue protocol: FIFO, LIFO and dequeue protocol: one item, multiple items, all items. Particularly, `<DataPort_*>` presents sampled data port connection, which is a specific port connection semantic for data ports and periodic threads.

Table 3. Transformation rule for AADL communication

Rule 3	

Port
 	
 - Types
  • data/event/event data
 - Properties
  • `Queue_Processing_Protocol`;
  • `Queue_Size`;
  • `Overflow_Handling_Protocol`;
  • `Dequeue_Protocol`;
  • `Dequeued_Items`.
	`process <EventPort_AADLIdentifier>`
	 `[Input : ChannelI,`
	 `Output : ChannelII]`
	 `(ConnectIDs : Connections,`
	 `Queue_Size : Nat,`
	 `Overflow_Handling_Protocol :`
	 `   Overflow_Handling_Protocol_Type,`
	 `Queue_Processing_Protocol :`
	 `   Queue_Processing_Protocol_Type,`
	 `Dequeue_Protocol :`
	 `   Dequeue_Protocol_Type,`
	 `Dequeued_Items : Nat)`

Port connections
 	
 - Port Connection Topology
  • n-to-n for event/event data port
  • 1-to-n for data port
 - Sampled Data Port Communication
  • Immediate
  • Delayed
	`process <DataPort_AADLIdentifier>`
	 `[Input : ChannelI,`
	 `Output : ChannelII]`

In LNT, gates are bidirectional. So we can present all AADL port directions: in, out and in out. The correspondence between in/out ports is ensured with identifiers, every connection (from out to in port) has an identifier. Sender includes a list of connection identifiers in its output. `<EventPort_*>` has a list of accepted connection identifiers (parameter `ConnectIDs`) to verify if its `<Thread_*>` is concerned by the received input. Thus, we can specify all AADL connection topologies. The Example presented in listings 1.3 and 1.4 transforms Producer/Consumer communication: `Producer` provides inputs to two consumers `Consumer1` and `Consumer2`. This is an 1-to-n topology and event data type AADL port connection. In LNT, we get five processes. `Process_Producer` sends messages. Each `EventPort_ConnPC*` identifies its concerned inputs with identifiers `Producer_D__Consumer*_D`.

3.3 Parallel Composition

Process and System AADL components are organized into a hierarchy of subcomponents: process may contain a composition of threads and system presents a composition of components. To preserve this structure, we translate these hierarchical organizations using `par` behaviour with rule 4 (table 4).

Listing 1.3. AADL initial model

```
system implementation S.Impl

subcomponents
    Producer : process A.Impl;
    Consumer1 : process B.Impl;
    Consumer2 : process B.Impl;
    -- code
connections

    -- code
    ConnPC1 : port
        Producer.D -> Consumer1.D;
    ConnPC2 : port
        Producer.D -> Consumer2.D;
    -- code
end S.Impl;
```

Listing 1.4. LNT obtained model

```
par
    Process_Producer  [..]  (
        -- parameters
        {Producer_D__Consumer1_D ,
         Producer_D__Consumer2_D })
    ||
    -- code
    EventPort_ConnPC1  [..]  (
        -- parameters
        {Producer_D__Consumer1_D })
    ||
    -- code
    EventPort_ConnPC2  [..]  (
        -- parameters
        {Producer_D__Consumer2_D })
end par
```

Table 4. Transformation rule for parallel composition

Rule 4	
Process - Features • data/event/event data port - Subcomponents • Thread - Connections • Port connection	```process <Process_AADLIdentifier> [` `-- AADL gate declarations` `] is` `par .. in` ` <Thread_AADLIdentifier> [..]` ` ||` ` <Thread_AADLIdentifier> [..]` ` || ..` `end par` `end process```
System - Subcomponents • Process • Processor • Bus - Connections • Port connection • Bus access	```process Main is` `par .. in` ` <Process_AADLIdentifier> [..]` ` ||` ` <Bus_AADLIdentifier> [..]` ` ||` ` <Processor_AADLIdentifier> [..` ` || ..` `end par` `end process```

For AADL process that contains a composition of threads. It becomes an LNT process containing a composition of <Thread_*>s. Else, there is no need to transform AADL process. Similarly, we apply rule 4 on AADL system component. It becomes the LNT "Main" process which composes process instances of transformed software and hardware subcomponents.

3.4   Synchronization

All transformed components should be synchronized to assemble the whole system. For synchronization, we define the following rules:

Rule 5 For each in/out communication, we apply two level of synchronization:
   I/ every in port of <Thread_*> is synchronized with an instance of <*Port_*> process;
   II/ the obtained composition from I/ is synchronized with <Thread_*> of out port.
   In listing 1.5 and 1.6, we give an example where we apply rule 4 for two communicating AADL threads ThreadA and ThreadB. We obtain three synchronized processes: a first "par" composition (Thread_threadB in global synchronization with DataPort_ConnAB on gate SyncI) is in synchronization with Thread_threadA (on gate SyncII).

Listing 1.5. AADL initial model

```
thread  ThreadA
features
    D : out data port DataAB;
end  ThreadA;
thread  ThreadB
features
    D : in data port DataAB;
end  ThreadB;

process implementation P.Impl
subcomponents
    threadA : thread ThreadA;
    threadB : thread ThreadB;
connections
    ConnAB : data port
    threadA.D -> threadB.D;
end  P.Impl;
```

Listing 1.6. LNT obtained model

```
process  Process_P_Impl [
    -- gate declarations
]
is
-- code
par SyncII in
    Thread_threadA [SyncII]
    ||
    par SyncI in
        Thread_threadB [SyncI]
        ||
        DataPort_ConnAB
            [SyncII, SyncI]
    end par
end par
-- code
end process
```

Rule 6 (table 5) Gates are synchronized in competition access or simultaneous access: all <Thread_*> are in competition access to <Bus_*> for sending messages (respectively to <Processor_*> for sending requests) and in simultaneous access for receiving messages (respectively for receiving responses).

3.5   Other Transformation Rules

In this section, we complete the presentation of our transformation description. It concerns Data, Subprogram and Bus AADL components. Due to the lack of space, we expose briefly the rest of rules.

Rule 7. *Data* is considered as a simple data type without features. It is translated to a suitable LNT type <Data_*> in order to present the exchanged data between threads. In addition, we add corresponding channels for gate communications.

Table 5. Bus and Processor binding transformation

Rule 6	

Bus access
 	
- Properties
  • Actual_Connection_Binding;
 	
Processor binding
 	
- Properties
  • Actual_Processor_Binding;
	par
	  inBus, outBus ->
	    <Bus_> [inBus, outBus]
	  ||
	  Rq, Rs -> <Processor_> [Rq, Rs]
	  ||
	  Rq, Rs, inBus, outBus ->
	    par Rs in
	      par
	        <Thread_> [Rq, Rs, inBus]
	        || ..
	      end par
	      ||
	      par Rs, outBus in
	        <Thread_> [Rq, Rs, outBus]
	        || ..
	      end par
	    end par
	end par

Rule 8. *Subprogram* becomes an LNT process without gates, containing the same parameters as AADL subprogram. We can translate code given in the programming language of the source text (Ada or C). Thus, subprogram calls are translated into a simple process instantiation in the corresponding <Thread_*>.

Rule 9. *Bus* becomes an LNT process <Bus_*>, with two ports (input, output) modeling a queue with a capacity determined by a parameter. <Bus_*> uses the push type where the communication is initiated by the sender. It allows the bound of any connection category: data/event/event data connection and immediate/delayed connection. <Bus_*> exchanges a message contained the following information: sender identifier, list of connection identifiers, exchanged data and data sending interval time.

4   Tools

Our contribution benefits from a couple of powerful tools Ocarina for modeling and CADP for analyzing:

Ocarina is a tool set designed in Ada for AADL modeling. It provides syntactic and semantic analysis, verification and code generation from AADL models in Ada and C languages. Ocarina compiler has two parts a frontend and a backend. Frontend analyzes AADL model and presents it as Abstract Syntax Tree (AST). Backend treats AADL AST to produce all types of generation.

We began our implementations in Ocarina backend (implementation details will be exposed in a forthcoming paper). We do not use model transformation languages for our generation. We apply directly transformation rules on AADL AST to generate an LNT AST. Then, we scan this tree in order to produce the corresponding LNT code file.

CADP is a toolbox for the design and verification of concurrent systems. It supports several specification languages (Lotos, Fsp, LNT, etc). It includes many tools for formal analyzing and bug detection like model checking, equivalence checking, simulation, performance evaluation, etc.

We consider CADP like a black-box. Yet, we should provide all inputs: our translation generates LNT file, additional inputs must be presented depending on the concerned tool. For example, model-checker tool verifies if LNT specification satisfies a property expressed in temporal logic. In this case, we also specify a set of properties as a second input. After analyzing, CADP gives useful results for the correction of the initial model. For example, model-checker gives a false/true response for every checked property.

5   Case Study

In this section, we test our contribution with the "Flight Control System" case study. We apply our transformation rules on the given AADL model to obtain an LNT specification which can be compiled and checked with CADP toolbox.

5.1   Flight Control System

This system allows the control of the altitude, the speed and the trajectory of an airplane. It consists of seven periodic threads grouped in one process binding to a processor. Threads, shown in figure 1, communicate directly and exchange data. FL thread acquires the state of the system (angles, position, acceleration) and computes the feedback law of the system. The order is then sent to the flight control surfaces. PL and PF threads determine the acceleration to apply. NL and NF determine the position to reach.

Flight Control System in LNT. After transformation, we obtain an LNT specification which is formed of 19 composite processes. In this example, threads communicate without bus and exchange data. So the obtained specification uses DataPort_* for inputs and Processor_CPU for RMS scheduling.

The listing 1.7 contains an extract from the Process_FCS specification, showing the instantiation of Thread_NL and Thread_NF (without parameters) in synchronization with Processor_CPU (Rule 6). For example, Thread_NL has three connections (Rule 5.I): output with acc_c gate; input 1 through synchronization with DataPort_Posc; and input 2 through synchronization with DataPort_Poso. Also it is in synchronization with Thread_NF for pos_o input (Rule 5.II).

Fig. 1. Flight control system

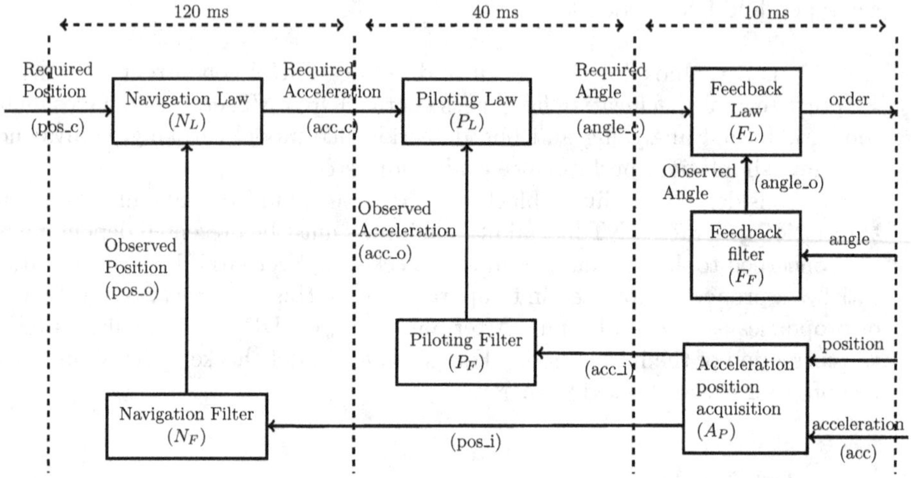

Listing 1.7. Flight control system in LNT

```
1   process Process_FCS [Rq : Response , Rs : Request ,
2       pos_c : Channelpos_c , order : Channelorder , acc : Channelacc ,
3       position : Channelposition , angle : Channelangle
4       ] is
5   -- code
6       par Rs in
7           acc_c , pos_o ->
8           par
9               SyncI_i , SyncI_j -> Tread_NL [Rq,Rs,SyncI_i ,SyncI_j ,acc_c ](..)
10              ||
11              SyncI_i -> DataPort_Posc [pos_c , SyncI_i ]
12              ||
13              pos_o , SyncI_j -> DataPort_Poso [pos_o , SyncI_j ]
14          end par
15          ||
16          pos_o , pos_i ->
17          par SyncI_k in
18              NF [Rq, Rs, SyncI_k ,pos_o ](..)
19              ||
20              pos_i -> DataPortAADL [pos_i , SyncI_k ]
21          end par
22          ||
23          -- code
24      end par
25  end process
```

5.2   Verification with CADP

The generated LNT specification can be analyzed with different tools in CADP. CADP transforms the obtained LNT specification into an LTS (Labeled transition system). In addition, CADP offers an automated reduction which allows

Table 6. "Flight Control System" LTS

	LTS	Reduced LTS
states	569 740	59 648
transitions	4 140 014	506 791

a strong reduction in the state space. We include, in table 6, the state space statistics of the generated LTS for our case study.

We can simulate LNT specification with CADP simulators like OCIS (Open/-Caesar Interactive Simulator). We can check various constraints with CADP model-checkers. In our case study, we use the Evaluator 3 model-checker [12] and we express properties in Rafmc (Regular Alternation-Free Mu-Calculus) language. For example, we verify the deadlock freedom:

$[true\ ]\ <true>\ true$

We can check the reachability of any state, for example, the following property verifies if the order is finally sent by FL thread:

$<\ true\ .\ "ORDER\ !FL\ "\ >\ true$

To check the schedulability of the AADL system, we add a specific LNT gate Is_Schedulable. If the execution ends successfully, the <Thread_*> writes TRUE in Is_Schedulable gate. Else, it writes FALSE when it detects an exceeding of deadline. Then, the model-checker verifies if this gate has the value FALSE. In our case study, this property is expressed in Rafmc as following:

$[true\ .\ "IS\_SCHEDULABLE\ !Thread\_NL\ !FALSE"]\ false\ and$
$[true\ .\ "IS\_SCHEDULABLE\ !Thread\_\ \ !FALSE"]\ false\ and$
$...$
$[true\ .\ "IS\_SCHEDULABLE\ !Thread\_AP\ !FALSE"]\ false$

We model-checked the "Flight Control System" case study, and ensure that it is well scheduled and has no deadlocks.

6   Related Work

Several work in formal verification of AADL models have been made by translating AADL with or without its annex into several specification languages: (i)transformation into Petri nets for example the symmetric net in [9] for model-checking; (ii) transformation into automata for example the use of timed automata in [8] and [10] to connect to the model-checker UPPAAL and the use of the linear hybrid automata in [7] for schedulability analysis; and (iii) transformation into different process algebras.

Our work is included in group (iii) with others approach, such as, the translation into Bip [13] to connect with Bip framework. This translation generates timed Bip models which should be transformed into non-timed models to be analyzed.

[4] transforms AADL model into Fiacre model for behavioral verification with Tina tool set or CADP toolbox. For the second alternative, AADL model is firstly converted into a Fiacre model and then transformed into a Lotos specification with the need of manual improvements. This work ignores hardware components and it is restricted on no preempted thread without scheduling execution.

[14] uses the Real-Time Maude language for transformation and the Maude framework for verification. However, this work focuses only on the software AADL components and ignores scheduling information.

Authors in [15] present a verified transformation of AADL model to TASM language using TASM Toolset, Coq and UPPAAL. This work considers only a synchronous subset of AADL (periodic threads with data port communication).

In our approach, we provide an automated model transformation of AADL models. We consider a subset of AADL language implicating software and hardware components with a significant property set. We focus on thread scheduling execution and port communication mechanism with the definition of an explicit scheduler. We use directly LNT input language of the formal tool without additional transformation. For verification, our work allows the connection with the CADP toolbox which offers a various verification methods and avoids the state explosion problem with a compositional verification.

7   Conclusion and Future Work

We presented our approach in the context of the verification of distributed real-time systems. We proposed a solution that allows the verification of AADL models using formal methods known by their rigorous checking results. We translated an interesting subset of AADL model to an LNT specification to exploit the CADP toolbox. Our mapping abstracts AADL model as a set of scheduled threads in communication enriched with connection and timing properties.

This paper introduced a first step of our contribution and validated its feasibility. Currently, we are focusing on communication problems. We plan to describe specific properties for communication consistency verification. Also we aim to exploit the compositional verification offered by CADP. And we are working continuously in our implementations in Ocarina.

Acknowledgments. The idea of translating AADL to LNT was first explored by Hubert Garavel from the CADP group. We would like to thank him and Wendelin Serwe and Frédéric Lang for their help in using LNT and CADP.

References

1. ISO/IEC: LOTOS a formal description technique based on the temporal ordering of observational behaviour. International Standard 8807, International Organization for Standardization Information Processing Systems Open Systems Interconnection, Geneve (1989)

2. ISO/IEC: Enhancements to LOTOS (E-LOTOS). International Standard 15437:2001, International Organization for Standardization Information Technology, Geneve (2001)
3. AS5506A: Architecture Analysis and Design Language (AADL) Version 2.0 (2009)
4. Berthomieu, B., Bodeveix, J.-P., Dal Zilio, S., Dissaux, P., Filali, M., Gaufillet, P., Heim, S., Vernadat, F.: Formal verification of AADL models with Fiacre and Tina. In: ERTSS 2010 - Embedded Real-Time Software and Systems, TOULOUSE (31000), France, pp. 1–9, 9 pages, May 2010. DGE Topcased
5. Champelovier, D., Clerc, X., Garavel, H., Guerte, Y., Lang, F., McKinty, C., Powazny, V., Serwe, W., Smeding, G.: Reference manual of the LNT to LOTOS translator (2014)
6. Garavel, H., Lang, F., Mateescu, R., Serwe, W.: Cadp 2011: a toolbox for the construction and analysis of distributed processes. International Journal on Software Tools for Technology Transfer **15**(2), 89–107 (2013)
7. Gui, S., Luo, L., Li, Y., Wang, L.: Formal schedulability analysis and simulation for AADL. In: ICESS, pp. 429–435 (2008)
8. Hamdane, M.E.-K., Chaoui, A., Strecker, M.: Toolchain Based on MDE for the Transformation of AADL Models to Timed Automata Models (2013)
9. Hecht, M., Lam, A., Vogl, C.: A tool set for integrated software and hardware dependability analysis using the architecture analysis and design language (AADL) and error model annex. In: ICECCS, pp. 361–366 (2011)
10. Johnsen, A., Lundqvist, K., Pettersson, P., Jaradat, O.: Automated verification of AADL-specifications using UPPAAL. In: HASE, pp. 130–138 (2012)
11. Lasnier, G., Zalila, B., Pautet, L., Hugues, J.: Ocarina : an environment for AADL models analysis and automatic code generation for high integrity applications. In: Kordon, F., Kermarrec, Y. (eds.) Ada-Europe 2009. LNCS, vol. 5570, pp. 237–250. Springer, Heidelberg (2009)
12. Mateescu, R., Sighireanu, M.: Efficient on-the-fly model-checking for regular alternation-free mu-calculus. Science of Computer Programming **46**(3), 255–281 (2003)
13. Chkouri, M.Y., Robert, A., Bozga, M., Sifakis, J.: Translating AADL into BIP - application to the verification of real-time systems. In: Chaudron, M.R.V. (ed.) MODELS 2008. LNCS, vol. 5421, pp. 5–19. Springer, Heidelberg (2009)
14. Ölveczky, P.C., Boronat, A., Meseguer, J.: Formal semantics and analysis of behavioral AADL models in Real-Time Maude. In: Hatcliff, J., Zucca, E. (eds.) FMOODS 2010. LNCS, vol. 6117, pp. 47–62. Springer, Heidelberg (2010)
15. Yang, Z., Hu, K., Ma, D., Bodeveix, J.-P., Pi, L., Talpin, J.-P.: From AADL to Timed Abstract State Machines: A verified model transformation, vol. 93, pp. 42–68. Elsevier (2014)

Using Sensitivity Analysis to Facilitate the Maintenance of Safety Cases

Omar Jaradat[1]($\boxtimes$), Iain Bate[1,2], and Sasikumar Punnekkat[1]

[1] School of Innovation, Design, and Engineering, Mälardalen University,
Västerås, Sweden
{omar.jaradat,sasikumar.punnekkat}@mdh.se
[2] Department of Computer Science, University of York,
York, UK
iain.bate@york.ac.uk

Abstract. A safety case contains safety arguments together with supporting evidence that together should demonstrate that a system is
acceptably safe. System changes pose a challenge to the soundness and
cogency of the safety case argument. Maintaining safety arguments is
a painstaking process because it requires performing a change impact
analysis through interdependent elements. Changes are often performed
years after the deployment of a system making it harder for safety case
developers to know which parts of the argument are affected. Contracts
have been proposed as a means for helping to manage changes. There has
been significant work that discusses how to represent and to use them
but there has been little on how to derive them. In this paper, we propose a sensitivity analysis approach to derive contracts from Fault Tree
Analyses and use them to trace changes in the safety argument, thus
facilitating easier maintenance of the safety argument.

Keywords: Safety case · Safety argument · Maintenance · FTA ·
Sensitivity analysis · Safety contracts · Impact analysis

1 Introduction

Building a safety case is an increasingly common practice in many safety critical
domains [7]. A safety case comprises both safety evidence and a safety argument that explains that evidence. The safety evidence is collected throughout
the development and operational phases, for example from analysis, test, inspection, and in-service monitoring activities. The safety argument shows how this
evidence demonstrates that the system satisfies the applicable operational definition of acceptably safe to operate in its intended operating context.

A safety case should always justify the safety status of the associated system, therefore it is described as a living document that should be maintained
as needed whenever some aspect of the system, its operation, its operating context, or its operational history changes. However, safety goals, evidence, argument, and assumptions about operating context are interdependent and thus,

© Springer International Publishing Switzerland 2015
J.A. de la Puente and T. Vardanega (Eds.): Ada-Europe 2015, LNCS 9111, pp. 162–176, 2015.
DOI:10.1007/978-3-319-19584-1_11

seemingly-minor changes may have a major impact on the contents and struc-ture of the safety argument. Any improper maintenance in a safety argument has a potential for a tremendous negative impact on the conveyed system safety status by the safety case. Hence, a step to assess the impact of this change on the safety argument is crucial and highly needed prior to updating a safety argument after a system change.

Changes to the system during or after development might invalidate safety evidence or argument. Evidence might no longer support the developers claims because it reflects old development artefacts or old assumptions about opera-tion or the operating environment. In the updated system, existing safety claims might not make any sense, no longer reflect operational intent, or be contra-dicted by new data. Analysing the impact of a change in a safety argument is not trivial: doing so requires awareness of the dependencies among the argu-ment's contents and how changes to one part might invalidate others. In other words, if a change was applied to any element of a set of interdependent ele-ments, then the associated effects on the rest of the elements might go unnoticed. Without this vital awareness, a developer performing impact analysis might not notice that a change has compromised system safety. Implicit dependencies thus pose a major challenge. Moreover, evidence is valid only in the operational and environmental contexts in which it was obtained or to which it applies. Opera-tional or environmental changes might therefore affect the relevance of evidence and, indirectly, the validity and strength of the safety argument.

Predicting system changes before building a safety argument can be useful because it allows the safety argument to be structured to contain the impact of these changes. Hence, anticipated changes may have predictable and traceable consequences that will eventually reduce the maintenance efforts. Nevertheless, planning the maintenance of a safety case still faces two key issues: (1) system changes and their details cannot be fully predicted and made available up front, especially, the software aspects of the safety case as software is highly changeable and harder to manage as they are hard to contain, and (2) those changes can be implemented years after the development of a safety case. Part of what we aim for in this work is to provide system developers a list of system parts that may be more problematic to change than other parts and ask them to choose the parts that are most likely to change. Of course our list can be augmented by additional changeable parts that may be provided by the system developers.

Sensitivity analysis helps the experts to define the uncertainties involved with a particular system change so that those experts can judge on the potential change based on how reliable they feel the consequences are. The analysis can deal with what aim for since it allows us to define the problematic changes. More specifically, we exploit the Fault Tree Analyses (FTAs) which are supposed to have been done by developers through the safety analysis phase and apply the sensitivity analysis to those FTAs in order to identify the sensitive parts in them. We define a sensitive part as one or multiple events whose minimum changes have the maximal effect on the FTA, where effect means exceeding reliability targets due to a change.

In spite of the assumption we make that the safety arguments logic is based on the causal pathways described in the FTAs, tracking the changes from the FTAs of a system down to its safety argument still requires a traceability mechanism between the two. To this end, we use the concept of contract to highlight the sensitive parts in FTAs, and to establish a traceability between those parts and the corresponding safety argument. In our work, we assume that safety arguments are recorded in the Goal Structuring Notation (GSN) [6]. However, the approach we propose might (with suitable adaptations) be compatible for use with other graphical assurance argument notations.

Combining the sensitivity analysis together with the concept of contracts to identify the sensitive parts of a system and highlight these parts may help the experts to make an educated decision as to whether or not apply changes. This decision is in light of beforehand knowledge of the impact of these changes on the system and its safety case. Our hypothesis in this work is that it is possible to use the sensitivity analysis together with safety contracts to (1) bring to developers' attention the most sensitive parts of a system for a particular change, and (2) manage the change by guiding the developers to the parts in the safety argument that might be affected after applying a change. However, using contracts as a way of managing change is not a new notion since it has been discussed in some works, such as [2][5], but deriving the contracts and their contents have received little or even no support yet. The main contribution of this paper is to propose a safety case maintenance technique. However, we focus on the first phase of the technique and explain how to apply the sensitivity analysis to FTAs and derive the contracts and their contents. We also explain how to associate the derived arguments with safety argument goals. The paper illustrates the technique and its key concepts using the a hypothetical aircraft Wheel Braking System (WBS).

The paper is structured as follows: in Section 2 we present background information. In Section 3 we propose a technique for maintaining safety cases using sensitivity analysis. In Section 4 we use the WBS example to illustrate the technique. In Section 5 we present the related work. Finally, we conclude and derive future works in Section 6.

2   Background and Motivation

This section gives background information about (1) the GSN, (2) the concept of contract, (3) some of the current challenges that are facing safety case maintenance including a brief review of the state-of-the-art, and (4) the sensitivity analysis including some possible applications.

2.1   The Goal Structuring Notation (GSN)

A safety argument organizes and communicates a safety case, showing how the items of safety evidence are related and collectively demonstrate that a system is acceptably safe to operate in a particular context. GSN [6] provides a graphical

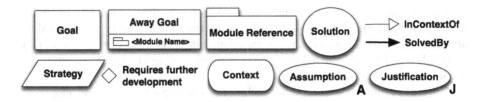

Fig. 1. Notation Keys of the Goal Structuring Notation (GSN)

means of communicating (1) safety argument elements, claims (goals), argument logic (strategies), assumptions, context, evidence (solutions), and (2) the relationships between these elements. The principal symbols of the notation are shown in Figure 1 (with example instances of each concept).

A goal structure shows how goals are successively broken down into (solved by) sub-goals until eventually supported by direct reference to evidence. Using the GSN, it is also possible to clarify the argument strategies adopted (i.e., how the premises imply the conclusion), the rationale for the approach (assumptions, justifications) and the context in which goals are stated.

2.2   The Concept of Safety Contracts

The concept of contract is not uncommon in software development and it was first introduced in 1988 by Meyer [12] to constrain the interactions that occur between objects. Contract-based design [3] is defined as an approach where the design process is seen as a successive assembly of components where a component behaviour is represented in terms of assumptions about its environment and guarantees about its behavior. Hence, contracts are intended to describe functional and behavioral properties for each design component in form of assumptions and guarantees. In this paper, a contract which describes properties that are only safety-related is referred to as a safety contract.

2.3   Safety Case Maintenance and Current Practices

A safety case is a living document that should be maintained as the system, its operation, or its operating context changes. In this paper, we refer to the process of updating the safety case after implementing a change as safety case maintenance. Developers are experiencing difficulties with safety case maintenance, including difficulty identifying the direct and indirect impact of change. Two main causes of this difficulty are a lack of traceability between a system and its safety case and a lack of documentation of dependencies among the safety cases contents. Systems tend to become more complex, this increasing complexity can exacerbate safety case maintenance difficulties. The GSN is meant to reduce these difficulties by providing a clear, explicit conceptual model of the safety cases elements and interdependencies [10].

Our discussion of documenting interdependencies within a safety case refers to two different forms of traceability. Firstly, we refer to the ability to relate safety argument fragments to system design components as component traceability (through a safety argument). Secondly, we refer to evidence across system's artefacts as evidence traceability.

Current standards and analysis techniques assume a top-down development approach to system design. When systems that are built from components, mismatch with design structure makes monolithic safety arguments and evidence difficult to maintain. Safety is a system level property; assuring safety requires safety evidence to be consistent and traceable to system safety goals [10]. One might suppose that a safety argument structure aligned with the system design structure would make traceability clearer. It might, but safety argument structures are influenced by four factors: (1) modularity of evidence, (2) modularity of the system, (3) process demarcation (e.g., the scope of ISO 26262 items [7]), and organisational structure (e.g., who is working on what). These factors often make argument structures aligned with the system design structure impractical. However, the need to track changes across the whole safety argument is still significant for maintaining the argument regardless of its structure.

2.4 Sensitivity Analysis

Sensitivity analysis helps to establish reasonably acceptable confidence in the model by studying the uncertainties that are often associated with variables in models. There are different purposes for using sensitivity analysis, such as, providing insight into the robustness of model results when making decisions [4]. The analysis can be also used to enhance communication from modelers to decision makers, for example, by making recommendations more credible, understandable, compelling or persuasive [13]. The analysis can be performed by different methods, such as, mathematical, graphical, statistical, etc.

In this paper, we use sensitivity analysis to identify the sensitive parts of a system that might require unnecessary painstaking maintenance. More specifically, we apply the sensitivity analysis on FTAs to measure the sensitivity of outcome A (e.g., a safety requirement being true) to a change in a parameter B (e.g., the failure rate in a component). The sensitivity is defined as $\Delta B/B$, where ΔB is the smallest change in B that changes A (e.g., the smallest increase in failure rate that makes safety requirement A false). Hence, a sensitive part is defined as one or multiple FTA events whose minimum changes have the maximal effect on the FTA, where effect means exceeding failure probabilities (reliability targets) to inadmissible levels due to the change. The failure probability values that are attached to the FTA events are considered input parameters to the sensitivity analysis. A sensitive event is the event whose failure probability value can significantly influence the validity of the FTA once it increases. A sensitive part of a FTA is assigned to a system design component that is referred to as sensitive component in this paper. Hence, changes to a sensitive component cause a great impact to system design.

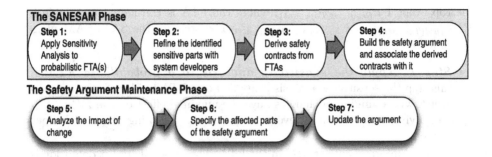

Fig. 2. Process diagram of the proposed technique

3   Using Sensitivity Analysis to Facilitate the Maintenance of a Safety Case

In this section, we build on the background information provided in Section 2 to propose a technique that aims to facilitate the maintenance of a safety case. The technique comprises 7 steps that are distributed between the Sensitivity ANalysis for Enabling Safety Argument Maintenance (SANESAM) phase and the safety argument maintenance phases as shown in Figure 2. The steps of the SANESAM phase are represented along the upper path, whilst the lower path represents the steps of the safety argument maintenance phase. The SANESAM phase, however, is what is being discussed in this paper.

A complete approach to managing safety case change would include both (a) mechanisms to structure the argument so as to contain the impact of predicted changes and (b) means of assessing the impact of change on all parts of the argument [8]. As discussed in Section 1, system changes and their details cannot be fully predicted and made available up front. Predicting potential changes to the software aspects of a safety case is even harder than other parts because software is highly changeable and harder to manage. Consequently, considering a complete list of anticipated changes is difficult. What can be easier though is to determine the flexibility (or compliance) of each component to changes. This means that regardless of the type of changes the latter will be seen as factors to increase or decrease a certain parameter value. Thus system developers can focus more on predicting those changes that might make the parameter value inadmissible.

The rationale of our technique is to determine, for each component, the allowed range for a certain parameter within which a component may change before it compromises a certain system property (e.g., safety, reliability, etc.). To this end, we use the sensitivity analysis as a method to determine the range of failure probability parameter for each component. Hence, the technique assumes the existence of a probabilistic FTA where each event in the tree is specified by an actual (i.e., current) failure probability $FP_{Actual|event(x)}$. In addition, the technique assumes the existence of the required failure probability for the top event $FP_{Required(Topevent)}$, where the FTA is considered unreliable if: $FP_{Actual(Topevent)} > FP_{Required(Topevent)}$. The steps of the SANESAM phase are as follows:

- **Step 1. Apply the sensitivity analysis to a probabilistic FTA**: In this step the sensitivity analysis is applied to a FTA to identify the sensitive events whose minimum changes have the maximal effect on the $FP_{Topevent}$. Identifying those sensitive events requires the following steps to be performed:

  1. Find minimal cut set MC in the FTA. The minimal cut set definition is: *"A cut set in a fault tree is a set of basic events whose (simultaneous) occurrence ensures that the top event occurs. A cut set is said to be minimal if the set cannot be reduced without losing its status as a cut set"[14].*
  2. Calculate the maximum possible increment in the failure probability parameter of event x before the top event $FP_{Actual(Topevent)}$ is no longer met, where $x \in MC$ and
  $$(FP_{Increased|event(x)} - FP_{Actual|event(x)}) \nRightarrow FP_{Actual(Topevent)} > FP_{Required(Topevent)}.$$
  3. Rank the sensitive events from the most sensitive to the less sensitive. The most sensitive event is the event for which the following equation is the minimum:
  $$(FP_{Increased|event(x)} - FP_{Actual|event(x)})/FP_{Actual|event(x)}$$

- **Step 2. Refine the identified sensitive parts with system developers**: In this step, the generated list from Step 1 should be discussed with system developers (e.g., safety engineers) and ask them to choose the sensitive events that are most likely to change. The list can be extended to add any additional events by the developers. Moreover, it is envisaged that some events may be removed from the list or the rank of some of them change.

- **Step 3. Derive safety contracts from FTAs**: In this step, the refined list from Step 2 is used as a guide to derive the safety contracts, where each event in the list should have at least one contract. The main objective of the contracts is to 1) highlight the sensitive events to make them visible up front for developers attention, 2) to record the dependencies between the sensitive events and the other events in the FTA. Hence, if any contracted event has received a change that necessitates increasing its failure probability where the increment is still within the defined threshold in the contract, then it can be said that the contract(s) in question still holds (intact) and the change is containable with no further maintenance. The contract(s), however, should be updated to the latest failure probability value. On the contrary, if the change causes a bigger increment in the failure probability value than the contract can hold, then the contract is said to be broken and the guaranteed event will no longer meet its reliability target. We create a template to document the derived safety contracts as shown in Figure 3a, where G and A stand for Guarantee and Assumption, respectively. Furthermore, each safety contract should contain a version number (it is shown as **V** in Figure 3a). The version number of the contract should match the *artefact version number* (as described in the next step), otherwise it will be considered out of date. We also introduce a new notation to the FTA to annotate the contracted events where every created contract should have a unique identifier, see Figure 3b.

- *Step 4. Build the safety argument and associate the derived contracts with it*: In this step, a safety argument should be built and the derived safety contracts should be associated with the argument elements.

  In order to associate the derived safety contracts with GSN arguments, we reuse our previous work [8]. The essence of that work is storing additional information in the safety argument to facilitate identifying the evidence impacted by change. This is done by annotating each reference to a development artefact (e.g. an architecture specification) in a goal or context element with an *artefact version number*. Also by annotating each solution element with:

  1. An *evidence version* number
  2. An *input manifest* identifying the inputs (including version) from which the evidence was produced
  3. The *lifecycle phase* during which the evidence obtained (e.g. Software Architecture Design)
  4. A *safety standard reference* to the clause in the applicable standard (if any) requiring the evidence (and setting out safety integrity level requirements)

  However, the approach description, just as it is, does not support associating our derived safety contracts in *Step 3* with the safety argument without proper adjustments. Hence, a set of rules are introduced to guide the reuse of the approach in the work of this paper, as follows:

  1. GSN element names should be unique.
  2. At least one GSN goal should be created for each guarantee (i.e., for each safety contract). Moreover, the contract should be annotated in the

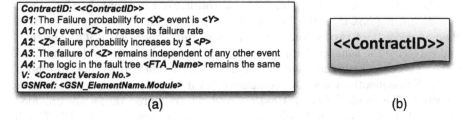

ContractID: <<ContractID>>
G1: The Failure probability for **<X>** event is **<Y>**
A1: Only event **<Z>** increases its failure rate
A2: **<Z>** failure probability increases by ≤ **<P>**
A3: The failure of **<Z>** remains independent of any other event
A4: The logic in the fault tree **<FTA_Name>** remains the same
V: **<Contract Version No.>**
GSNRef: **<GSN_ElementName.Module>**

<<ContractID>>

(a)   (b)

Fig. 3. (a) Safety Contract Template (b) Safety Contract Notation for FTA

goal which is made for it. The annotation should be done by using the contract ID and the notation in Figure 3b.

3. Assumptions in each safety contract should be restricted to one event only. If the guarantee requires assumptions about another event, a new contract should be created to cover these assumptions.

4. An event in the assumptions list of a safety contract may be also used as a goal in the argument. In this case, the goal name should be similar to the event name.

5. Each safety contract should contain the GSN reference within it. The reference is the unique name of the GSN element followed by a dot and the name of the GSN module (if modular GSN is used). It is worth noting that while documenting the safety contracts, the GSN references might not be available as the safety argument itself might not be built yet. Hence, whenever GSN references are made available, system developers are required to revisit each contract and add the corresponding GSN reference to it. GSN reference parameter is shown as **GSNRef** in Figure 3a.

It is worth saying that the technique shall not affect the way GSN is being produced but it brings additional information for developers' attention.

4   An Illustrative Example: The Wheel Braking System (WBS)

In this section, we illustrate the proposed technique and its key concepts using the hypothetical aircraft braking system described in Appendix L of Aerospace Recommended Practice ARP-4761 [1]. Figure 4 shows a high-level architecture view of the WBS

4.1   Wheel Braking System (WBS): System Description

The WBS is installed on the two main landing gears. The main function of the system is to provide wheel braking as commanded by the pilot when the aircraft is on the ground. The system is composed of three main parts: Computer-based part which is called the Brake System Control Unit (*BSCU*), *Hydraulic* part, and *Mechanical* part.

The *BSCU* is internally redundant and consists of two channels, *BSCU System 1 and 2* (*BSCU* is the box in the gray background in Figure 4). Each channel consists of two components: *Monitor* and *Command*. *BSCU System 1 and 2* receive the same pedal position inputs, and both calculate the command value. The two command values are individually monitored by the *Monitor 1 and 2*. Subsequently, values are compared and if they do not agree, a failure is reported. The results of both *Monitors* and the compared values are provided to a the *Validity Monitor*. A failure reported by either system in the *BSCU* will cause that system to disable its outputs and set the *Validity Monitor* to invalid

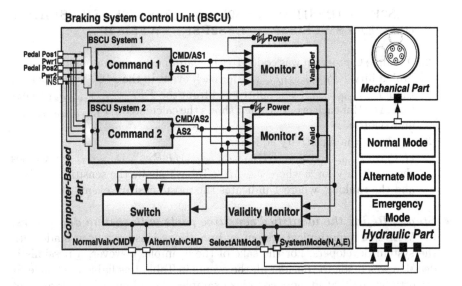

Fig. 4. A high-level view of the WBS

with no effect on the mode of operation of the whole system. However, if both monitors report failure the $BSCU$ is deemed inoperable and is shut down [11].

It worth noting that Figure 4 shows high-level view of the $BSCU$ implementation and it omits many details. However, the figure is still sufficient to illustrate key elements of our technique. More details about the $BSCU$ implementation can be found in ARP-4761 [1].

4.2   Applying the Technique

Before we can apply the technique, both the required and actual failure probabilities of the top event should be clearly defined, where $FP_{Required(Topevent)} > FP_{Actual(Topevent)}$. Appendix L of the ARP-4761 states, as a safety requirement on the $BSCU$, that: *"The probability of BSCU fault causes Loss of Braking Commands shall be less than 3.30E-5 per flight"*. This means that: $FP_{Required(Topevent)}$ < **3.30E-5**. In line with this, we assumed that the $FP_{Actual(Topevent)} \approx$ **1.50E-6**. Figure 5 shows the "Loss of Braking Commands" probabilistic FTA.

- *Step 1. Apply the sensitivity analysis to the "Loss of Braking Commands" probabilistic FTA*: the following steps were performed to apply the sensitivity analysis:
  1. Find minimal cut set MC in the FTA: there are several algorithms to find the MC. We apply Mocus cut set algorithm [14], as follows:

  MC = {BSVMIRFCSTA + SWFSIIP + (BSS1EF ∗ BSS2EF) + (BSS1EF ∗ BSS2PSF) + (BSS1EF ∗ SWFSIS1P) + (BSS1PSF ∗

BSS2EF) + (BSS1PSF * BSS2PSF) + (BSS1PSF * SWFSIS1P) + (BSS2EF * SWFSIS2P) + (BSS2PSF * SWFSIS2P)}.

2. A simple C program was coded to calculate the maximum possible failure probability $FP_{Increased|event(x)}$ for each event in the MC. Subsequently, the $FP_{Actual|event(x)}$ was subtracted from the $FP_{Increased|event(x)}$ to obtain ΔFP for each event. Table 1 shows the calculated $FP_{Increased|event(x)}$ and ΔFP.

3. Applying the sensitivity equation:
$(FP_{Increased|event(x)} - FP_{Actual|event(x)})/FP_{Actual|event(x)}$ determines the sensitivity for x where $x \in MC$. Table 1 shows the sensitivity values and the ranking, where 1 indicates the most sensitive event.

- **Step 2. Refine the identified sensitive parts with system developers**: the WBS is a hypothetical system and no discussions have been made with the system developers. For the sake of the example, however, a pessimistic decision was made to consider all the events in Table 1 as liable to change. It is worth noting that in more complex examples the volume of sensitive event lists will be quite big. Hence, discussing those lists with system developers

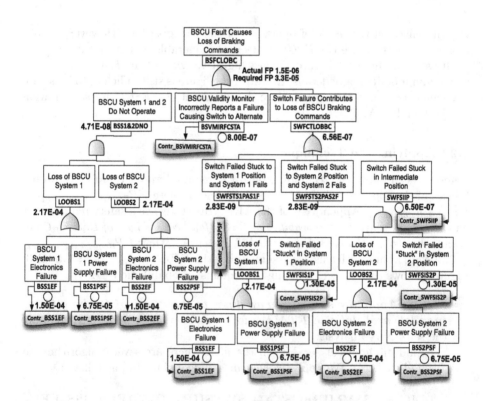

Fig. 5. Loss of Braking Commands FTA

Table 1. The results of the sensitivity analysis

Event	$FP_{Actual|event(x)}$	$\approx \Delta FP$	$FP_{Increased|event(x)}$	Sensitivity	Rank
BSVMIRFCSTA	8.00E-07	3.150E-05	3.2304E-05	39	1
SWFSIIP	6.50E-07	3.150E-05	3.2154E-05	48	2
SWFSIS1P	1.30E-05	1.448E-01	1.4484E-01	51182	5
SWFSIS2P	1.30E-05	1.448E-01	1.4484E-01	51182	5
BSS1EF	1.50E-04	1.448E-01	1.4498E-01	965	3
BSS1PSF	6.75E-05	1.448E-01	1.4490E-01	2145	4
BSS2EF	1.50E-04	1.448E-01	1.4498E-01	965	3
BSS2PSF	6.75E-05	1.448E-01	1.4490E-01	2145	4

can lead to more selective events and thus alleviating the number of safety contracts.

- **Step 3. Derive safety contracts from "Loss of Braking Commands" FTA**: based on the list of the sensitive events from Step 2, a safety contract was derived for each event in the list. The introduced safety contract template in Figure 3a was used to demonstrate the derived safety contracts. For lack of space, we show only one example of the eight derived safety contracts (see Figure 6).

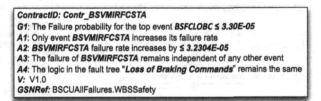

Fig. 6. A derived safety contract

- **Step 4. Build the safety argument for the BSCU and associate the derived contracts with it**: a safety argument fragment was built as shown in Figure 7. The derived safety contracts are associated with the derived safety contracts according to **Steps 4** in Section 3. *BSCUAllFailures* claims that *BSCU* faults cause Loss of Braking commands are sufficiently managed. The possible faults of *BSCU*, based on "Loss of Braking Commands" FTA, are addressed by the subgoals below the *ArgAllCaus* strategy. Hence, *BSCUAllFailures* represents the top event of the FTA and thus the derived safety contracts are associated with it. The single black star on the left refers to the notation that is used to associate the contracts with *BSCUAllFailures*. It is important to note that goals in the gray color background represent assumptions in the safety contract. Each goal of those has the same name of the event in the assumptions list of the corresponding contract. For instance, *BSVMIRFCSTA* is a goal that represents an assumption within *Contr_BSVMIRFCSTA* contract which, in turn, guarantees a property for another event.

The double black stars in the lower right corner refer to that annotation which is described in Section 3. It is important to make sure that contracts, related artefacts and items evidence have the same version number. The main idea of having the information within this notation is to pave the way to highlight the impact of changes. However, this idea will be described for the last three steps of the technique which is left for future work.

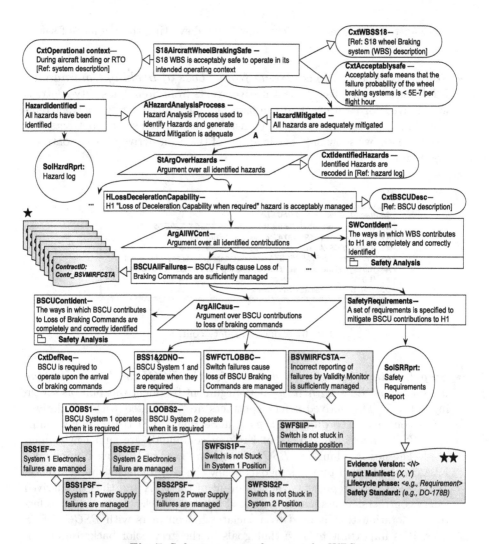

Fig. 7. Safety argument fragment for WBS

5   Related Work

A consortium of researchers and industrial practitioners called the Industrial Avionics Working Group (IAWG) has proposed using modular safety cases as a means of containing the cost of change. IAWGs Modular Software Safety Case (MSSC) process facilitates handling system changes as a series of relatively small increments rather than occasional major updates. The process proposes to divide the system into a set of blocks [2][5]. Each block may correspond to one or more software components but it is associated to exactly one dedicated safety case module. Engineers attempt to scope blocks so that anticipated changes will be contained within argument module boundaries. The process establishes component traceability between system blocks and their safety argument modules using Dependency-Guarantee Relationships (DGRs) and Dependency-Guarantee Contracts (DGCs). Part of the MSSC process is to understand the impact of change so that this can be used as part of producing an appropriate argument. The MSSC process, however, does not give details of how to do this. The work in this paper addresses this issue.

Kelly [9] suggests identifying preventative measures that can be taken when constructing the safety case to limit or reduce the propagation of changes through a safety case expressed in goal-structure terms. For instance, developers can use broad goals (goals that are expressed in terms of a safety margin) so that the these goals might act as barriers to the propagation of change as they permit a range of possible solutions. A safety case therefore, interspersed with such goals at strategic positions in the goal structure could effectively contain "firewalls" to change. Some of these initial ideas concerning change and maintenance of safety cases have been presented in [15]. However, no work was provided to show how these thoughts can facilitate the maintenance of safety cases.

6   Conclusion and Future Work

Changes are often only performed years after the initial design of the system making it hard for the designers performing the changes to know which parts of the argument are affected. Using contracts to manage system changes is not a novel idea any more since there has been significant work discusses how to represent contracts and how to use them. However, there has been little work on how to derive them. In this paper, we proposed a technique in which we showed a way to derive safety contracts using the sensitivity analysis. We also proposed a way to map the derived safety contracts to a safety argument to improve the change impact analysis on the safety argument and eventually facilitate its maintenance. Future work will focus on describing the last three steps of the technique. Also, creating a case study to validate both the feasibility and efficacy of the technique is part of our future work.

Acknowledgments. We acknowledge the Swedish Foundation for Strategic Research (SSF) SYNOPSIS Project for supporting this work. We thank Patrick Graydon for his help and fruitful discussions of this paper.

References

1. SAE ARP4761 Guidelines and Methods for Conducting the Safety Assessment Process on Civil Airborne Systems and Equipment, December 1996
2. Modular software safety case (MSSC) – process description, November 2012. https://www.amsderisc.com/related-programmes/
3. Benvenuti, L., Ferrari, A., Mazzi, E., Vincentelli, A.L.S.: Contract-based design for computation and verification of a closed-loop hybrid system. In: Egerstedt, M., Mishra, B. (eds.) HSCC 2008. LNCS, vol. 4981, pp. 58–71. Springer, Heidelberg (2008)
4. Cullen, A., Frey, H.: Probabilistic techniques in Exposure assessment. Plenum Press, New York (1999)
5. Fenn, J.L., Hawkins, R.D., Williams, P., Kelly, T.P., Banner, M.G., Oakshott, Y.: The who, where, how, why and when of modular and incremental certification. In: Proceedings of the 2nd IET International Conference on System Safety, pp. 135–140. IET (2007)
6. GSN Community Standard: Version 1; (c) 2011 Origin Consulting (York) Limited. http://www.goalstructuringnotation.info/
7. ISO 26262:2011. Road Vehicles – Functional Safety, Part 1–9. International Organization for Standardization, November 2011
8. Jaradat, O., Graydon, P.J., Bate, I.: An approach to maintaining safety case evidence after a system change. In: Proceedings of the 10th European Dependable Computing Conference (EDCC), August 2014
9. Kelly, T.: Literature survey for work on evolvable safety cases. Department of Computer Sceince, University of York, 1st Year Qualifying Dissertation (1995)
10. Kelly, T.P., McDermid, J.A.: A systematic approach to safety case maintenance. In: Felici, M., Kanoun, K., Pasquini, A. (eds.) SAFECOMP 1999. LNCS, vol. 1698, pp. 13–26. Springer, Heidelberg (1999)
11. Lisagor, O., Pretzer, M., Seguin, C., Pumfrey, D.J., Iwu, F., Peikenkamp, T.: Towards safety analysis of highly integrated technologically heterogeneous systems - a domain-based approach for modelling system failure logic. In: The 24th International System Safety Conference (ISSC), Albuquerque, USA (2006)
12. Meyer, B.: Object-Oriented Software Construction, 1st edn. Prentice-Hall Inc, Upper Saddle River (1988)
13. Pannell, D.J.: Sensitivity analysis of normative economic models: theoretical framework and practical strategies. Agricultural Economics 16(2), 139–152 (1997)
14. Rausand, M., Høyland, A.: System Reliability Theory: Models, Statistical Methods and Applications. Wiley-Interscience, Hoboken (2004)
15. Wilson, S.P., Kelly, T.P., McDermid, J.A.: Safety case development: current practice, future prospects. In: proc. of Software Bases Systems - 12th Annual CSR Workshop. Springer-Verlag (1997)

Multicore and Distributed Systems

Challenges in the Implementation of MrsP

Sebastiano Catellani[1], Luca Bonato[1(✉)], Sebastian Huber[2],
and Enrico Mezzetti[1]

[1] Department of Mathematics, University of Padua, Padua, Italy
{scatella,lbonato,emezzett}@math.unipd.it
[2] Embedded Brains GmbH, Puchheim, Germany
sebastian.huber@embedded-brains.de

Abstract. The transition to multicore systems that has started to take
place over the last few years, has revived the interest in the synchronization protocols for sharing logical resources. In fact, consolidated solutions
for single processor systems are not immediately applicable to multiprocessor platforms and new paradigms and solutions have to be devised.
The Multiprocessor resource sharing Protocol (MrsP) is a particularly
elegant approach for partitioned systems, which allows sharing global
logical resources among tasks assigned to distinct scheduling partitions.
Notably, MrsP enjoys two desirable theoretical properties: optimality and
compliance to well-known uniprocessor response time analysis. A coarse-
grained experimental evaluation of the MrsP protocol on a general-
purpose operating system has been already presented by its original
authors. No clear evidence, however, has been provided to date as to
its viability and effectiveness for industrial-size real-time operating systems. In this paper we bridge this gap, focusing on the challenges posed
by the implementation of MrsP on top of two representative real-time
operating systems, RTEMS and LITMUS^{RT}. In doing so, we provide a
useful insight on implementation-specific issues and offer evidence that
the protocol can be effectively implemented on top of standard real-time
operating system support while incurring acceptable overhead.

Keywords: Real-time systems · Multiprocessor systems · Resource
sharing protocols · Empirical evaluation

1 Introduction

Cost, performance and availability considerations increasingly push application
developers towards the adoption of multiprocessor platforms even in the traditionally conservative domains of embedded real-time systems [14], [1]. The
migration to multicores, however, threatens to disrupt all the analysis approaches
and solutions that are consolidated practices on single processors. Despite the
notable progress achieved in this direction in recent years [13], scheduling algorithms and schedulability analyses of multiprocessor systems have not reached
the same degree of maturity as single processors yet.

In fact, the transition from uniprocessor to multiprocessor continues
unabated in spite of the arguably insufficient expertise to master the latter

© Springer International Publishing Switzerland 2015
J.A. de la Puente and T. Vardanega (Eds.): Ada-Europe 2015, LNCS 9111, pp. 179–195, 2015.
DOI:10.1007/978-3-319-19584-1_12

targets in numerous application domains. Under this scenario, *partitioned approaches* to multiprocessor scheduling offer a gentler slope by allowing the user to break down the problem into smaller uniprocessor sub-problems, on which standard consolidated techniques can still be applied. A known drawback of partitioned approaches is that they must undergo the so called *partitioning phase*: an initial step where the system load is broken down in small units, each fitting into a single processor. Partitioning is an NP-hard problem in the general case [18] and has been proved to waste, in the worst case, half of the platform's processing power [3]. The partitioning of a system is not only a problem of sharing processor resources: it should not disregard the implicit constraints stemming from logical resource sharing throughout the system. Prioritizing on system feasibility may enforce a partitioning where two or more logically-dependent tasks are assigned to different partitions, which complicates inter-task interactions.

The conflicting requirements of feasibility (grouping tasks based on a quantitative value – typically their utilization) and program logic (clustering tasks based on their actual collaborative patterns) can be accommodated by adopting a resource sharing protocol. Also in this respect, however, state-of-the-art uniprocessor resource sharing protocols cannot be directly applied as they cannot handle resources shared by tasks allocated to different partitions. A specific global resource sharing protocol for multiprocessor systems must be used.

Several global resource sharing protocols have been proposed in the literature. Although capable of guaranteeing mutually exclusive accesses to global resources, not all the proposed solutions are fully satisfactory with respect to the induced costs, both as theoretical and runtime overhead. The induced costs vary enormously between uniprocessor and multiprocessor protocols. In the uniprocessor case, when using an optimal resource sharing protocol, such as the Stack Resource Protocol (SRP) [4], the theoretical overhead stems from the priority inversion suffered by tasks, which is bounded by the length of the critical section. In the multiprocessor case, instead, the simple fact that a resource can be contended for in parallel (and not simply concurrently) intrinsically amplifies the effects of priority inversion. Moreover, in partitioned systems, it is necessary to determine a criterion to assign urgency of tasks using or waiting for global resources on different processors: we may want to reduce as much as possible the time a remote task waits for an already locked resource while delaying other tasks not interested in that resource.

These same concepts are recalled by the principle of optimality for resource sharing protocols for global [9] and partitioned systems [11],[7]. When it comes to partitioned systems, optimal solutions exploit ordered queues to avoid starvation while serializing the access to shared resources. A *helping mechanism* is advocated to speed up the release of a resource without hindering unrelated tasks. This mechanism can consist in permitting migration of tasks across partitions[1]: when a task holding a resource is not executing, it migrates to a partition

---

[1] Migration here is determined by the protocol and not due to a general scheduling decision, as in globally scheduled systems.

where there is a task waiting for the same resource and that has the possibility to execute but cannot progress until the task relinquishes the resource.

Contributions. Sometimes elegant theoretical solutions show unexpected drawbacks when evaluated against a realistic implementation as they may unveil viability issues and exhibit untenable runtime overheads. In this paper we focus on the Multiprocessor resource sharing Protocol (MrsP) [11], an optimal multiprocessor resource sharing protocol which explicitly targets partitioned systems. Our goal is to gather evidence that such a protocol can be efficiently implemented in standard RTOS. Specifically, in this work we try to point out difficulties and problems hidden behind the theoretical definition of the protocol and that must be addressed for a reference implementation of MrsP. As a complementary objective, we aim at assessing the protocol with respect to the incurred runtime overhead, so as to understand the induced costs (as compared to not having MrsP) and to obtain sound figures to feed into schedulability tests.

The remainder of this paper is organized as follows: in Section 2 we briefly introduce MrsP and the real-time operating systems (RTOS) on which we implemented and evaluated the effectiveness of the protocol. In Section 3 we point out the main challenges and issues encountered in the implementation of MrsP: we discuss possible design choices and detail on the specific solutions adopted on each RTOS. In Section 4 we assess the runtime overheads and performances of our implementations. Section 5 discusses relevant related works. Finally, in Section 6 we summarize our efforts and outline our future lines of work.

2   Background on MrsP and Target RTOSes

Before delving into the subject matter, we provide first a high-level description of the MrsP protocol and briefly introduce LITMUS^{RT} and RTEMS, the RTOS we used as targets in our implementation and evaluation.

MrsP. MrsP [11] is an optimal resource sharing protocol for multiprocessor systems, explicitly developed with the intent of being fully compatible (analyzable) with the standard response time analysis (RTA) framework, similarly to SRP [4] in single processor systems. The timing effects of the protocol can be simply fed into the RTA iterative equation as an additive factor, whose order of magnitude is proportional to the potential parallel contention incurred by global resources.

The core concept of MrsP is closely inspired by SRP: a resource request triggers a change of priority for the requesting task (to the local ceiling) and the task busy waits until it is granted the resource. Requests are organized (and satisfied) according to a FIFO ordering, as represented in Figure 1. A ceiling is defined within each processor, corresponding to the highest priority among all the tasks that may require access to a resource within the partition. This preserves independence of all tasks with priority higher than the ceiling. In order to contain the waiting time, MrsP provides a helping mechanism to enable a task waiting for a resource already locked by a preempted task on a different partition, to allow the lock holder to progress within its critical section: this way the resource can be relinquished faster and used by the next-in-order task. In [11], two solutions are suggested: (i) if the critical section is stateless, then it is sufficient that one waiting task executes in place of the actual resource holder; (ii) in the more general case, with stateful resources, the resource holder should be allowed to migrate to and then to execute in the partition where there is a task busy-waiting for the same resource.

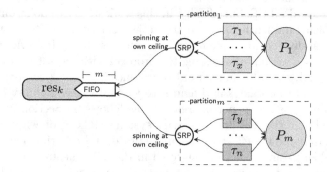

Fig. 1. Visual representation of MrsP

From a theoretical point of view, the contribution of SRP to the RTA equation for a fixed-priority scheduler has been given in [11]. The MrsP algorithm allows each partition to be regarded as a plain uniprocessor system, with the sole exception that the RTA equations need to be updated to account for parallel contention on global resources:

$$R_i = C_i + B_i + \sum_{\tau_j \in lhp(i)} \left\lceil \frac{R_i}{T_j} \right\rceil C_j \qquad (1)$$

where the response time R_i for task τ_i is defined as the sum of three terms. The execution time contribution of τ_i itself (first term), the maximum blocking time induced by SRP, that is determined by the maximum computation time of all resources that are shared between a lower priority task and a task with priority greater or equal to τ_i (second term) and the interference caused by *local* higher priority tasks ($lhp(i)$ in the third term). The worst-case execution time C_i of τ_i can be broken down to explicitly represent the time spent to execute within each resource and the effect of serialization:

$$C_i = WCET_i + \sum_{r^j \in F(\tau_i)} n_i e^j \qquad (2)$$

where n_i represents the number of times τ_i uses r_j (in the set of accessed resources $F(\tau_i)$), and e^j represents the effect of serialization (the cost of executing within the resource for each processor whose tasks may access the global resource). As shown in equation 1, a task can be delayed by lower priority tasks for a total duration of B_i. Since this quantity is bounded by the number of processors m, MrsP can therefore be considered an optimal resource sharing protocol [9] since the maximum blocking incurred by a task is $O(m)$.

LITMUS^{RT}. The LInux Testbed for MUltiprocessor Scheduling in Real-Time system [12], [20], abbreviated as LITMUS^{RT}, is a real-time extension of the Linux kernel, aiming at providing a configurable testbed for the implementation of multiprocessor real-time scheduling policies and locking protocols. The LITMUS^{RT} framework adds an abstraction layer to the execution domain, which provides a set of functionalities and data structures that are compatible with the underlying Linux kernel, regardless of the specific version.

From a scheduling point of view, Linux relies on a list of classes of processes with increasing priority. A specific scheduling policy is associated to each class and a process can execute only if there is no ready process in the higher priority classes. On top of this framework, LITMUS^{RT} adds a scheduling class at the top of the scheduling hierarchy – thus characterized by the highest priority – and provides an interface to implement the scheduling logic. Through such interface, it is possible to define a specific behavior for each scheduling event (dispatch, job release, blocking, etc.) via a set of primitives. LITMUS^{RT} also provides a generic interface for implementing locking protocols (based on primitives as lock, unlock, etc.). The system overrides the primitives of a class with those provided by the given implementation.

RTEMS. The Real-Time Executive for Multiprocessor Systems (RTEMS) [23] is an open-source fully featured RTOS that supports a variety of open standard application programming interfaces (API) and interface standards such as POSIX and BSD sockets. In this work we specifically focus on the symmetric multiprocessor (SMP) support in RTEMS, in particular on its scheduling framework. The SMP scheduling framework is structured as a plugin: a set of operations must be provided (e.g., yield, change priority) that are called from within the implementation of the API (e.g, start task). This plugin-like structure makes it possible to assign different schedulers to distinct processors (or partitions).

A fundamental entity that is replicated on each scheduler is the *scheduler node*. Scheduler nodes are used to build up the sets of scheduled and ready tasks and are used to guide the scheduling decisions: each scheduler node corresponds to a specific task and maintains the task's priority with respect to the scheduler. For this last reason a scheduler node is local to a specific scheduler instance and therefore cannot migrate. A scheduler node can be viewed as a box containing a task, a box residing on a specific shelf (a scheduler instance) with other boxes. If a task must migrate then the content of the box is moved from one box to a box of another scheduler instance.

3   Implementation Issues

As summarized in Section 2, MrsP offers an optimal solution for logical resource sharing in partitioned systems that is fully compatible with the standard uniprocessor response time analysis framework. From a practical standpoint, the desirable properties offered by MrsP builds on the provision of three items: (1) a FIFO ordering of global requests; (2) a busy wait mechanism at ceiling priority (until a task reaches the head of the FIFO queue); and (3) a helping mechanism, to speed up the fulfillment of global requests. These three mechanisms together guarantee a nice bound on the effects of serialization. With respect to their actual implementation, some high-level considerations are provided in [11]. However, the focus in [11] is set on the theoretical traits of MrsP and most implementation-specific details were intentionally omitted. Although the three MrsP requirements are relatively simple to accomplish, the way they are actually implemented could largely affect the performance of the protocol.

In the following sections we discuss the main challenges we faced while implementing those three key mechanisms on top of LITMUS^{RT} and RTEMS, and discuss possible solutions. It is worth noting that among the theoretical helping mechanisms proposed in [11], we decided to stick to the one relying on job migration to support stateful logical resources.

3.1   FIFO Ordering

FIFO ordering for global requests can easily be implemented as an ordered list, either dynamic or static. It is worth noting that MrsP can do with simple fixed-length lists because the maximum length of the FIFO queue is known a-priori, independently from the specific application, as the number of processors available determines the maximum degree of parallelism for the platform. The use of a dynamic list is also a viable option: since each task can participate at most in one FIFO queue, it is possible to statically allocate a node for each task, and then add or remove it from a specific resource list when required.

A more interesting design choice consists in how to organize the FIFO queues in case of nested resources as it may have considerable consequences at run time. With nested resources, as depicted in Figure 2, the helping mechanism will undergo a look-up procedure along several queues to look for an available spinning task to help: clearly, the search space is no more bounded by the length of a single queue. The more intuitive way to combine queues of nested resources is to create a sort of hierarchy (e.g., a tree). The possibility to avoid a deep search is heavily coupled to the busy-waiting technique and the amount of additional information saved in this hierarchy. However, frequent updates to this additional information could end up being even more onerous than sporadic deep searches.

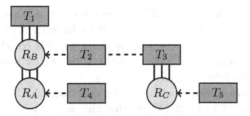

Fig. 2. Scenario with nested resources: the property of being a "task offering help" must be transitive. In this example, task T_5 which is waiting for resource R_C, can help both task T_3, which is directly preventing its execution, *and* task T_1, which is instead doing it indirectly, through R_B. Symmetrically, a helper for T_1 is to be searched within the set of tasks it is directly or indirectly blocking.

RTEMS implementation: the FIFO queues are implemented as dynamic lists where their nodes are created (at system start time) for each task. In case of nested resources these queues naturally form a tree, where all operations performed on resources are bounded by the size of the tree, which could be quite onerous. However, the choice of using the tree finds its motivation in the desire to have a more general structure that could be used to implement several types of semaphores (e.g., using the same structure for both MrsP and OMIP [7]).

LITMUS^{RT} implementation: the FIFO queue is implemented as a list of statically allocated nodes that are dynamically added/removed at need. The current implementation of the protocol does not support nested resources as their implementation would have required a major refactoring of MrsP data structures on LITMUS^{RT}. Anyway, LITMUS^{RT} provides an optimized implementation of binary heaps that may enable low-latency solutions to this problem.

3.2   Busy Waiting

Busy-waiting is commonly associated to *spinning*, for which several implementations are possible [2], [21]. From our standpoint, the most interesting design decision here is related to whether spinning should be used just to delay the task until it becomes the owner of the resource (i.e., the head of the FIFO queue) or it should be used to check whether the task holding the resource is in need of help (i.e., the resource holder is being preempted and no other task has still offered help). In the first scenario, it is possible to organize the spinning mechanism locally to each task, thus minimizing the interference incurred on shared hardware resources (e.g., bus). In the second scenario, instead, the helping mechanism can be made simpler, at the expenses of a global state for all spinning tasks. Since every spinning task must peek the state of the resource holder, this latter approach could lead to higher contention on hardware resources.

It is worth noting that busy-waiting is not strictly necessary to achieve the intent of MrsP: we only need to prevent all tasks with a priority lower than the ceiling of a partition from resuming execution. This could be achieved, for example, also by suspending all lower priority tasks, or by rising the priority of the idle thread to the ceiling level.

RTEMS implementation: busy wait is implemented as a MCS (Mellor-Crummey and Scott) queue-based locks [21] exploiting the memory hierarchy of the platform: spinning is performed on a local flag, easily fitting inside L1 cache (no bus accesses), whose value is updated only once by the remote task that is releasing the resource (just one bus access).

LITMUS^{RT} implementation: in the baseline implementation a global state is shared among all spinning tasks. A waiting task repeatedly polls the semaphore data structure, which causes high contention on the hardware bus.

3.3   Helping Mechanism

The helping mechanism is surely the most challenging part of the protocol as it is expected to interact with the nominal scheduling operations. The very fact that MrsP introduces job migration into a partitioned system introduces unexpected issues and corner cases.

The strict correlation of the helping mechanism with the scheduling primitives stems from the necessity to enforce the invariant of MrsP, stating that an helping mechanism shall be in place whenever the following conditions hold: (i) a resource holder is not executing; (ii) there is at least one task that is spinning while waiting for the same resource. This invariant must be enforced not only when the resource holder is going to be preempted (and therefore it is necessary to look for a candidate available to help it), but at any scheduling decision. In fact, it may be the case that a spinning task is being resumed while both the resource holder and all other spinning tasks are not executing, and in such case the resumed spinning task must be able to help the resource holder. In practice, this means that the spinning task itself must be able to realize that the holding task is not executing nor already being helped (and then help it) or that a super-partes entity (i.e., the scheduler) recognizes the situation and acts accordingly to enforce the MrsP invariant.

Another problem caused by the helping protocol regards job migrations. A freshly migrated task (the resource holder) is coming from a different partition, with a priority that likely has no meaning in the new partition. Moreover, such task must be able to execute in place of the spinning task (i.e., must be able to preempt it). The solution to this issue is strictly related to the scheduling framework of the RTOS. However, as noted by the authors of MrsP, the issue can be easily solved by updating the priority of the migrated task to a level higher than the priority of the spinning task (which must be equal to the ceiling priority of the resource in that partition). This workaround postulates that the priorities used by the tasks in each partition grows by steps of 2 (so that a migrated task will never hinder a higher priority task of that partition).

A third, possibly subtler problem, is raised by the possibility to migrate tasks while enforcing the ceiling priority in each partition. The definition of MrsP states that a task can execute in a partition different from its own only if it has been preempted in its own partition. This means that whenever the partition of the holding task can execute it, the holding task must be executing there. Therefore, if the holding task is being helped and executes in another partition while in its own partition a local scheduling event makes it available to execute, it should be migrated back. However, this can be less efficient than letting the holding task execute where it migrated to. Even in case the task holding the resource does not migrate back to its own partition, it is still fundamental to preserve the ceiling priority property in that partition: no lower priority tasks should be able to execute. A possible solution to this problem consists in blocking all lower priority tasks until the resource holder completes, which, however, would cause a non-strictly-necessary disturbance to the nominal scheduling operation. A more elegant and efficient way to ensure the ceiling priority property is to let a dummy placeholder execute at the priority of the resource holder. Such placeholder can be created to this end, but the idle thread could be used as well. *RTEMS implementation:* all these issues are managed by the built-in scheduler. The helping mechanism is strictly coupled with the procedures that change the scheduler state. A task that is going to be preempted is moved to another partition by the scheduler to enforce the MrsP invariant. Interestingly, the schedulable entity inside RTEMS are the *scheduler nodes*, which are always updated to point to the task that must be executing (e.g., if the resource holder or the spinning task must execute). Hence, whenever a task is resumed, it is not necessary to check for the MrsP invariant since it is already enforced by the operations that update the scheduler nodes (i.e., obtain and release resource, block, unblock).

Scheduler nodes also simplify the management of priorities of migrated tasks: it is not necessary to change the priority of tasks when they migrate. In fact, the priority of the task with respect to the scheduler is maintained inside a scheduler node, and these nodes do not migrate, only their tasks do. A migrated task takes control of a remote scheduler node and automatically uses the priority of that node (which will be the partition-specific ceiling priority of the resource that the task holder is using since the node belongs to a spinning task, waiting for the same resource). Moreover, scheduler nodes are also used by the idle tasks whenever the rightful owner of a node is executing in another partition: in this way the per-partition ceiling is not violated and the holding task is not forced to migrate back as soon as possible.

LITMUS^{RT} implementation: the invariant of MrsP is enforced in LITMUS^{RT} by a combination of scheduling and locking primitives. The migration of a preempted resource owner cannot be performed contextually within the context switch: scheduling primitives cannot directly access the list of tasks waiting on a semaphore since both scheduling structures and semaphores are protected through dedicated spin locks, which cannot be simultaneously acquired. Migrations are handled at the end of the scheduling primitive, where the state of the resource holder is checked: if a partition becomes available and the task is not running, a migration will occur. A partition becomes available when a waiting task is resumed or when the processor of the resource owner becomes idle.

These mechanisms are not sufficient to guarantee the MrsP invariant requiring that a (preempted) task holding a resources makes progress whenever at least a task is running and waiting to access the same resource. This is accomplished within the lock and unlock primitives: within the lock primitive, when a task requires the resource and the resource holder is preempted, the protocol triggers a migration; within the unlock, the state of the next resource holder is checked and, if it is not running, the protocol searches an available partition for the migration. This mechanism reduces both the workload of the waiting tasks and the burden of ensuring the invariant of the protocol is charged to the scheduler. In case of migration, the lock holder inherits a priority level above the ceiling of the new partition (destination) in order to preempt the waiting task and to prevent the execution of lower-priority tasks. To this end, each partition uses a specific data structure to keep track of the highest "active" local ceiling, which is equal to the lowest priority available or to the local ceiling of a resource.

4   Evaluation

In this work we focused on the implementation of MrsP on top of two representative RTOSes to assess the protocol in terms of performance and induced overheads. To this end, we performed two groups of experiments on both platforms: on the one hand, we wanted to measure the explicit cost of the primitives involved in the realization of the resource access protocols; on the other hand, we wanted to evaluate the intrusiveness of MrsP, in terms of the additional overhead incurred simply by having the protocol implemented but not used. To complement our evaluation, we conducted a further experiment specific to RTEMS to assess the variation in the cost incurred by the tree-shaped structure used to represent nested resources, with the increase of the nesting depth. Our experiments were conducted on different platforms and execution stacks, according to the support offered by the respective RTOS. For LITMUS^{RT}, experiments were performed on an Intel Quad Core i7-2670QM, running at 2.2GHz. Each core is equipped with a 64KB L1 and 256KB L2 caches, and all four share a 6MB L3 one. The platform includes an internal bus (100MHz) and a serial bus, 5GT/s. The system execution is supported by a Kernel-based Virtual Machine (KVM), providing direct access to the hardware platform without a virtualization middleware, on top of which the LITMUS^{RT} environment is executed (4 physical processors and 512MB of RAM). For RTEMS, the experiments were performed on a Freescale T4240, a 24-processor PowerPC system with 32KB L1 caches and 2MB L2 caches (where 8 processors share one L2 cache) running at 1667MHz.

4.1   Overhead of MrsP Primitives

A first important metric is the cost of the primitives involved in the use of MrsP resources. Such overhead gives a threshold under which it is not convenient to use the protocol: if the use of the resource is less than the overhead of the protocol, a simple non-preemptive section is a better approach. The overhead we report is by no means an absolute value (since it depends on both the OS and the hardware), but it can give an idea of the general cost of using MrsP resources. Results are summarized in Table 1. All the experiments were performed in the scenario where resources are not nested.

Table 1. Overhead of conceptually similar primitives in RTEMS and LITMUS^{RT}

	RTEMS	LITMUS^{RT}	
obtain	$5,376\ ns$	$8,800\ ns$	lock
release	$5,514\ ns$	$8,500\ ns$	unlock
ask for help	$1,827\ ns$	$35,000\ ns$	finish switch

Results on RTEMS. In RTEMS there are three main procedures in which MrsP performs its work: *obtain resource*, *release resource* and *ask for help*. The experiments are performed incrementing up to 23 the number of tasks that act as rivals on a specific resource (one task per partition). The thread dispatch was intentionally disabled in order to evaluate the cost of the procedure while avoiding the cost of preemptions and migrations.

Obtain resource updates the necessary data structures (e.g., raise the priority of the task to the ceiling) and, if necessary, initializes the MCS lock. The maximum observed value is $5,376\ ns$.

Release resource: it restores the state of the used data structures (e.g., restore the priority to the task) and, if necessary, updates the resource tree to point to the next resource holder. The maximum observed value is $5,514\ ns$.

Ask for help looks inside the resource tree (since there is no nesting, the tree equals a list) and finds a possible spinning task that is available to help. The worst case is met when all 23 threads are queued but no one of them is actually spinning, and its maximum observed value is $1,827\ ns$.

The release resource and help procedures are subjected to variability. In fact, both these procedures need to inspect the resource tree: the bigger it is, the costly the primitive. A valid upper bound for these procedures depends on the available number of processors, that is, the maximum degree of parallelism available.

Results on LITMUS^{RT}. MrsP operates using three LITMUS^{RT} primitives: *resource lock*, *resource unlock* and *finish switch*.

Resource lock manages the ceiling and the FIFO queue in $800\ ns$, when it is necessary to yield the processor to the resource holder it updates the remote partition and perform the migration in $8,000\ ns$, and each spinning cycle costs $500\ ns$ (maximum delay to stop spinning).

Resource unlock restores priorities and releases the resource in $500\ ns$; the operations on remote processors, to migrate back or to migrate the new resource holder in another partition (when necessary) cost $8,000\ ns$.

Finish switch operates under different scenarios to enforce the MrsP invariant. If the lock holder is preempted and there is at least one running task waiting for the resource, the task migrates to that partition. This requires to search for a spinning task and to perform a migration, for a cost of 35, 000 ns. If the resource owner migrated to a remote processor but it is not running any more, then it needs to migrate back. The notify mechanism involved requires 6, 000 ns.

Part of the observed overheads are intrinsic to the implementation of MrsP and they reflect the need to share the data structures of the protocol. The high cost of migrations (an average of 6, 000 ns per migration) is to be attributed to different sources (e.g., the operations that Linux uses to enforce consistency before and after a migration, the internal state of the partitions). Our experiment shows anyhow that in absence of migrations the protocol adds a small overhead: in the average case where no migration is needed to obtain or release a resource, the protocol overhead is less than 1 μs.

4.2   Intrusiveness of MrsP

This second experiment evaluates the net cost of the MrsP framework when no MrsP resources are actually used. The experiment highlights how much the implementation of MrsP must interact with normal scheduling operations.

Results on RTEMS. Figure 3 shows the maximum observed time to perform three of the main procedures used by the FP scheduler in RTEMS while the MrsP protocol is or is not implemented. The simple fact of having available MrsP inside RTEMS even while not using it, causes an overhead (approximately 100 instructions) to the main scheduling procedures. This stems from the need to modify the internals of the scheduler to correctly manage the migration of tasks (in an environment that normally does not permit it) as well as to perform part of the checks required to enforce the MrsP invariant.

Results on LITMUS^{RT}. Figure 4 shows the maximum observed time to perform the main scheduling primitives in the partitioned fixed-priority scheduler (PFP): schedule, job release and finish switch. The experiment reveals that the integration of MrsP has a low impact when not in use, despite the support required by the helping mechanism: the complexity of the Linux kernel far outweighs the operations needed to enforce the MrsP invariant.

4.3   Cost of Supporting Nested Resources

As highlighted in Section 3.1, the implementation of MrsP in RTEMS uses a resource tree. Since the tree grows dynamically and its size is proportional to the number of tasks partaking in the protocol, and since it is scanned in order to find tasks available to help, we performed and experiment to understand how much overhead the use of the tree induces. Each sampled value in Figure 5 represents the maximum time that it takes to look inside a full tree of height x, with no task available to help. Each level of the tree contains 23 tasks.

It comes without surprise that the overhead induced by the inspection of the resource tree is linear to its size. This shows an implementation flaw in the MrsP implementation of RTEMS. Unrelated high priority tasks can suffer from excessive resource nesting of unrelated lower priority tasks. A possible

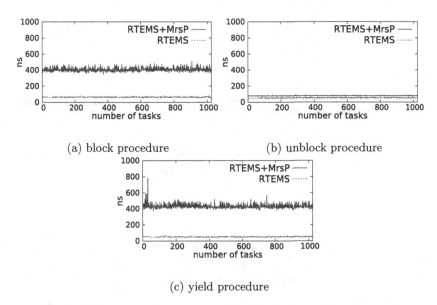

(a) block procedure   (b) unblock procedure

(c) yield procedure

Fig. 3. Max observed behavior of relevant primitives on RTEMS

improvement would be to pre-compute the highest priority tasks available for help in each partition. This would limit the cost of the search by the number of partition in the system. However, the obtain and release operations would be more expensive since such information must be kept updated.

5   Related Work

A large majority of state-of-the-art multiprocessor resource sharing protocols were originally conceived as an extension of well-known uniprocessor techniques to a new scenario where resource accesses can happen in parallel and task priorities (used by ceiling-based protocols) are not comparable when tasks belong to different partitions. Simpler multiprocessor protocols [22], [19] use some kind of *priority boosting* mechanism to speed up the use (and release) of global resources and to reduce the time spent by tasks waiting for remotely locked global resources. Concepts that are very similar to priority boosting are also exploited by more advanced approaches, e.g.,[17], [9], [5]. The main drawback of priority boosting mechanism and its derivatives, however, is that they indiscriminately interfere with all local tasks. A possible solution to this problem has been identified in the use of a *helping mechanism*: a mechanism that lets tasks waiting on a global resource "help" (take care of the execution of) a remote preempted resource holder. A helping mechanism is used, for example, in the Multiprocessor Bandwidth Inheritance Protocol (M-BWI) [15], in the $O(m)$ Independence-preserving Protocol (OMIP) [7] and in the Server Based Locking Protocol (SBLP) [6]. All these approaches, however, do not lend themselves to an easy integration in the classic RTA framework, which instead MrsP does.

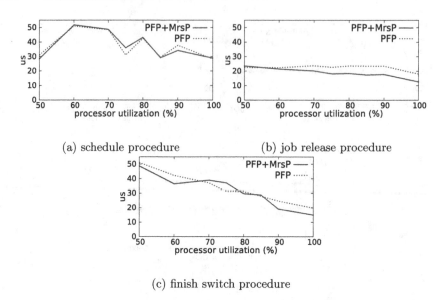

(a) schedule procedure   (b) job release procedure

(c) finish switch procedure

Fig. 4. Max observed behavior of relevant primitives on LITMUS[RT]

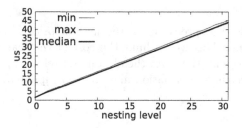

Fig. 5. Overhead induced by traversing the whole resource tree. Each level of the tree has 23 elements: the size of the tree is $(x + 1) * 23$.

To the best of our knowledge, only few works in literature address the problem of implementing and evaluating a multiprocessor resource sharing protocol with a strong emphasis on low-level design and implementation issues. The work in [8] offers two main contributions: an improved analysis to accurately account for the blocking contributions of several multiprocessor resource sharing protocols (MPCP[19], DPCP[22] and FMLP+[5], among others) and an extensive empirical evaluation of such protocols, spanning from their algorithmic comparison to the evaluation of their implementations in LITMUS[RT]. The evaluation is however limited to the *lock* and *unlock* procedures, since the studied protocols make no use of a helping mechanism. Consequently, the induced overhead on other scheduling procedures is almost null. The same work also discusses the algorithmic principles for multiprocessor resource sharing protocols, giving some coarse grained guidelines about queueing resource requests (either FIFO or priority ordered) and the opportunity of executing critical sections through remote agents or locally.

The same protocols have been also evaluated in a previous work [10], whose main goal was to describe their implementation on top of LITMUS^{RT}. A first contribution in [10] consists in the exploration of a number of design issues, arising from practically implementing non-trivial resource sharing protocols. In contrast with our work, such issues are largely related to the provision of an efficient and robust support for resource sharing in LITMUS^{RT} (e.g, where to store the priority for inheritance/ceiling protocols, how to generalize the Linux wait queues to allow ordering elements). The implemented protocols were also compared based on their runtime performances. An important conclusion drawn from the authors is that the algorithmic performance of a multiprocessor resource sharing protocol dominates its runtime performance: the general overhead induced from the *lock* and *unlock* procedures is small compared to the advantages that stem from the determinism that the use of such protocols give.

The work in [16] deals with the construction, implementation and evaluation of M-BWI protocol. Similar to the work in [10], the discussion on the implementation of the M-BWI protocol focuses on explaining the specific solution used by the authors to adapt the protocol inside LITMUS^{RT} without exploring other possible designs, but still exposing (hidden) corner cases that must be addressed to soundly implement the protocol. The evaluation of M-BWI that the authors propose in their work, share similar traits with our work. Similar to our evaluation, they compared the cost of the three main primitives involved in the use of global resources (i.e., *schedule*, *lock* and *unlock*) when (i) the system does not support the protocol, (ii) the system support the protocol but no global resource is used, and (iii) global resources are used. Their results depict the same trend of our implementation of MrsP in LITMUS^{RT}: the overhead induced by the protocol in the scheduling decision, besides the *lock* and *unlock* primitives, is negligible as compared to the cost induced by the Linux kernel primitives.

6   Conclusions

With this work we provide evidence that MrsP can effectively be implemented on standard RTOS. In our implementation effort we identified and addressed some design issues, spanning from the data structures to be used, to the management of particularly subtle corner cases in the scheduling operations. Arguably, these implementation issues were not explicitly in the original formulation of MrsP [11] because they are strictly coupled with the kernel support and structures provided by the specific RTOS.

We also performed some experiments to evaluate the runtime behavior of the protocol. The overheads incurred by our implementation of MrsP are generally acceptable, assuming critical sections of non-negligible length. A limited increase in the execution time of the kernel primitives is compensated by the improvement in the response time of tasks sharing global resources, with no interference on independent tasks [11]. In future work, we are interested in further analyzing the various contributions (in terms of kernel overhead) that MrsP induces at runtime. We are particularly interested in evaluating the costs of job migration. Finally, we aim at taking all the overheads into account within the RTA framework.

References

1. Abella, J., Cazorla, F., Quinones, E., Grasset, A., Yehia, S., Bonnot, P., Gizopoulos, D., Mariani, R., Bernat, G.: Towards improved survivability in safety-critical systems. In: 17th IEEE International On-Line Testing Symposium (IOLTS) (2011)
2. Anderson, T.: The performance of spin lock alternatives for shared-money multiprocessors. IEEE Transactions on Parallel and Distributed Systems (1990)
3. Andersson, B., Jonsson, J.: The utilization bounds of partitioned and pfair static-priority scheduling on multiprocessors are 50%. In: 15th Euromicro Conference on Real-Time Systems (ECRTS) (2003)
4. Baker, T.: A stack-based resource allocation policy for realtime processes. In: 11th IEEE Real-Time Systems Symposium (RTSS) (1990)
5. Block, A., Leontyev, H., Brandenburg, B., Anderson, J.: A flexible real-time locking protocol for multiprocessors. In: 13th IEEE Embedded and Real-Time Computing Systems and Applications (RTCSA) (2007)
6. Bonato, L., Mezzetti, E., Vardanega, T.: Supporting global resource sharing in RUN-scheduled multiprocessor systems. In: 22nd International Conference on Real-Time Networks and Systems (RTNS) (2014)
7. Brandenburg, B.: A fully preemptive multiprocessor semaphore protocol for latency-sensitive real-time applications. In: 25th Euromicro Conference on Real-Time Systems (ECRTS) (2013)
8. Brandenburg, B.: Improved analysis and evaluation of real-time semaphore protocols for P-FP scheduling. In: 19th IEEE Real-Time and Embedded Technology and Applications Symposium, RTAS, pp. 141–152 (2013)
9. Brandenburg, B., Anderson, J.: Optimality results for multiprocessor real-time locking. In: 31st IEEE Real-Time Systems Symposium (RTSS) (2010)
10. Brandenburg, B.B., Anderson, J.H.: An lmplementation of the PCP, SRP, D-PCP, M-PCP, and FMLP real-time synchronization protocols in LITMUS^{RT}. In: 14th IEEE International Conference on Embedded and Real-Time Computing Systems and Applications, RTCSA, pp. 185–194 (2008)
11. Burns, A., Wellings, A.: A schedulability compatible multiprocessor resource sharing protocol - MrsP. In: 25th Euromicro Conference on Real-Time Systems (ECRTS) (2013)
12. Calandrino, J., Leontyev, H., Block, A., Devi, U., Anderson, J.: LITMUS^{RT}: a testbed for empirically comparing real-time multiprocessor schedulers. In: 27th IEEE Real-Time Systems Symposium (RTSS) (2006)
13. Davis, R., Burns, A.: A survey of hard real-time scheduling for multiprocessor systems. ACM Comput. Surv. **43**(4) (2011)
14. Edelin, G.: Embedded systems at THALES: the artemis challenges for an industrial group. In: Invited Talk at the ARTIST Summer School in Europe (2009)
15. Faggioli, D., Lipari, G., Cucinotta, T.: The multiprocessor bandwidth inheritance protocol. In: 22nd Euromicro Conference on Real-Time Systems (ECRTS) (2010)
16. Faggioli, D., Lipari, G., Cucinotta, T.: Analysis and implementation of the multiprocessor bandwidth inheritance protocol. Real-Time Systems **48**(6), 789–825 (2012)
17. Gai, P., Natale, M.D., Lipari, G., Ferrari, A., Gabellini, C., Marceca, P.: A comparison of MPCP and MSRP when sharing resources in the janus multiple-processor on a chip platform. In: 9th IEEE Real-Time and Embedded Technology and Applications Symposium (2003)

18. Garey, M.R., Johnson, D.S.: Computers and Intractability: A Guide to the Theory of NP-Completeness. W. H. Freeman & Co. (1979)
19. Lakshmanan, K., De Niz, D., Rajkumar, R.: Coordinated task scheduling, allocation and synchronization on multiprocessors. In: 30th IEEE Real-Time Systems Symposium (RTSS) (2009)
20. LITMUS^{RT}. http://www.litmus-rt.org/
21. Mellor-Crummey, J.M., Scott, M.L.: Algorithms for scalable synchronization on shared-memory multiprocessors. ACM Transactions on Computer Systems (1991)
22. Rajkumar, R.: Synchronization in Real-Time Systems: A Priority Inheritance Approach. Kluwer Academic Publishers (1991)
23. RTEMS. http://www.rtems.org/

An Execution Model
for Fine-Grained Parallelism in Ada

Luís Miguel Pinho[1(✉)], Brad Moore[2], Stephen Michell[3], and S. Tucker Taft[4]

[1] CISTER/INESC-TEC, ISEP, Polytechnic Institute of Porto, Porto, Portugal
lmp@isep.ipp.pt
[2] General Dynamics, Ottawa, ON, Canada
brad.moore@gdcanada.com
[3] Maurya Software Inc, Ottawa, ON, Canada
stephen.michell@maurya.on.ca
[4] AdaCore, New York, NY, USA
taft@adacore.com

Abstract. This paper extends the authors earlier proposal for providing Ada with support for fine-grained parallelism with an execution model based on the concept of abstract executors, detailing the progress guarantees that these executors must provide and how these can be assured even in the presence of potentially blocking operations. The paper also describes how this execution model can be applied to real-time systems.

1 Introduction

This work is part of an ongoing effort to incorporate fine-grained parallelism models and constructs into existing programming languages, such as CPLEX (for C Parallel Language Extensions) [1], the C++ "Technical Specification for C++ Extensions for Parallelism" [2], or, the topic of this work, the tasklet model for Ada [3,4,5].

The current proposal to extend Ada with a fine-grained parallelism model is based on the notion of tasklets, which are non-schedulable computation units (similar to Cilk [6] or OpenMP [7] tasks). However, in contrast to the C and C++ work, the principle behind this model is that the specification of parallelism is an abstraction that is not fully controlled by the programmer. Instead, parallelism is a notion that is under the control of the compiler and the run-time. The programmer uses special syntax to indicate where parallelism opportunities occur in the code, whilst the compiler and runtime co-operate to provide parallel execution, when possible.

The work in [3] introduced the notion of a Parallelism OPportunity (POP). This is a code fragment or construct that can be executed by processing elements in parallel. This could be a parallel block, parallel iterations of a **for** loop over a structure or container, parallel evaluations of subprogram calls, and so on. That work also introduced the term tasklet to capture the notion of a single execution trace within a POP, which the programmer can express with special syntax, or the compiler can implicitly create.

© Springer International Publishing Switzerland 2015
J.A. de la Puente and T. Vardanega (Eds.): Ada-Europe 2015, LNCS 9111, pp. 196–211, 2015.
DOI: 10.1007/978-3-319-19584-1_13

This model is refined in [4], where each Ada task is seen as an execution graph of execution of multiple control-dependent tasklets using a fork-join model. Tasklets can be spawned by other tasklets (fork), and need to synchronize with the spawning tasklet (join). The concept is that the model allows a complete graph of potential parallel execution to be extracted during the compilation phase. Together with the Global aspects proposed in [5], it is thus possible to manage the mapping of tasklets and data allocation, as well as prevent unprotected parallel access to shared variables. Although not a topic addressed in this paper, the work considers that issues such as data allocation and contention for hardware resources are key challenges for parallel systems, and therefore compilers and tools must have more information on the dependencies between the parallel computations, as well as data, to be able to generate more efficient programs.

Tasklets as defined are orthogonal to Ada tasks and execute within the semantic context of the task from which they have been spawned, whilst inheriting the properties of the task such as identification, priority and deadline. The model also specifies that calls by different tasklets of the same task into the same protected object are treated as different calls resulting in distinct protected actions; therefore synchronization between tasklets could be performed using protected operations (in [5] it was restricted to non-blocking operations)[1].

As tasklets compete for the (finite) execution resources, an execution model is then necessary. This paper provides the specification of the execution behavior of tasklets based on the notion of abstract executors, which carry the actual execution of Ada tasks in the platform. The goal of this abstraction is to provide the ability to specify the progress guarantees that an implementation (compiler and runtime) need to provide to the parallel execution, without constraining how such implementation should be done. This abstraction is then used to demonstrate how tasklet synchronization can be supported using potentially blocking operations.

The paper also shows how the approach can be applied for use in real-time systems (under certain assumptions), and how a finer control of the tasklet execution can be made available to the programmer.

The structure of the paper is as follows. Section 2 provides a short summary of the previously proposed tasklet model for fine-grained parallelization of Ada code. Then, Section 3 proposes the underlying executing model for tasklets, whilst Section 4 shows how this model can be used in real-time systems and mentions some currently open issues. Finally, Section 5 provides some conclusions.

2   The Tasklet Model

This work considers a model where an Ada task is represented as a fork-join Directed Acyclic Graph (DAG) of potentially parallel code block instances (denoted as tasklets). The DAG of a task represents both the set of tasklets of the task, as well as the control-flow dependencies between the executions of the tasklets.

---

[1] Note that this is consistent with the current standard which already supports multiple concurrent calls by a single task in the presence of the asynchronous transfer of control capability [8, section 9.7.4].

An Ada application can consist of several Ada tasks, each of which can be represented conceptually by a DAG. Therefore, an application might contain multiple (potentially data dependent) DAGs. Dependencies between different DAGs relate to data sharing and synchronization between Ada tasks (e.g. using protected objects, suspension objects, atomic variables, etc.).

An Ada task might correspond to several different DAGs, but the actual execution of the task will correspond to only one. Control-flow constructs indicate multiple different paths within the code, each one a different DAG, but during execution a single flow is created.

Within this DAG, a terminology of relation between tasklets is defined, as follows:

The spawning tasklet is referred to as the *parent* tasklet;

The spawned tasklets are referred to as the *children*;

Tasklets spawned by the same tasklet in the same POP are denoted *siblings*;

Ancestor and *descendant* denote the nested hierarchical relationships, since spawned tasklets may themselves spawn new tasklets.

Figure 1 shows code representing the body of execution of an Ada 202X task (according to the syntax proposal in [5]), whilst Figure 2 provides its associated DAG.

```
task body My_Task is
begin
   -- tasklet A, parent of B, C, F and G, ancestor of D and E

   parallel
      -- tasklet B, child of A, parent of D and E
      parallel
         -- D, child of B, descendent of A, sibling of E
      and
         -- E, child of B, descendent of A, sibling of D
      end;
   and
      -- tasklet C, child of A, sibling of B, no relation to D and E
   end;

   -- tasklet A again

   parallel
      -- tasklet F, child of A, no relation to B,C,D and E
   and
      -- tasklet G, child of A, no relation to B,C,D and E
   end;

   -- tasklet A again
end;
```

Fig. 1. Task body example (Ada 202X)

This model of tasklet execution is a *fully strict* fork-join, where new tasklets spawned by the execution of a tasklet are required to complete execution before the spawning tasklet is allowed to complete [2]. Note that this model is mandatory for

---

[2] A *terminally* strict fork join for implicit parallelization is left for future work. This is a model where a spawned tasklet is required to join with one ancestor, but not forcibly the parent.

explicit parallel constructs, such as parallel blocks and parallel loops, where the sibling tasklets are required to complete at the parallel construct "**end**" keyword, before the spawning (parent) tasklet is allowed to continue past this construct.

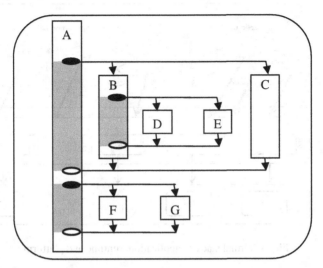

Fig. 2. Task DAG example (rectangles denote tasklets, dark circles fork points, and white circles join points)

In Figure 2, although there is no direct relation between F/G and B/C/D/E, the execution of F and G can actually only start after the completion of the latter. Implicit parallelization by the compiler (as proposed in [5]) introduces additional fork-join points (as if an explicit parallel block was being created). The grey parts within the tasklets A and B represent the fact that the tasklet is waiting for the execution of its children. As discussed later in this paper, this does not imply tasklet (or task) blocking.

3   The Tasklet Execution Model

The proposal of this paper is to define the DAG's execution based on a pool of abstract executors (Figure 3), which are required to serve the execution of tasklets while guaranteeing task *progress*, under certain assumptions.

An *executor* is an entity which is able to carry the execution of code blocks (the notion of an executor entity is common to many systems, and can be traced back to the SunOS lightweight processes [9]). Although we consider that most likely executors would be operating system threads, the definition gives freedom to the implementers to provide other underlying mechanisms to support this model. The justification for this abstraction is that it allows implementations to provide the minimum functionality to execute parallel computation, without requiring the full overhead associated with thread management operation. In an extreme case, an executor can be the core itself, continually executing code blocks placed in a queue.[3]

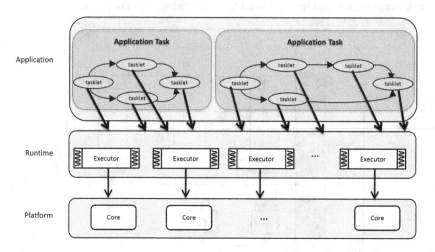

Fig. 3. Virtual stack of application, runtime and platform

The model presumes that the allocation of tasklets to executors, and of executors to cores is left to the implementation. More flexible systems, that are compatible with this model, might decide to implement a dynamic allocation of tasklets to executors, and a flexible scheduling of these in the cores, whilst static approaches might determine an offline-fixed allocation of the tasklets to the executors, and utilize partitioned scheduling approaches for the executors within the cores. Also, in the general case it is left to the implementation whether executor pools are allocated per task or globally to a given dispatching domain or to the entire application.

The model of tasklet execution by the executors is a limited form of run-to-completion, i.e., when a tasklet starts to be executed by one executor, it is executed by this same executor until the tasklet finishes. Limited because the model allows executing tasklets to migrate to a different executor, but only in the case where the tasklet has performed an operation that would require blocking or suspension. It would be too restrictive to force the executor to also block or suspend. Before starting to execute, tasklet migration is unrestricted.

Note that run-to-completion does not mean that the tasklet will execute uninterruptedly or that it will not dynamically change the core where it is being executed, since the executor itself might be scheduled in a preemptive, or quantum-based scheduler, with global or partitioned scheduling.

---

[3] Note that an executor cannot explicitly be an Ada Task, as it was proposed in earlier works [10]. This would defeat the separation between the design model of concurrency around Ada Tasks, and the platform model of parallelism around executors.

3.1   Progress

The progress of a task is defined such that a task progresses if at least one of its tasklets is being executed. Only if all tasklets of a task DAG are not being executed then the task is considered not to be progressing. It might not be blocked, as it might simply be prevented from being executed by other higher priority tasks being executed.

A task is only blocked when all its tasklets are blocked or have self-suspended. Tasklets are considered to be blocked when they are waiting for a resource, which is not an executor nor a core (e.g. executing an entry call) [4].

Considering this, we can identify different progress classes, and use them to define the execution model, rather than the actual implementation [11] (our definition differs from [11] in that we relate progress to tasklet execution and not to thread equivalence). Implementations must guarantee one class of *progress*, as defined below:

> *Immediate progress* – when cores are available, tasklets which are ready to execute can execute to completion in parallel (limited only by the number of free cores);
>
> *Eventual progress* – when cores are available, ready tasklets might need to wait for the availability of an executor, but it is guaranteed that one will become available so that the tasklet will eventually be executed.
>
> *Limited progress* – even if cores are available, ready tasklets might need to wait for the availability of an executor, and the runtime does not guarantee that one will be eventually available. This means a bounded number of executors, which may block when tasklets block.

Immediate progress is the strongest progress model, but it might require the implementation to create new executors, even if this would not be needed for progress. The main difference from immediate to eventual progress, is that in the former, if no executor is available, a new executor needs to be created (the implementation needs to be work-conserving). In the latter, the implementation is allowed some freedom, as long as it guarantees that tasklets will not starve.

Limited progress does not guarantee there will be an executor available. It is defined for the cases where a bounded number of executors needs to be pre-determined, and the implementation is such that executors block when tasklets block. In this case, offline static analysis (considering the actual mapping of the tasklet DAG to the underlying executors' implementation) is needed to guarantee tasklets neither starve nor deadlock.

3.2   Use of Potentially Blocking Operations

The work in [5] left as an open issue whether to support potentially blocking operations within tasklets, limiting parallelism to invoking subprograms where the `Potentially_Blocking` aspect was set to `False`. Nevertheless, although the work considers

---

[4]   There are cases where the compiler is able to guarantee that this blocking is actually bounded (e.g. a delay operation). It may be possible to allow an implementation in this case to consider the tasklet not to be blocked. Nevertheless, in order to be consistent with the Ada standard, these operations are also considered to be potentially blocking [8, section 9.5.1].

the use of locking in a parallel setting as heavily impacting performance, there are reasons to support (but not recommend) the use of protected operations, such as supporting the need to synchronize "stitching" operations where the results of computations of neighboring regions are combined in the proper order. Moreover, parallel tasks themselves might need to wait for data or delay while within parallel constructs. In any case, lock-free approaches [12] such be considered.

The use of blocking synchronization between tasklets introduces further risks of deadlock, which is dependent on the method of tasklet allocation to the underlying executor. For example, the execution of the code in Figure 4 is safe if all iterations are executed in real parallelism, or with some interleaving of iterations, but will deadlock if all iterations of the loop are sequential and executed in order. The code in Figure 5 might appear to be safe for any order of iterations, but in fact it is not safe if the compiler aggregates several iterations in the same tasklet [5]. If, for instance, in a platform with two cores, the compiler generates a DAG of 2 tasklets to execute the loop, both tasklets will call the entry Wait in their first iteration, and will wait there indefinitely.

```
protected Obj is
   entry Wait;
   procedure Release;
private
   Open: Boolean := False;
end Obj;
protected body Obj is
   entry Wait when Open is
   begin
      null;
   end Wait;
   procedure Release is
   begin
      Open := True;
   end Release;
end Obj;

-- ...
begin
   for I in parallel 1..10 loop
      -- Phase 1 Work
      if I < 10 then
         Obj.Wait;
      else
         Obj.Release;
      end if;
      -- Phase 2 Work
   end loop;
end;
```

Fig. 4. Deadlock example

---

[5]   "Chunking" of several iterations in the same tasklet is an optimization which is usually done to reduce the parallelism overhead when each iteration in isolation is computationally small,

```
protected Obj is
  entry Wait;
private
  Open: Boolean := False;
end Obj;
protected body Obj is
  entry Wait when Wait'Count = 10 or Open is
  begin
     Open := True;
  end Wait;
end Obj;

-- ...

begin
  for I in parallel 1..10 loop
     -- Phase 1 Work
     Obj.Wait;
     -- Phase 2 Work
  end loop;
end;
```

Fig. 5. Deadlock example

It is possible for tasklets to synchronize with protected operations (tasklets are the "caller" as specified in the standard [8, section 9.5]), as long as the following conditions are satisfied: (i) the implementation guarantees that all tasklets will eventually be allowed to execute, and (ii) the implementation ensures that the behavior is as if each call to a potentially blocking operation was allocated to a single tasklet.

Condition (i) is satisfied in implementations that provide immediate or eventual progress. In the limited progress model, condition (i) needs to be satisfied by complementing the implementation with offline analysis.

Condition (ii) is satisfied by the compiler that generates an individual tasklet whenever a call could be performed to a potentially blocking operation [8, section 9.5.1] or to a subprogram which has the `Potentially_Blocking` aspect set to `True` (note that according to the rules specified in [5] this is the default value of the aspect). As tasklets can be logical entities only, implementations may provide other means to guarantee (ii), as long as the behavior is equivalent.

3.3 Implementation Issues

The model does not stipulate how an implementation provides these guarantees. Nevertheless, this section discusses a few usage approaches, knowing that experience of use may lead to more efficient mechanisms to implement the model.

The implementation may allocate multiple tasklets to the same executor, allowing these tasklets to be executed sequentially by the executor (under a run-to-completion model). As soon as a tasklet starts to be executed by a specific executor it continues to be executed by this executor, until it completes, or blocks. It is nevertheless possible that tasklets that are ready and that have not yet begun execution (but queued for one executor), to be re-allocated (e.g. with work-stealing [13]) to a different executor.

In the general case it is implementation defined whether or not a tasklet, when it blocks, releases the executor. The implementation may also block the executor, creating a new executor, if needed, to serve other tasklets and guarantee the progress of the task, or it may queue the tasklet for later resumption (in the same or different executor). In the latter case, the implementation releases the executor to execute other tasklets but maintain the state of the blocked tasklet in the executor, for later resumption.

In the immediate and eventual progress models, the implementation must allow a blocked tasklet to resume execution, either by allocating it to an existing or new executor as soon as the tasklet is released, or by resuming it in the original executor (if it is available). In the case of resuming in a different executor than the one that started the computation, the implementation must guarantee that any tasklet-specific state that is saved by the executor is migrated to the new executor.

Note that when a tasklet needs to join with its children (wait for the completion of its children), it is not considered to be blocked, as long as one of its children is executing (forward-progressing). Regardless of the implementation, the executor that was executing the parent tasklet may suspend it and execute one or more of its children, only returning to the parent tasklet when all children have completed.

Note that in a fork-join model it is always safe to suspend a parent tasklet when it forks children, releasing the executor to execute the children tasklets, and resuming the parent tasklet in the same executor when all children tasklets have completed (since the parent can only resume once the children complete). It might happen that other executors take some of the children tasklets. In that case, it might happen that the executor that was executing the parent finishes the execution of children tasklets while other executors are still executing other children of the same parent. In this case, the parent needs to wait for other children tasklets still being executed in other executors, and the implementation may spin, block or suspend the executor, or release it to execute other unrelated tasklets (as described above).

Implementations may also use some form of parent-stealing [13]. In this case, the suspended parent tasklet might be reallocated to a different executor, or its continuation might be represented by a different tasklet. As before, the implementation must guarantee that tasklet-specific state is also migrated.

3.4　Tasklets and Protected Actions

When executing in protected actions, it is possible to allow tasklets to spawn new tasklets, if we are able to guarantee that deadlock will not arise from different executors accessing the same locks.

This is possible if: (i) the executor that is executing the parent tasklet (which owns the lock of the protected action) is only allowed to execute children tasklets, suspending or spinning if none are available for execution (this guarantees that the same executor will not acquire another non-nested lock); and (ii) fully-strict fork-join is used thus all nested children tasklets need to join with the ancestor that entered the protected action, before it leaves the protected action; and (iii) executors for children tasklets inherit the lock from the executor executing the parent, and do not acquire it again.

Note that protected operations are supposed to be very short. The time needed to spawn tasklets might exceed the recommended time inside a protected operation.

3.5   Use of Atomics and Programmer Specific Synchronization

If the programmer uses atomic variables or some specific synchronization code outside of the Ada synchronization features, then no guarantees can be provided as is the case for the use of these mechanisms in the presence of concurrent Ada tasks.

4   Real-Time

4.1   Model

We propose a model of real-time parallel programming where real-time tasks map one-to-one with Ada tasks. The execution of the Ada task generates a (potentially recurrent) DAG of tasklets, running on a shared memory multiprocessor. [6]

The use of enhanced parallel programming models such as this one proposed for Ada, will allow for the compiler (with optional parameters/annotations provided by the programmer) to generate the task graphs (similar to the Parallel Control Flow Graphs [14]) which can be used to perform the required schedulability analysis [15].

As specified in the model [4] and presented in the introduction, tasklets run at the priority (and/or with the deadline) of the associated task. We consider that each Ada task (or priority) is provided with a specific executor pool, where all executors carry the same priority and deadline of the task and share the same budget and quantum. Tasklets run-to-completion in the same executor where they have started execution, although the executor can be preempted by higher-priority (or nearer deadline) executors, or even the same priority/deadline if the task's budget/quantum is exhausted.

The executors and the underlying runtime guarantee progress as defined in section 3, and if only limited progress is available, offline analysis is able to determine the minimum number of executors required for each task.

Each task, and therefore its DAG of tasklets, execute within the same dispatching domain [8, section D.16.1]. A dispatching domain is a subset of the processors that is scheduled independently from all other processors. Henceforth we focus on a single

---

[6] We recognize that it is difficult if not impossible to scale shared memory to hundreds or thousands of cores. One possibility is to address scalability through clustering, where cores are divided into shared memory clusters (current architectures use 4/8/16 cores per cluster), with clusters communicating through a network on chip. Scalability is dependent on data placement: if the problem is such that the compiler can partition the data into the local memory of each core, the number of cores can actually increase. The communication can be explicit or transparent (depending on design decisions, and the availability of tools to partition the data set and create the required communication patterns).

dispatching domain, and when we talk of *global* scheduling we mean that the (on-line) scheduling (dispatching) algorithm allows any given tasklet of a task to be scheduled on any processor within the task's dispatching domain, while fully *partitioned* scheduling means that the on-line scheduling algorithm relies on tasklets being pre-assigned to individual processors by some off-line analysis. We also can consider intermediary strategies where some tasklet migration is permitted, but not necessarily sufficient to ensure an absence of priority inversion within the domain. We consider part of being a *global* scheduling approach that there is no priority inversion within the domain: at any given time, there is never a tasklet running on a processor in the dispatching domain if there are tasklets of tasks with a higher priority (or earlier deadline) awaiting execution.

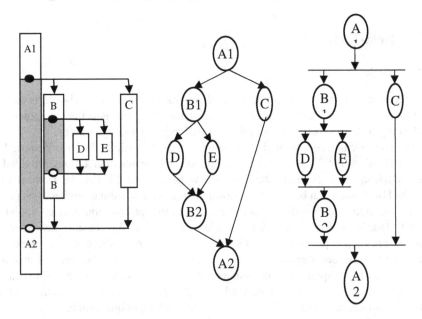

Fig. 6. Mapping of tasklet DAG (left) to a general DAG (middle) and synchronous fork-join (right)

This model allows for the tasklet DAG to be converted (Figure 6) to a DAG of sub-tasks (Figure 6 middle) as commonly used in the real-time systems domain [16, 17, 18]. Response-time analysis techniques can also be used [19, 20] (restricted to non-nested tasklets), as the tasklet model is actually more restricted than the general real-time DAG model, as it considers a fully-strict fork-join, thus a synchronous model can be used [18] (Figure 6 right).

It is important to note that the challenges of providing high-reliability systems with real-time guarantees in the presence of parallelized execution are still far from being solved. When the number of processors increases, it is no longer possible to separate schedulability and timing analyses. Execution time is highly dependent on the interference on accessing hardware resources (e.g. memory) from other parallel tasks, which is dependent on how these are mapped and scheduled. The analysis becomes potentially unfeasible or extreme pessimism must be incorporated.

The work in this paper recognizes this challenge. The path of the work is to allow the compiler, static tools and the underlying runtime to derive statically known tasklet graphs and use this knowledge to guide the mapping and scheduling of parallel computation, reducing the contention at the hardware level. Co-scheduling of communication and computation [21] can further remove contention, and requires knowledge from the application structure. But with the increased complexity and non-determinism of processors, it is not easy to recognize a solution in the near future.

For less time-critical firm real-time systems, the model allows for more flexible implementations, using less pessimistic execution time estimates (e.g. measurement-based), and work-conserving scheduling approaches.

We note finally that, as described in section 2, an Ada task might potentially generate several different DAGs (actual execution will only generate one), and therefore the offline schedulability analysis needs to take into consideration all potential DAGs. Works that consider the general workload of a graph can still be used, by taking the maximum workload and critical path length among all the potential graphs (with a less optimal result), or approaches that use a single tighter worst-case graph can be considered [22], which allow one to reduce the complexity of the interference analysis.

4.2   Blocking Issues and Real-Time

Common real-time models assume that tasks execute an infinite number of iterations of the same code (each iteration being called a *job*), with each release of the code being performed with specific time intervals (cyclic or periodic tasks), or triggered by an event (aperiodic or sporadic). It is also common that blocking (or voluntary-suspension) is not allowed inside the iteration of the loop. Blocking calls (such as delay-until or entry calls) are only allowed at each iteration start, to suspend the task until release.

For such cases, parallel execution should follow the same rules as sequential, and parallel code should not block or self-suspend during execution. However, as shown in section 3, the notion of blocking in the parallel model is not as straightforward as in sequential. In particular, calling a closed entry, which blocks a task in a sequential setting, might not block the task in a parallel setting if the call is executed in the context of a tasklet when other tasklets of the same task are progressing in parallel.

Another issue is that spawning tasklets might cause the executor of the parent tasklet to need to wait for some of its children tasklets to finish before being able to proceed. Although this is not considered blocking (see section 3), it is nevertheless a voluntary suspension of execution.

Therefore, in order to simplify, we propose that for these systems, the following additional rules apply: (i) potentially blocking operations are not allowed when executing in a potentially parallel setting (i.e. if more than one tasklet exists); and (ii) an executor that spawns children tasklets, such as in a parallel block, or loop, is required to execute children tasklets, if available, or spin as if executing the parent tasklet.

4.3 How to Control Parallelization

For the general case, the compiler is assumed to have the ability to make the best decisions on how to manage the parallelism associated with each POP. For real-time systems however, it may be necessary to allow the programmer to have more control of the parallelism, since the analysis might need to consider how the parallelism is implemented in greater detail. Certain types of analysis might not work well with the default choices made by the compiler, but by giving more control to the programmer, the programmer can guide the compiler to produce an implementation that supports the best available analysis methods, in particular for more restricted models.

Table 1 summarizes a set of controls for the programmer to fine tune the parallelism, and control its implementation, while Figure 7 presents examples of their use.

Table 1. Parallelism Controls

Control	Interpretation	Typical Specification
`Executors` aspect of task or task type	Restricts number of executors for task or task type, unless Unbounded is specified	Number of cores plus number of tasklets that might undergo unbounded blocking
`Max_Executors` parameter for dispatching domain `Create` operation	Restricts total number of executors that may be allocated to the domain; sum of `Executors` aspects must not exceed this value	Sum of `Executors` aspects for tasks in domain
`Potentially_Unbounded_Blocking` aspect of subprogram	When False, disallows untimed, unconditional entry calls; defaults to same value as Potentially_Blocking aspect	Specifying False allows a tasklet to perform delays but not potentially unbounded entry calls.
`No_Executor_Migration` restriction	Disallows executor migration from one processor to the next during its execution	Can be specified in a Restrictions pragma to restrict scheduling mechanisms
`Tasklet_Count` aspect of a discrete subtype, an array type, an iterator type, or an iterable container type	Limits number of tasklets that may be spawned in a single iteration	Typically the number of processors, or the number of executors for the enclosing task.
`No_Implicit_Parallelism` restriction	Restricts the compiler from inserting parallelism at places not explicitly identified as **parallel**	Can be specified in a Restrictions pragma to ensure tasklets are only spawned at programmer-defined points
`No_Nested_Parallelism` restriction	Restricts the programmer from using nested explicitly **parallel** constructs, and disallows the compiler from implicitly inserting such constructs	Can be specified in a Restrictions pragma to ensure tasklet DAGs remain one-level structures, to simplify analysis

```
task My_Task with Executors => 4;

function Create (First, Last   : CPU;
                 Max_Executors : Natural) return Dispatching_Domain;
...
My_Domain : Dispatching_Domain := Create (1, 4, Max_Executors => 8);

procedure P with Potentially_Blocking => True,
                 Potentially_Unbounded_Blocking => False;

subtype Loop_Iterator is Natural range 1 .. 1000
   with Tasklet_Count => 10;
...
for I in parallel Loop_Iterator loop
   Array (I) := Array (I) + I;
end loop;

pragma Restrictions (No_Implicit_Parallelism, No_Nested_Parallelism);
```

Fig. 7. Examples of Parallelism Controls

4.4   Other Real-Time Issues

4.4.1   Mixed Priorities and Per-Task Deadlines

There are approaches that require setting different priorities/deadlines for parallel computation (e.g. some decomposition methods [18]), but the model considers all tasklets to inherit the priority/deadline of the Ada task that contains the POP. It both simplifies the creation and scheduling of tasklets (all tasklets share all attributes of the parent task, including ID and priority), and allow for priority and deadline to represent the relative urgency of the job executing. If priority/deadline boosting is required, it is only the executor that is actually affected that will have this change.

4.4.2   Changing Task Priority and Other Task Attributes

Under the rules proposed above, when a tasklet in a DAG executes Set_Priority, it is the base priority of the parent task and all tasklets of that task currently executing that are changed. Under Ada rules [8, section D.5.1], this change happens as soon as the task is outside a protected action. Care should be taken that calls to change a priority or deadline are executed by only a single tasklet, and ideally when it is the only active tasklet. It is likely an error to let multiple tasklets change the priority or deadline, especially if with different values. The same applies to changing other task attributes.

4.4.3   Timing Events

A timing event [8, section D.15] is handled by a protected object, with a protected procedure called if the event occurs, and a protected procedure or entry used to handle the event. Care is needed to ensure that the presence of multiple tasklets does not result in multiple event creations, nor in multiple tasklets attempting to handle the same event.

4.4.4 Execution Time Timers

Execution time timers measure the amount of time that a single task (or group of tasks or interrupt routine) uses and notifies a handler if that time is exceeded. Under our proposal, the execution of a tasklet is reflected in the budget of its task. The overhead of managing the parallel update of the budget may make this unfeasible, except if larger quanta are used or budget updates are not immediate (which may lead to accuracy errors). Specific per core quanta may be used to address this issue.

5 Conclusion

This paper presented an execution model for the execution of tasklet graphs (previously proposed for fine-grained parallelism in Ada), based on the abstract notion of executors, which allows reasoning about the execution model in terms of progress guarantees, rather than on the actual implementation. The paper also shows how this model can be used for real-time systems, complementing the model with a proposal for mechanisms the programmer can use to explicitly specify the parallel behavior.

Although no implementation exists of the complete proposal, parallelism only makes sense to provide faster computation. This work brings to the Ada world models which are widely used in other fine-grained parallelization approaches, where for the general case efficient solutions exist. For the case of real-time systems, addressing parallelism is still a challenge, and more research and experimentation is needed.

Acknowledgements. The authors would like to thank Ted Baker and the anonymous reviewers for the valuable comments and suggestions. This work was partially supported by General Dynamics, Canada, the Portuguese National Funds through FCT (Portuguese Foundation for Science and Technology) and by ERDF (European Regional Development Fund) through COMPETE (Operational Programme 'Thematic Factors of Competitiveness'), within project FCOMP-01-0124-FEDER-037281 (CISTER) and ref. FCOMP-01-0124-FEDER-020447 (REGAIN); by FCT and EU ARTEMIS JU, within project ARTEMIS/0001/2013, JU grant nr. 621429 (EMC2), and European Union Seventh Framework Programme (FP7/2007-2013) grant agreement n° 611016 (P-SOCRATES).

References

1. CPLEX, C Parallel Language EXtensions study group. http://www.open-std.org/mailman/listinfo/cplex (last accessed March 2015)
2. Working Draft: Technical Specification for C++ Extensions for Parallelism. http://www.open-std.org/jtc1/sc22/wg21/docs/papers/2014/n3960.pdf (last accessed March 2015)
3. Michell, S., Moore, B., Pinho, L.M.: Tasklettes – a fine grained parallelism for Ada on multicores. In: Keller, H.B., Plödereder, E., Dencker, P., Klenk, H. (eds.) Ada-Europe 2013. LNCS, vol. 7896, pp. 17–34. Springer, Heidelberg (2013)
4. Pinho, L.M., Moore, B., Michell, S.: Parallelism in Ada: status and prospects. In: George, L., Vardanega, T. (eds.) Ada-Europe 2014. LNCS, vol. 8454, pp. 91–106. Springer, Heidelberg (2014)

5. Taft, T., Moore, B., Pinho, L.M., Michell, S.: Safe parallel programming in Ada with language extensions. In: High-Integrity Language Technologies Conference (October 2014)
6. Intel Corporation: Cilk Plus. https://software.intel.com/en-us/intel-cilk-plus (last accessed March 2015)
7. OpenMP Architecture Review Board: OpenMP Application Program Interface, Version 4.0, July 2013
8. ISO IEC 8652:2012. Programming Languages and their Environments – Programming Language Ada. International Standards Organization, Geneva, Switzerland (2012)
9. Eykholt, J., Kleiman, S., Barton, S., Faulkner, R., Shivalingiah, A., Smith, M., Stein, D., Voll, J., Weeks, M., Williams, D.: Beyond multiprocessing: multithreading the SunOS kernel. In: Proceedings of the Summer USENIX Conference (June 1992)
10. Moore, B., Michell, S., Pinho, L.M.: Parallelism in Ada: general model and ravenscar. In: 16th International Real-Time Ada Workshop (April 2013)
11. Riegel, T.: Light-Weight Execution Agents (October 2014). http://www.open-std.org/jtc1/sc22/wg21/docs/papers/2014/n4156.pdf (last accessed March 2015)
12. Bosch, G.: Lock-free protected types for real-time Ada. In: 16th International Real-Time Ada Workshop (April 2013)
13. Blumofe, R.D., Leiserson, C.E.: Scheduling multithreaded computations by work stealing. J. ACM **46**, 720–748 (1999)
14. Huang, L., Eachempati, D., Hervey, M.W., Chapman, B.: Extending Global Optimizations in the OpenUH Compiler for OpenMP. Open64 Workshop at CGO (2008)
15. Pinho, L.M., Quiñones, E., Bertogna, M., Marongiu, A., Carlos, J., Scordino, C., Ramponi, M.: P-SOCRATES: a parallel software framework for time-critical many-core systems. In: Euromicro Conference on Digital System Design (August 2014)
16. Baruah, S.: Improved multiprocessor global schedulability analysis of sporadic DAG task systems. In: 26th Euromicro Conference on Real-Time Systems (July 2014)
17. Li, J., Chen, J.J., Agrawal, K., Lu, C., Gill, C., Saifullah, A.: Analysis of federated and global scheduling for parallel real-time tasks. In: 26th Euromicro Conference on Real-Time Systems (July 2014)
18. Saifullah, A., Li, J., Agrawal, K., Lu, C., Gill, C.: Multi-core real-time scheduling for generalized parallel task models. Real-Time Systems, **49**(4) (July 2013)
19. Maia, C., Bertogna, M., Nogueira, L., Pinho, L.M.: Response-time analysis of synchronous parallel tasks in multiprocessor systems. In: 22nd International Conference on Real-Time Networks and Systems (October 2014)
20. Axer, P., Quinton, S., Neukirchner, M., Ernst, R., Dobel, B., Hartig, H.: Response-time analysis of parallel fork-join workloads with real-time constraints. In: 25th Euromicro Conference on Real-Time Systems (July 2013)
21. Pellizzoni, R., Betti, E., Bak, S., Yao, G., Criswell, J., Caccamo, M., Kegley, R.: A predictable execution model for COTS-based embedded systems. In: 17th IEEE Real-Time and Embedded Technology and Applications Symposium (April 2011)
22. Fonseca, J., Nélis, V., Raravi, G., Pinho, L.M.: A multi-DAG model for real-time parallel applications with conditional execution. In: 30th ACM Symposium on Applied Computing (April 2015)

AFDX Emulator for an ARINC-Based Training Platform

Jesús Fernández, Héctor Pérez, J. Javier Gutiérrez[✉],
and Michael González Harbour

Software Engineering and Real-Time Group, Universidad de Cantabria,
39005 Santander, Spain
{fsainzj,perezh,gutierjj,mgh}@unican.es
http://www.istr.unican.es/

Abstract. AFDX (Avionics Full Duplex Switched Ethernet) is a standard communication network for avionics based on Ethernet links and special-purpose switches. This paper proposes an AFDX emulator based on standard Ethernet hardware (cards and switches) to build a low cost AFDX network for training or basic research purposes. We also propose the integration of the emulator within an ARINC-653 platform to allow the development of real-time Ada applications. Finally, a performance evaluation has been done in order to show the usability of the emulator.

Keywords: AFDX network · Distributed systems · Partitioned systems · Real-time · Ada applications · Education

1 Introduction

The partitioning paradigm is becoming very popular in the development of high-integrity or safety-critical systems as an evolution of the cyclic executive traditionally used in this kind of systems. Different domains such as aerospace, avionics or automotive are currently using this paradigm in which an operating system or other hardware abstraction layer (e.g., a hypervisor) provides a set of protected time windows arranged in partitions, which also ensure memory isolation. Each partition contains one or more time windows that define the intervals during which the application allocated to that partition may execute. This time and space isolation allows applications to be certified separately, even if they have been developed by different companies. An example of partitioned system can be found in ARINC-653 [1], a standard for avionics that defines the interface of a partition-based operating system allowing multiple applications to execute in the same hardware platform, while maintaining time and space isolation among them.

This work has been funded in part by the Spanish Government and FEDER funds under grant number TIN2011-28567-C03-02 (HI-PARTES).

J.A. de la Puente and T. Vardanega (Eds.): Ada-Europe 2015, LNCS 9111, pp. 212–227, 2015.
DOI: 10.1007/978-3-319-19584-1_14

Distributed systems based on ARINC-653 partitions can be built by interconnecting two or more single core or multicore partitioned systems through special purpose networks. AFDX (Avionics Full Duplex Switched Ethernet) is the communication network defined for ARINC systems as the ARINC-664, Part 7 standard [2]. It is based on the use of point-to-point full-duplex Ethernet links and special-purpose switches in which the routing of messages is preconfigured so that the discovery of routing addresses through network protocols does not interfere with the transmission of application messages.

Working with AFDX networks requires special purpose hardware at a very high cost that can be paid by companies developing real applications, but that is prohibitive for small or medium size research groups or academics that want to introduce this technology in their respective environments for research or teaching. Thus, this paper proposes the development of an open source AFDX emulator implemented in Ada and based on standard Ethernet hardware with the objective of enabling a low cost access to ARINC technology for training or proof of concepts purposes. To this end, we also propose the integration of the AFDX emulator into an ARINC platform based on GPL software: XtratuM [3] as a hypervisor providing the ARINC-653 interface and partitioning, and MaRTE OS [4] as a real-time operating system allowing the development of partitions written in Ada.

The document is organized as follows. Section 2 presents the motivation of this research along with related work. In Section 3, the AFDX network is introduced and its relevant characteristics are described. The design of our proposal for the AFDX emulator is presented in Section 4. Section 5 deals with the implementation details of the emulator. The integration of the proposed emulator within an ARINC-based platform is described in Section 6. Section 7 presents some overhead and performance estimations. Finally, Section 8 draws the conclusions.

2   Motivation and Related Work

Since the publication of the AFDX standard [2] a lot of research works have appeared mostly related to the calculation of the latency in the network by proposing techniques based on the application of Network Calculus [5][6], the Trajectory Approach [7][8], or response time analysis [9]. Other research works, such as the ones in [10][11], propose changes to the current AFDX standard in order to reduce latencies. However, contrary than in the analysis of tasks in processors, it is not common that theoretical latency calculations in the AFDX network were compared with real measurements on AFDX hardware, mainly due to cost reasons. Thus, having an AFDX emulator based on standard Ethernet hardware could allow low cost experiments and obtaining some quantitative results, which are interesting even if they lack absolute precision. Assuming that the emulator is integrated in a partitioned platform it could also be useful for education purposes, allowing students to be trained in the development of partitioned distributed systems.

To the best of our knowledge, there are few works related to AFDX simulators or emulators. The work in [12] presents an AFDX network simulation based on NS2

(Network Simulation 2), where both the end system and the switch are simulated. Similarly, the work in [13] also simulates the end systems and the switch based on QNAP2 (Queuing Network Analysis Package), which has specific facilities for building, handling and solving queuing network models. Another work [14] uses a component-based design methodology to simulate the behavior of the network, and proposes a stochastic abstraction that allows simplifying the complexity of the verification process by providing quantitative information on the protocol. The work in [15] presents an implementation of the AFDX network up to the MAC layer for OMNET++, a component-based C++ simulation library and framework for building network simulators. All these works are based on a complete simulation of the network without the use of real communication hardware. On the other hand, there are specialized options to emulate part of the equipment connected to an AFDX network for testing purposes [16].

In our proposal, we emulate the whole AFDX network. The behavior in the end system is emulated over a standard Ethernet card, and we also use a standard Ethernet switch with traffic prioritizing features [17]. The use of real hardware is interesting for educational purposes and makes it possible to integrate the emulator with a real ARINC-653 platform.

3   An Introduction to the AFDX Network

The usual way for applications to exchange messages in AFDX is through the communication ports defined in the ARINC-653 standard [1], which in turn are connected to AFDX ports [2]. There are two different types of ports: sampling or queuing. From the transmission point of view, there is no difference in the management of both types. The generated messages are directly queued in the corresponding transmission buffer. For message reception, the behavior of these ports is different:

- *Sampling Port*: the incoming message overwrites the current message stored in the buffer. This kind of port is limited to single-packet messages.
- *Queuing Port*: the incoming message is appended to a FIFO queue. This kind of port is required to manage at least 8Kbytes of data and allows messages to be fragmented into several packets, so a fragmentation service may be needed.

The ARINC-653 API includes operations to send or receive messages to or from these communication ports. The messages are driven through the AFDX network by using a transport stack based on the UDP/IP protocol, and they might be fragmented into packets according to traffic regulation parameters. AFDX sends the packets through two redundant networks at the same time. The redundancy management is made by specific Ethernet hardware at both ends, transmission or reception.

Traffic regulation is made via *Virtual Links* (VL), which are defined as objects to establish a logical unidirectional connection from one source end system to one or more destination end systems crossing one or more AFDX switches. Each VL has a dedicated maximum bandwidth that is characterized by two parameters:

- *Lmax*: the largest Ethernet frame, which is a value in bytes. Since message fragmentation is not allowed for sampling ports, this parameter should be adjusted to accommodate the complete message in that case.
- *BAG*: the Bandwidth Allocation Gap, which is a power of 2 value in the range [1,128] ms. The BAG represents a minimum interval in milliseconds between Ethernet frames transmitted on the VL.

Each VL has a dedicated FIFO queue for all the fragmented packets to be transmitted through it with the appropriate bandwidth. In a partitioned system using ARINC-653, several AFDX ports can share the same VL to transmit their packets as long as they belong to the same partition, as shown in Fig. 1.

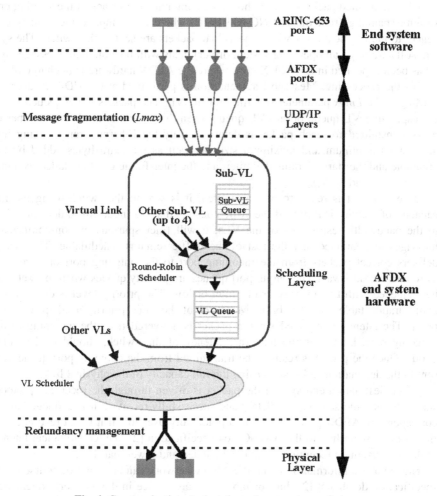

Fig. 1. Communication stack at the end system transmission

The VL scheduler is in charge of selecting the next packet to be transmitted according to the allocated bandwidth for each VL. This scheduler selects the first packet from a VL queue with packets ready to be transmitted. When several VLs are ready to transmit then they are selected in turns until all of their messages have been transmitted. This choice introduces jitter for the transmission over any of the VLs, which is bounded by a maximum value of 500 µs at the output of the end system according to the standard [2]. The way to calculate this jitter for a sending end system is also defined by the standard, along with limiting cases to mathematically treat the allowed latency in the end system transmission.

A VL can optionally have up to four *Sub-Virtual Links* (sub-VLs), all of them having a dedicated FIFO queue which is read by the VL scheduler on a round-robin basis over IP fragmented packets. Fig. 1 shows the communication stack at the sending end system, spanning from the ARINC-653 ports, where the complete message is managed, to the physical layer where individual packets are sent to the switch. The system software (e.g., an operating system driver) deals with the complete message until it has been deposited in the AFDX port, where the AFDX hardware is in charge of the rest of the processing. Message fragmentation is performed at the UDP/IP layer according to the *Lmax* parameter specified for the VL. The packets are enqueued in the corresponding VL queue or sub-VL queue when this option is used. The number of bytes transmitted for each packet is determined by the Ethernet frame, taking into account its minimum and maximum sizes as well as the extra bytes added by the preamble and the start of frame delimiter, and the inter-frame gap (a detailed explanation can be found in [9]).

Once a packet is ready to be transmitted, it is sent to the switch using the full capacity of the physical link. If the switch detects that the input traffic does not obey to the bandwidth restrictions of the VLs, it will filter spurious or non-conformant messages to guarantee that the rest of the traffic remains schedulable. The switch delivers correct packets from the incoming port to the outgoing port or ports in a store-and-forward way. The output port queues are priority queues where packets can be enqueued with two priority levels, high or low. The priority level is defined in a configuration table on a VL basis. Messages of the same priority are kept in FIFO order. The latency introduced when a packet is delivered from the incoming to the outgoing port, known as the hardware latency of the switch, should be less than 100µs. Once the packet is ready to be transmitted from the outgoing port queue, it is sent to the destination end system using the full capacity of the physical link.

At the destination end system the packet is driven through the reception protocol stack. When a message is completely and successfully received, it is enqueued at the corresponding AFDX port, which could potentially overflow if it is not read at a sufficient rate. According to the ARINC-664 specification [2], the technological latency of the end system in reception should be bounded and lower than 150µs.

The complete information about the AFDX network can be found of course in the specification document [2], but for those who are novice in this network, interesting details can be found in the tutorial in [18].

4   Design of the AFDX Emulator

In the design of the emulator we assume that the bandwidth restrictions in the switch are obeyed, so no message filtering is needed and non-conformant traffic is not considered, assuming a correct operation of all the end systems. Thus, the frames are time spaced by the BAG of their respective VL and sent in the right order. This assumption is reasonable in our emulated environment, as the end systems are real-time platforms where the timing requirements can be guaranteed.

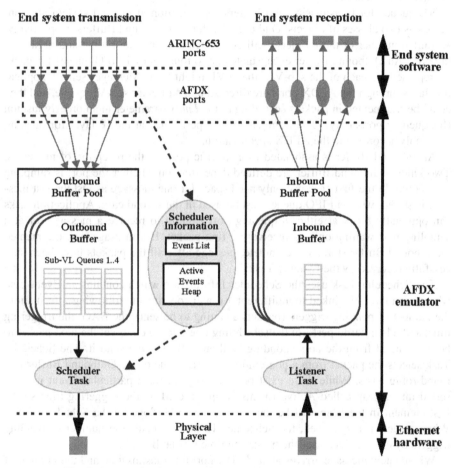

Fig. 2. Communication stack of the AFDX emulator at the end system

We also assume that the switch shall be compatible with the IEEE 802.1p protocol [17] in order to guarantee traffic prioritization, and that it shall provide static routing so that non-conformant traffic, such as ARP requests, is minimized. Prioritization of VLs can be set in two ways: at the end system level by specifying the priority when the VL is created; or by configuring the switch associating each UDP destination port with the priority queue to be used at the outgoing port (this latter option is closer to real AFDX behavior). Furthermore, no network redundancy is used and the emulator will be only able to deliver messages from one VL to one end system, so multicast operations are not supported.

The architecture of the AFDX emulator in relation with the end system is depicted in Fig. 2. Its operation is controlled by two tasks: the Scheduler Task is responsible of sending data through the VLs according to the AFDX specification, while the Listener Task is in charge of receiving and propagating data upwards the UDP/IP stack upon the arrival of packets.

VL queues for transmission and buffers for reception at the end system are conceived as two classes of objects: Outbound Buffers and Inbound Buffers, respectively. A limited number of these objects will be created at compilation time and organized in pools. An Outbound Buffer encapsulates up to four internal FIFO queues for packets representing each of the sub-VLs that a VL might have. Messages sent by application tasks through the AFDX ports are directed to a particular sub-VL queue, and they could be fragmented in packets according to the *Lmax* parameter in an orderly fashion (for queuing ports only). The fragmentation is performed at the IP layer for queuing ports only according to the AFDX specification.

An Inbound Buffer is associated to a specific port for the reception of messages. Two kinds of Inbound Buffer are defined depending on whether the port is sampling or queuing. In the first case, we only need space for one message as just the last message is stored, while a FIFO queue must be used in the second case. Application tasks can optionally block at either a queuing port waiting to receive a message, or at a sampling port waiting only to receive the first packet. If a message was fragmented the Inbound Buffer stores the complete message after all the packets have been successfully received by the Listener Task.

The Scheduler Task uses the Scheduler Information which contains an Event List, where each Event is linked to a different VL and contains the following information: the number of pending triggers (packets awaiting to be sent), the BAG, the triggering time, and a handler to perform the scheduling operation, i.e., to get the next packet to be transmitted from the corresponding Outbound Buffer and send it. The Scheduler Task selects the packet from a non-empty sub-VL queue of the Outbound Buffer in a round-robin basis. While there exist pending triggers for a particular Event it is inserted into a heap called Active Events Heap, ordered by the triggering time so the first element in the heap will be the next action to be done by the Scheduler Task. When an action is executed, the Scheduler Task decrements the number of pending triggers by one and increases the triggering time by one BAG.

When a new message arrives at an AFDX port for transmission, and the number of pending triggers is consequently increased by the number of packets enqueued in the Outbound Buffer, two cases have to be considered:

- The Event had pending triggers: no action is required since this Event is already in the Active Events Heap.
- The Event did not have pending triggers: we have to put the Event into the Active Events Heap and we have to schedule the new triggering time by taking into

account the instant when the event was triggered the last time, increased by one BAG. Then:

- If this new triggering time has not been reached yet, the new triggering time is scheduled.
- If this new triggering time has expired, the Event has to be triggered immediately.

In the case when a new Event reaches the top of the Active Events Heap, the Scheduler Task has to be rescheduled.

```
package AFDX.Config is
  procedure Add_ES
   (ID                 : in End_Systems.ID_Range;
    MAC                : in String;
    IP                 : in String);
  procedure Add_VL
   (ID                 : in Virtual_Links.ID_Range;
    BAG                : in Virtual_Links.BAG_Enum;
    Priority           : in Virtual_Links.Prio_Enum;
    Lmax               : in Positive;
    Source             : in End_Systems.ID_Range;
    Destination        : in End_Systems.ID_Array;
    SubVLQ_Size        : in Virtual_Links.SubVLQ_Size_List);
  procedure Add_Transmission_Port
   (Port               : in Ports.Port_Range;
    Virtual_Link       : in Virtual_Links.ID_Range;
    Sub_Virtual_Link   : in Virtual_Links.SubVL_Range:=0);
  procedure Add_Reception_Port
   (Port               : in Ports.Port_Range;
    Mode               : in Ports.Port_Type;
    Virtual_Link       : in Virtual_Links.ID_Range;
    Buffer_Size        : in Stream_Element_Count);
end AFDX.Config;
```

Fig. 3. Package AFDX.Config

5   Implementation of the AFDX Emulator

The AFDX emulator has been implemented in Ada and presents two different APIs: one for the configuration of the network (end systems, VLs, and communication ports); the other one to allow the application tasks to send and receive messages through the emulated AFDX network. Furthermore, the standard Ethernet switch used needs to be configured to properly route the traffic coming from the VLs.

5.1   Configuration API

A configuration API (see Fig. 3) is provided in the package AFDX.Config where a set of procedures are given in order to declare the information related to the configuration of the network for end systems, VLs and AFDX ports. This information will be statically defined at compilation time in order to obtain a more efficient behavior of the emulator. The definition of the network configuration has to be done in a child package called AFDX.Config.Definitions. It is recommended to create a common definition package and share it among all the running end systems, since each node will identify itself with an end system based on the MAC address, so that the appropriate set of VLs and AFDX ports will be automatically created.

In a real AFDX network, end systems and switches contain static tables that we try to replicate with this API. Thus, we have to define each of the running end systems in the network with the procedure Add_ES. Each of these elements is identified with a number and shall be constructed upon a unique MAC and IP addresses.

```
package AFDX.System is
  type Access_Mode is (Blocking, Non_Blocking);
  type AFDX_Port is new Root_Stream_Type with private;
  procedure Write
        (This  : in out AFDX_Port;
         Item  : in  Stream_Element_Array);
  procedure Read
        (This  : in out AFDX_Port;
         Item  : out Stream_Element_Array;
         Last  : out Stream_Element_Offset);
  procedure Bind
        (This  : in out AFDX_Port;
         Mode  : in Access_Mode;
         Port  : in Ports.Port_Range);
  function Freshness   (This : in AFDX_Port) return Time;
  function Is_Readable (This : in AFDX_Port) return Boolean;
  function Is_Writable (This : in AFDX_Port) return Boolean;
  function Is_Queueing (This : in AFDX_Port) return Boolean;
  function Is_Sampling (This : in AFDX_Port) return Boolean;
  function Mode        (This : in AFDX_Port) return Access_Mode;
private
  ...
end AFDX.System;
```

Fig. 4. Package AFDX.System

The properties of the VLs are declared by means of the procedure Add_VL. A number to identify the VL, the BAG and *Lmax* parameters, the identifier of the sending end system, and a list of receiving end systems identifiers (only one destination is supported for the moment) should be provided. We also have to provide the priority that will be used at the outgoing port of the switch; this method allows avoiding the configuration of priorities at the switch level. The configured priority will be set by the implementation in the Ethernet frame so that the switch can manage it properly. The last parameter to be specified is the size of each sub-VL queue (up to four) that a VL might have. Sub-VLs configured with a size of zero are not used.

Finally, AFDX ports are defined through the procedures Add_Transmission_Port and Add_Reception_Port, which respectively create a sending AFDX port at the sending end system and a receiving AFDX port at the receiving end system. We have to provide an identifier, the kind of port (sampling or queuing), the VL and sub-VL used for transmission, and the size of the Inbound Buffer at the receiving end system. In order to simplify the mapping of transmission and reception ports, we use the port number to make this mapping. Ports with the same number are linked together.

5.2 Communications API

Applications can use the AFDX emulator through the communications API (see Fig. 4) defined in the package AFDX.System, which enables accessing the AFDX ports in order to send or receive data depending on whether the end system is a source or a destination. The class AFDX_Port is defined by inheritance from Ada's Root_Stream_Type and Read and Write procedures exchange messages with the AFDX ports declared in the configuration package AFDX.Config.Definitions. The Read operation can be configured as blocking or non-blocking by specifying the Mode parameter in the Bind procedure, which establishes the connection between AFDX_Port objects and the port identifiers defined in the configuration.

A set of additional functions are provided in this API to obtain information about the characteristics of AFDX_Port objects, in particular whether they support Read or Write operations, the kind of port (queuing/sampling), the Read operation mode (blocking/non-blocking), or the freshness of data in a sampling port. The value returned by the Freshness function corresponds to the last message obtained by Read. Time_First is returned for a queuing port, or if Read has never been called for the specific port.

5.3 Switch Configuration

The AFDX emulator requires configuring the network switch to be as deterministic as possible. To this end, the internal traffic associated with third-party protocols must be disabled: for instance, both the Spanning Tree protocol and the Neighbor Discovery Protocol must be disabled, and the ARP protocol should be statically configured. Furthermore, support for network traffic prioritization is also required to differentiate VLs with different priorities. Nowadays, most of the high-end switches support traffic prioritization features based on the Class of Service/Quality of Service (CoS/QoS) technologies [17][19]. On the one hand, the association of VLs with priorities at the switch level can be configured by means of the UDP destination port, thus allowing different priorities to be used for the same VL when the packet has to cross more than one switch; on the other hand, if the priority specified in VL at the end system level is used, all the switches will handle the VL with the same priority.

6 ARINC-Based Platform

The ARINC-653 architecture [1] is built upon the concept of *partition,* a kind of container for applications whose execution is both spatially and temporally isolated. Partitioning eases the verification, validation and certification of heterogeneous applications executed in the same hardware platform [20], which may feature different levels of criticality and/or may even be developed by different companies.

In the context of our partitioned platform, space and time partitioning are provided through XtratuM [3], an ARINC-653-like hypervisor especially designed for real-time embedded systems and developed at the Real-Time System Group of the Instituto de Automática e Informática Industrial of the Universitat Politècnica de València

(Spain). Among other services, this hypervisor provides partition management, scheduling or inter-partition communications.

Inter-partition communication is performed through the ARINC-653 transport mechanism. This transport is based on the definition of sampling and/or queuing ports which are statically connected by means of communication channels. All these communication entities are entirely defined through a configuration file, and the same configuration scheme can be used for ports allocated to the same or a different node. Therefore, this process decouples applications from system and partition configuration.

In the context of XtratuM, device drivers are not implemented at the hypervisor level so shared devices are managed by means of special partitions called *I/O partitions* or *pseudo-partitions* (see Fig. 5). In a distributed system multiple partitions may require access to the AFDX network, being the corresponding pseudo-partition responsible for handling the contention in the network device. Under this approach, all the partitions belonging to the same node are interconnected through the standard ARINC transport mechanism; and communications between partitions allocated to different nodes must be performed via the pseudo-partition, which will be responsible for redirecting messages to the communications network as shown in Fig. 5.

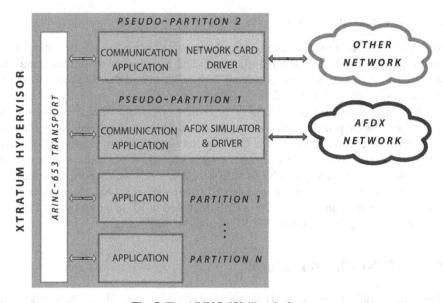

Fig. 5. The ARINC-653-like platform

A prototype for the proposed approach has been developed as a proof of concepts, focusing on the validation of the proposed AFDX emulator. Other important aspects such as the use of safety-related hardware or implementation efficiency are planned for future work.

7   Overhead and Latency Measurements

The complete characterization of the proposed approach would be too extensive to be included in this paper. Instead, this section presents a representative test to validate the AFDX emulator and the developed platform.

The hardware platform used for the test is composed of two PCs (Intel Pentium 3 single-core processor with a clock rate of 2.8 Ghz) connected through a 100 Mbps network using a 3COM 5500G switch. The software platform consists of one single partition running on top of MaRTE OS v1.9 and XtratuM v3.7.

Latency measurements associated with the AFDX emulator require configuring the network switch as was commented in Section 5.3, i.e., disabling extra network traffic and specifying priorities. The 3COM 5500G switch allows the network traffic coming from third-party protocols to be disabled, and it provides eight priority queues for traffic prioritization. Finally, the switch also presents a store-and-forward switching latency lower than 10 µs.

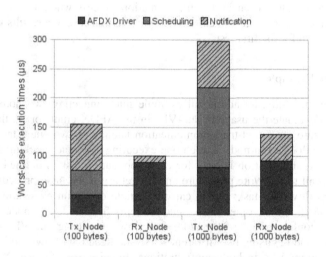

Fig. 6. Overheads of the AFDX emulator

7.1   Characterization of the AFDX Emulator

For the estimation of overheads in the AFDX emulator, a simple test connecting two nodes with one VL is executed. The test is executed 10,000 times to obtain the worst-case execution time for the different operations executed in the emulator in relation with the size of the network packet. In particular, the following metrics have been measured: (1) *AFDX driver*, which measures the time associated with the operations related to the creation and handling of AFDX frames; (2) *scheduling*, which measures the time associated with the scheduling decisions and the delivery of the AFDX frame to the NIC (Network Interface Card) driver provided by the operating system; and (3) *notification*, which measures the handling and notification of events between the *AFDX driver* and the application at the receiving end system, or between the *AFDX driver* and the Scheduler Task at the sending end system.

Table 1. Performance metrics for the usage example (times in μs)

CONFIGURATION	APPLICATION TASK	MAX.	MIN.	STD. DEV.
VIRTUAL LINKS	CLIENT 1	1956	1605	101
	CLIENT 2	1932	1607	95
SUB-VIRTUAL LINKS	CLIENT 1	2614	1606	462
	CLIENT 2	3374	1606	865

The results based on the frame size are shown in Fig. 6. As can be observed, the transmission of 100 bytes using the AFDX emulator takes a maximum of 150μs, while the reception is below 100μs. When the frame size is incremented to 1000 bytes, the time associated with the scheduling layer is substantially increased, as this layer is in charge of the delivery of frames to the underlying NIC driver. Finally, the test has been repeated to check the fragmentation process when a message of 1000 bytes is fragmented into ten packets of 100 bytes. In this case, the results were similar to those obtained for the first test.

7.2   Usage Example

To complete the study, an additional example interconnecting two nodes has been developed to evaluate the usage of sub-VLs in the AFDX emulator. In this case, the test will measure the round-trip communication latency of two client tasks, Client 1 and Client 2, allocated in node 1, each one executing a remote blocking operation in node 2. The communication latency for each application task is defined as the time between the call to the Write procedure and the return of the Read procedure. We define two data flows per task: one to call the remote operation by sending data from node 1 to node 2, and the other one to send the reply from node 2 to node 1. We study two possible configurations of the Write data flows: (1) using one VL composed of two sub-VLs, and (2) using two different VLs. The Read data flows are implemented by using different VLs in both configurations. In this example, AFDX frames are restricted to an *Lmax* value of 98 bytes, and the BAG is configured to 1 ms for all the VLs. Furthermore, the payloads for the calling and reply messages are bounded to 120 and 56 bytes respectively, and thus fragmentation is required for the former.

Table 1 shows the results of the measurements for the example. When two different VLs are used for the calling message, the round-trip latency associated with both client tasks is quite similar. However, the maximum latency is notably increased for the configuration with sub-VLs, as a round-robin scheduler is used when multiple packets are ready to be transmitted (see Section 3).

Finally, Fig. 7 shows the configuration of the example using the proposed API for the configuration with sub-VLs. In this case, the use of sub-VLs is allowed by associating them to different AFDX ports, as can be seen in the figure.

```
package body AFDX.Config.Definitions is
begin
  Add_ES (ID        =>1, MAC => "00:02:44:3C:08:21", IP => "192.168.85.1");
  Add_ES (ID        =>2, MAC =>"00:02:44:3B:6A:DE", IP => "192.168.85.2");
  Add_VL
    (ID             =>1, BAG => Virtual_Links.BAG1,
     Priority       => Virtual_Links.Prio_HIGH,
     Lmax           =>98, Source => 1, Destination => ( 1 =>2),
     SubVLQ_Size    =>(0 => 1*8*1024*1024, 1 => 1*8*1024*1024, 2 =>0, 3 => 0));
  Add_VL
    (ID             => 2, BAG => Virtual_Links.BAG1,
     Priority       => Virtual_Links.Prio_HIGH,
     Lmax           => 98, Source => 2, Destination => (1 => 1),
     SubVLQ_Size    => (0 => 1024*1024, 1 => 0, 2 =>  0, 3 => 0));
  Add_VL
    (ID             => 3, BAG => Virtual_Links.BAG1,
     Priority       => Virtual_Links.Prio_LOW,
     Lmax           => 98, Source => 2, Destination => (1 => 1),
     SubVLQ_Size    => (0 => 1024*1024,1 => 0, 2 => 0, 3 => 0));
  Add_Transmission_Port
    (Port           => 1, Virtual_Link => 1, Sub_Virtual_Link => 0);
  Add_Transmission_Port
    (Port           => 2, Virtual_Link => 1, Sub_Virtual_Link => 1);
  Add_Transmission_Port
    (Port           => 3, Virtual_Link => 2, Sub_Virtual_Link => 0);
  Add_Transmission_Port
    (Port           => 4, Virtual_Link => 3, Sub_Virtual_Link => 0);
  Add_Reception_Port
    (Port           => 1, Mode => Ports.QUEUEING, Virtual_Link => 1,
     Buffer_Size    => 1*8*1024*1024);
  Add_Reception_Port
    (Port           => 2, Mode => Ports.QUEUEING, Virtual_Link => 1,
     Buffer_Size    => 1*8*1024*1024);
  Add_Reception_Port
    (Port           => 3, Mode => Ports.QUEUEING, Virtual_Link => 2,
     Buffer_Size    => 1024*1024);
  Add_Reception_Port
    (Port           => 4, Mode => Ports.QUEUEING, Virtual_Link => 3,
     Buffer_Size    => 1024*1024);
end AFDX.Config.Definitions;
```

Fig. 7. Configuration with sub-VLs for the usage example

7.3   Overall Evaluation

The AFDX emulator proposed here has basic functionality for transmission and re-ception of messages at the end systems through the ARINC ports (sampling and queuing), allowing the configuration of VLs and also sub-VLs, which are scheduled according to the traffic regulation rules specified by the standard (*Lmax* and BAG parameters for VLs, and round-robin policy for sub-VLs in a VL). Messages that cannot be sent in an Ethernet frame of length *Lmax* are split in packets. Redundant networks are not supported.

The functionality of the switch allows the usage of the up to eight priorities, so the two priority levels specified in the AFDX standard are supported, and they can be configured in two ways: at the switch level by means of the UDP destination port, or at the end system level via the API provided. Multicast and filtering are not sup-ported.

As can be observed, the emulator overheads make it difficult to comply with some timing requirements specified by the standard, such as transmission jitter or technological latency in reception, while the hardware latency of the switch can be comfortably fulfilled. However the overheads evaluation allows modeling the AFDX emulator within the platform and the whole application by using a modeling framework such as MAST 2 [21] for example. Once the application has been modeled, the MAST schedulability analysis tools [22] could be applied to obtain response times and latencies in the AFDX network by using the technique in [9] (not yet implemented in MAST). The calculated latencies can be compared with those values measured in the real application using the AFDX emulator.

8   Conclusions

Although the usage of partitioned systems is increasing in some domains such as aerospace, avionics or automotive, this technology is expensive to be used in education or research. So, we have proposed an AFDX emulator built on top of standard Ethernet hardware suitable for training or research purposes. We have also integrated this emulator into an ARINC platform based on GPL software consisting of XtratuM as an ARINC-like hypervisor, and MaRTE OS as the operating system allowing the development of Ada applications.

The AFDX emulator allows complex AFDX configuration capabilities at the end system: definition of VLs and sub-VLs with sampling and queuing ports, and message fragmentation. Priorities are also supported at the switch, but message filtering has not been implemented as the switch cannot be programmed to do this. Redundancy management has not been included, as it does not add any extra value to the emulator purposes. The evaluation of the emulator shows that it can be used under certain load restrictions due to the overheads. It is worth noting that this emulator can be used within an ARINC-based platform as proposed in this paper, but it can also be executed on top of the operating system without any hypervisor underneath. The AFDX emulator is offered as open source and will be available at the MaRTE OS web page (http://marte.unican.es/).

References

1. Airlines Electronic Engineering Committee, Aeronautical Radio INC: Avionics Application Software Standard Interface. ARINC Specification 653-1 (March 2006)
2. Airlines Electronic Engineering Committee, Aeronautical Radio INC: ARINC Specification 664 P7-1: Aircraft Data Network, Part 7 - Avionics Full Duplex Switched Ethernet Network, September 23, 2009
3. Masmano, M., Ripoll, I., Crespo, A., Metge, J.J.: Xtratum a hypervisor for safety critical embedded systems. In: Proc. of the 11th Real-Time Linux Workshop, Dresden, Germany (2009)
4. Aldea Rivas, M., González Harbour, M.: MaRTE OS: an Ada kernel for real-time embedded applications. In: Strohmeier, A., Craeynest, D. (eds.) Ada-Europe 2001. LNCS, vol. 2043, pp. 305–316. Springer, Heidelberg (2001)
5. Frances, F., Fraboul, C., Grieu, J.: Using network calculus to optimize the AFDX network. In: Proc. of the ERTS, Toulouse, France (2006)

6. Scharbarg, J.L., Ridouard, F., Fraboul, C.: A probabilistic analysis of end-to-end delays on an AFDX network. IEEE Transactions on Industrial Informatics **5**(1), 38–49 (2009)
7. Bauer, H., Scharbarg, J.L., Fraboul, C.: Improving the worst-case delay analysis of an AFDX network using an optimized trajectory approach. IEEE Transactions on Industrial Informatics **5**(4), 521–533 (2010)
8. Bauer, H., Scharbarg, J.L., Fraboul, C.: Applying trajectory approach with static priority queuing for improving the use of available AFDX resources. Journal of Real-Time Systems **48**, 101–133 (2012)
9. Gutiérrez, J.J., Palencia, J.C., González Harbour, M.: Holistic schedulability analysis for multipacket messages in AFDX networks. Journal of Real-Time Systems **50**(2), 230–269 (2014). Springer
10. Li, J., Guan, H., Yao, J., Zhu, G., Liu, X.: Performance enhancement and optimized analysis of the worst case end-to-end delay for AFDX networks. In: Proc. of the IEEE International Conference on Green Computing and Communications, GREENCOM, Besançon, France, pp. 301–310 (2012)
11. Zhang, J., Qiao, S., Li, D., Shi, G.: Modeling and simulation of EDF scheduling algorithm on AFDX switch. In: Proc. of the IEEE International Conference on Signal Processing, Communications and Computing (ICSPCC), pp. 1–4 (2011)
12. Dong, S., Xingxing, Z., Lina, D., Qiong, H.: The design and implementation of the AFDX network simulation system. In: Proc. of the International Conference on Multimedia Technology (ICMT), pp. 1–4 (2010)
13. Charara, H., Fraboul, C.: Modelling and simulation of an avionics full duplex switched ethernet. In: Proc. of the Advanced Industrial Conference on Telecommunications, pp. 207–212 (2005)
14. Basu, A., Bensalem, S., Bozga, M., Delahaye, B., Legay, A., Sifakis, E.: Verification of an AFDX infrastructure using simulations and probabilities. In: Barringer, H., Falcone, Y., Finkbeiner, B., Havelund, K., Lee, I., Pace, G., Roşu, G., Sokolsky, O., Tillmann, N. (eds.) RV 2010. LNCS, vol. 6418, pp. 330–344. Springer, Heidelberg (2010)
15. Hornig, R.: Avionics Full-Duplex Switched Ethernet for OMNeT++ (2012). https://github.com/omnetpp/afdx
16. Calluaud, J.M., Cloury, E.: Simulation and test system for at least one item of equipment on an AFDX network. US Patent 7,406,050 (2008)
17. IEEE Std 802.1Q. Virtual Bridged Local Area Networks. Annex G, IEEE Document (2006)
18. Condor Engineering: AFDX/ARINC 664 tutorial (May 2005). http://www.cems.uwe.ac.uk/~ngunton/afdx_detailed.pdf
19. Nichols, K., Blake, S., Baker, F., Black, D.: Definition of the differentiated services field (DS field) in the Ipv4 and Ipv6 headers. RFC-2474, RFC Editor (1998)
20. Prisaznuk, P.J.: ARINC 653 role in Integrated Modular Avionics (IMA). In: Proc. of the 27th IEEE/AIAA Digital Avionics Systems Conference (DACS), pp. 1.E.5 1–10 (2008)
21. González Harbour, M., Gutiérrez, J.J., Drake, J.M., López, P., Palencia, J.C.: Modeling distributed real-time systems with MAST 2. Journal of Systems Architecture **56**(6), 331–340 (2013). Elsevier
22. MAST web page. http://mast.unican.es/

Author Index